AF842646

Moroccan Women, Activists, and Gender Politics

Moroccan Women, Activists, and Gender Politics

An Institutional Analysis

By Eve Sandberg and Kenza Aqertit

LEXINGTON BOOKS
Lanham • Boulder • New York • London

EAC LIBRARY

Published by Lexington Books
An imprint of The Rowman & Littlefield Publishing Group, Inc.
4501 Forbes Boulevard, Suite 200, Lanham, Maryland 20706
www.rowman.com

16 Carlisle Street, London W1D 3BT, United Kingdom

Copyright © 2014 by Lexington Books

All rights reserved. No part of this book may be reproduced in any form or by any electronic or mechanical means, including information storage and retrieval systems, without written permission from the publisher, except by a reviewer who may quote passages in a review.

British Library Cataloguing in Publication Information Available

Library of Congress Cataloging-in-Publication Data

Sandberg, Eve Nan, author.
Moroccan women, activists, and gender politics : an institutional analysis / Eve Sandberg and Kenza Aqertit.
pages cm
ISBN 978-0-7391-8209-3 (cloth : alk. paper) -- ISBN 978-0-7391-8210-9 (electronic)
1. Women--Morocco--Social conditions. 2. Women political activists--Morocco. 3. Women--Legal status, laws, etc.--Morocco. 4. Women (Islamic law)--Morocco. 5. Sex discrimination--Morocco. I. Aqertit, Kenza. II. Title.
HQ1791.S35 2014\
305.420964--dc23
2014025389

™ The paper used in this publication meets the minimum requirements of American National Standard for Information Sciences—Permanence of Paper for Printed Library Materials, ANSI/NISO Z39.48-1992.

Printed in the United States of America

Eve Sandberg dedicates this book to her late, beloved Aunt, Ann Cohen, who offered Eve support in all its forms and who modeled how to live one's life so as to become enriched in every year, even at 107.

Kenza Aqertit dedicates this book to her mother, Halima Bouchfer, for her support and encouragement throughout Kenza's academic and professional years to think bigger, aim higher and challenge different political and cultural barriers to women.

Table of Contents

Preface

As participant observers to the work that Moroccan women gender activists were accomplishing 1985-2010, we felt we needed to tell their stories. Because Moroccan women met with such good success, we felt we all could learn from their strategies. To improve the status of women in any country is a difficult task. Moroccan women have worked for decades, achieving some major victories even though more work remains to be done. How they have achieved their victories is the subject of this book. Borrowing from the theoretical perspective of institutionalism, the book offers a template for change to those who theorize about gender advocacy and to those who practice it.

We, as authors, believe that our personal epistemologies have influenced the research methods we have chosen and the manner in which they are employed. That one of us is a Moroccan citizen of Berber descent and one of us is a citizen of the United States (a first generation citizen whose father came from a village in ByloRusso) means that our world theoretical understandings often are dissimilar in important ways. Our life experiences, also dissimilar in many ways, however, overlap in some ways so that, as researchers, we share enough epistemological understandings that we are able to collaborate on this project. We believe that acting as authors who come from different cultures but who seek to navigate each other's culture has provided our work with a richer multi-dimensional understanding of our subject matter than just one of us could have achieved alone.

Additionally, the "insider-outsider" research issue takes on an important dimension in our methodology because both authors have been participant observers in some aspects of the subject matter of this study. Beginning in early November 2001, the American author has been a participant observer, conducting training workshops for Moroccan women seeking public office, particularly parliamentary office. Also in 2001, the American author conducted workshops for the Executive Boards of a number of Morocco's political parties to assist with their planning, targeting, and messaging prior to the 2002 election. In December 2007, she offered a workshop module and then served as a facilitator for a dialogue between heads of Moroccan NGOs and representatives of Morocco's parliament. The American is a tenured academic with a Ph.D. in Political Science from Yale University. She Chairs the Politics Department and teaches at historic Oberlin College. She is the President of a small political consultancy firm based in Oberlin, Ohio U.S.A (Strategic Research Inc.), and a two-term locally elected official. Beyond conducting workshops and giving talks on various aspects of democratization in Morocco and the U.S., she has also worked on campaigns, advocacy training, and state-NGO relations in Jordan, South Africa, Namibia, Zambia, Tanzania, and Ethiopia, which informs her comparative framework and the questions she finds of interest. The American author's travels to Morocco in 2001, 2002, 2007, 2009, and 2012 have allowed her to study the evolving gender institution of Moroccan women over time.

The Moroccan author has been a democratization professional in Morocco and other Middle East North African (MENA), and West African and South Asian countries for most of her professional life. Most recently, she serves as Resident Country Director for the National Democratic Institute (NDI) in Nepal, a U.S. based organization that engages in democracy building around the world. Previously she served as Deputy Regional Director of Programs at the International Center for Human Rights and Democratic Development (Rights and Democracy) headquartered in Montreal, Canada, where she oversaw democracy development programs for the Center in Asia and Latin America. Working as a Moroccan national for NDI in Rabat, Morocco from 1997-2006, she organized and in some cases conducted workshops for political office holders, appointed officials, media practitioners, and political activists in Morocco, as well as other democratically transitioning countries, including Jordan, Kuwait, Iraq, Algeria, and Egypt. She earned a Masters Degree in the United States from the University of Pittsburgh on a Fulbright scholarship and a fellowship at Stanford University from the Center for Democracy Development and the Rule of Law (CDDRL). She speaks Arabic, Russian, English, French, and Berber fluently.

Together we have collaborated on researching, writing, and presenting conference papers, conducting workshops and on completing this manuscript. We have chosen to analyze the specific accounts of leading Moroccan women involved in the struggle for gender rights as a major component in our analysis of how a gender institution was altered. As authors, we came to believe that it was important to utilize a methodology that emphasized the human component of historical change with regard to the creation of institutions. It was not enough simply to offer an event-based account and track those events within the exogenous and endogenous structures that influenced Morocco's gender activists during a critical period in Moroccan history. We deemed understanding the choices debated and selected as a result of those exogenous and endogenous pressures equally important to our study.

Our research included: referencing our notes taken during years of practical observation—participant activities in Morocco's unfolding democratization initiatives; analyzing primary documents; reading the secondary literature on the topics of concern in this study; and conducting interviews with numerous key Moroccan women activists in order to understand their personal motivations and the context in which they undertook their political, social, and community work. Additionally, we interviewed or discussed Morocco and the multiple meanings of Moroccan gender advocacy and democratization with Moroccan women and men, foreign aid donors, and members of the diplomatic corps.

Acknowledgments

There are many people who contributed to the completion of this book and while we cannot thank them all, we do wish to thank those who had a direct hand in our access to the relevant Moroccan affairs that is the subject of this study and to those who assisted in supporting the writing and production of this manuscript.

Kenza and Eve would not have met and begun their collaboration had it not been for the work of the National Democratic Institute, its staff in Rabat and Washington D.C. and the teams led by Cathy Allen that were invited to Morocco by ADFM women and by other Moroccan women who were associated with their political parties. Thus we are indebted to Cathy Allen (Connections Group, Seattle) and the teams of women that traveled to Morocco. Team members included Sue Hammell of British Columbia joined by those from Washington state: Christine Gregoire, Jenny Durkan, Kathy Koelker, Maggie Ragland Neilson, Kathy Kreiter, Teresa Purcell, Cynara Lilly, Bobbe Bridge, Stanley Tsao, Linda Kelly, and Dorothy Mann.

Additionally, our initial work and our subsequent research would not have been possible without Kenneth Wollach (President, NDI), Les Campbell (NDI Director for Middle East Programs), those who directed the NDI Rabat offices—Gerard Latulippe and Maryam Montague, and those who worked there during our programmatic initiatives—Sarah Ezzy, Nadia Kamil, May Taylor, Osmae Otmani, Kristin Haffert, and assisting on special projects, Nora Mabkhouti and Maryem Ouedghiri. Eve also wants to recognize that Nadia Tahri and Narfissa Laphmil are translators extraordinaire. Additionally, Tahri and Laphmil generously shared their insights over time gleaned, in part, from serving as faculty in American Studies programs headquartered in Rabat.

The African Studies Association (ASA) generously administered a Ford Fouation grant that allowed Kenza to travel to the ASA annual conference to copresent a paper during an early period in this collaboration. Likewise we are grateful to Larry Diamond, Director of the Stanford Center on Democracy, Development and the Rule of the Law, who made it possible for Kenza to join Stanford's summer democracy program to reflect on the intersection of theory and practice in the context of a democratizing state. Eve benefitted multiple times from Oberlin College support especially through a Powers Travel Grant to Morocco.

Mostly we are grateful to the dozens of individuals who spoke to us about Moroccan politics, men and women, Moroccans and foreigners. We are especially grateful to the many, many Moroccan women who shared their views and thoughts on Morocco's evolving gender institution with us. We could not use all of their stories or name all of them in this text, but we are grateful for the work that they do and the insights that they offered.

Thanks to the many colleagues who were supportive of this project, in particular Benjamin Schiff who frequently stepped forward to take on institutional work to free up time for Eve to work on this manuscript. Additionally, Judith Brown offered her Tucson, Arizona home as a January hideaway and provided the support that only a close friend can to help Eve complete her writing.

Both Eve and Kenza are grateful to Jan Cooper, Molly Johnson, and Sandra Zagarell for all of their assistance with the production of the book, especially their bibliographic work, footnotes, and copy editing of various sections. We are also grateful to Sandy Austin for her technical assistance and help with the final draft.

Additionally, Eve notes that she is personally grateful to Sandra Zagarell for her encouragement and support during the writing of this book and on the many other projects of her life.

Kenza would like to acknowledge her gratitude to her husband Monsif Mzibri and son Hamza Mzibri for their support to Kenza during the writing of this book, and for their continuous encouragement and backing for her career.

All of these wonderful people encouraged, supported, and contributed to the completion of this manuscript. Any errors found within the text are ours alone. The final project is much improved, however, as a result of their support.

Chapter One
Institutional Theories, Feminist Theories, and Moroccan Women Activists

In 1992 in the Muslim Kingdom of Morocco, after several decades of official neglect regarding women's rights and their civil society organizations, Moroccan women and their male allies collected one million signatures that advocated for improving the status of women—by working through their civil society organizations and some through their associated political parties. Morocco's King Hassan II responded to this outpouring of social advocacy and offered some improvements for women, but the women did not receive all, or even many, of the rights they sought.

These activists, however, continued to organize for improvement in the status of Moroccan women and found a powerful ally when, on King Hassan II's death, his son Mohamed VI assumed the throne. Over time, during the reign of the new monarch, improvements for women were initiated in the Muslim kingdom. In 2002 a gender quota was added to the national parliament's election law that required that at least 10% of the members of parliament be female. Then in 2004, the women experienced an important victory when changes to Morocco's family code (the Moudawana) advanced the rights of women in the areas of inheritance, citizenship for Moroccan women's children even if the father was a foreigner, and ability to sue for divorce. By 2009 there was a significant increase in the number of women elected to municipal councils. In fact, women's representation increased from 0.5% to 12.3%; although the government had established a baseline quota of 12% for women in the 2009 municipal elections, women candidates managed to exceed the quota. Programs to advance women's education and health care also were promoted throughout the 2000s. In 2006, another reform that astonished many observers was enacted; women religious leaders were identified, trained, and certified to teach in the Muslim madrasas of Morocco. These women were no liberal feminists; rather they were religious practitioners of a religion that prescribed different roles for men and women. But now young religious men and women studied with female teachers and thus saw that women, too, understood and could guide others regarding Islam's tenets.

Not all of the changes that Moroccan gender activists had hoped for were achieved between the 1980s—when the initial efforts of post-independence gender activists put gender on the national agenda—and the first decade of the twenty-first century, a thirty year span that witnessed the reforms above. It appeared, however, that Moroccan women had gained many new rights despite strong resistance from the country's Islamic movement and conservative customary forces. New practices were being followed, and it was anticipated that improvements for Moroccan women would continue.

By the end of 2010, Moroccan women were to be found in all realms of the country's political economy: as parliamentarians in the National Assembly, as mayors and councilors in local elected political bodies, as cabinet ministers and deputies, as executive directors in the non-profit world, as senior corporate directors in the private sector, and in all the positions below those of such high authority and rank. In short, a young Moroccan girl looking around her in 2010 could aspire to any profession if she wondered what she might do when she grew up. Although Moroccan women remained in the minority in most professions, they were present and they were visible in all realms of society.

Such a rapid thirty-year transition from "burka to boardroom," as the *Economist* has called it, begs for an explanation.[1] A number of important scholars have offered insights into this phenomenon. Variations on at least two important theoretical approaches are given: 1) a domestic politics balancing approach argues that Morocco's monarch has used leftist parties and the women's movement to "balance" Morocco's Islamic forces (and vice versa); and 2) Moroccan women activists were/are part of a larger social movement, a domestic phenomenon that attached itself to an international women's movement and thus has achieved some success.

However, the former explanation seems to suggest that there would be relatively few positive gains to come for Moroccan women as the Monarchy would swing again towards the Islamists to balance against women and their leftist allies. Instead, Moroccans saw Mohammed VI continuing to work to improve the status of Moroccan women. Further, it appeared the King had little interest in the existing left political parties nor did he have any need to use them against the Islamists. Rather, many believed that the Monarch was involved in the effort to create a new political party in Morocco, the Party of Authenticity and Modernity (PAM) led by the King's friend and adviser, Fouad Ali El Himma, that was founded in 2008, and claimed to stand for reform and good governance. This party occupied the political center seeking to gain support from both the left and the right.

The second explanation has much to commend it. The civil society explanation focuses mainly on the civil society organizations that were created within Morocco and traces how Moroccan activists drew intellectual support from international initiatives and norms, especially from officials and activists at the United Nations, as well as drawing upon international resources. This approach offers many important insights to answer the question of how changes in the status of Moroccan women could transform so quickly in thirty years. Thus, this book will analyze the institutional transformation of gender in Morocco by building upon the foundation of civil society approaches. But it will expand the civil society explanation to include a more elaborated and interactive understanding of structure, agency, discursive behaviors, and resources—key attributes for understanding institutions and institutional participants.

We thus turn to an institutional theoretical framework to answer our research question "What accounts for the positive changes in the status of Moroccan women between 1980 and 2010?" We utilize an institutionalist approach because such a theoretical frame investigates questions of both structure and agency and argues that institutions are greater than the sum of their parts.[2] Institutionalist theory by itself, however, does not fully address the structures and agency of Moroccan women activists. To truly understand the changes in the status of Moroccan women, we must also investigate our subject through a feminist theoretical lens.

Feminist theory teaches us that women experience the dynamics in their societies, including (and especially) the gender institutions in their societies, differently than men do. Further, a feminist theoretical framework acknowledges that scholars perceive their subject matter from the perspective of their own cognitive schemas, and thus scholars must push the limits of their inquiries. In this study we utilize an institutionalist theoretical framework, but we combine that approach with the concerns of feminist theorizing to capture a more complex understanding of our subject matter.

Our research within these two theoretical frames uncovers specific independent variables that contribute to the improvement in the status of Moroccan women through changes in components of Morocco's gender institution over a thirty-year period. In Chapter Two, we map the four components of Morocco's gender institution shortly after independence. In the chapters that follow, we explicate how analyzing those four institutional components through a feminist lens allows us to track the independent variables within each component that altered the institution of gender in Morocco. Thus we offer a template and also model a case study for investigating the change in a country's gender institution over time. It is our hope that other scholars will find our template for analyzing changes in a country's gender institution useful and utilize it for work they are doing in other countries. The template we develop is our contribution to the theoretical literature while our case study is our contribution to the subject matters of gender studies, area studies, and the study of Morocco.

Based on our study, we hypothesize that, as demonstrated in our template, four variables must be achieved in order to promote change in a national institution of gender.

* **Hypothesis one** argues that women in a given country must utilize their agency to make demands for change.
* **Hypothesis two** argues that the women advocating for improving the status of women within their country must find ways to create new structures for action and follow new rules, both informal and formal.
* **Hypothesis three** proposes that these women and their male allies will engage in discursive initiatives designed with intentionality to engage the national alert public in a debate concerning the status of women and

to offer an alternative logic to underpin a new national institution of gender.

* **Hypothesis four** proposes that women activists will find resources within their country and external to their country to pursue the changes they demand in their country's institution of gender.

To utilize our template of change with regard to a country's gender institution, we analyze the Morocco case. We track the changes that comprise Morocco's gender institution which are derived primarily from the four hypotheses which serve as independent variables that promote change in a nation's institution of gender. Below, we identify the subunits within these hypotheses/variables that were found in the Moroccan case.

Component 1: The Agency of Moroccan women

- the rise of agency for women activists in the 1960s that was largely achieved with the support of male mentors and accelerated in the 1980s;
- the personal bravery and leadership of Morocco's women activists in the face of threats of violence and in response to endogenous and exogenous pressures;
- the strategic choices of gender activists for targeting and messaging that created legitimacy for gender change and marshaled concerns for women as a resource, not a hindrance to change; and
- a change in Morocco's key policy makers.

Component 2: Changing rules (informal and formal), structures of action, and paths within institutions

- the changing international norms for women and the socialization of a younger Moroccan elite within those norms creating new schemas of informal action and legitimating claims of activists to change formal rules;
- the creation of new norms of consultation among Moroccan policy makers and the resulting structures that included an expansion of access by women to policy makers;
- the creation of new civil society organizations dedicated to the advancement of women;
- the strategic choice of Moroccan gender activists across party and organizational lines who were knowledgeable enough to choose to network with each other in order to achieve their goals, rather than to balkanize their initiatives; and
- the outreach initiatives to structures in all aspects of society—judicial, religious, economic, sport, political, etc. that regulate values.

Component 3: Discursive initiatives

- the early involvement of many women activists within Morocco's student organizations, and political parties where they developed their own ideas, presentation skills, and abilities to reflect and strategize across many arenas; and
- the work of mainly women scholars, journalists, and publicists (i.e., knowledge bearers) who applied an alternative logic of gender to Morocco's national agenda and legitimized it.

Component 4: Resources

- the formation and maintenance of important political alliances;
- the support of external donors for government and civil society programs that supported an improvement in the status of women;
- the pressures by external foreign investing companies during difficult economic times in Morocco that sought a climate in which their female managers and workers would feel comfortable should they invest in Morocco; and
- the leadership structures of Moroccan elite women who could bring and secure resources to women's initiatives.
- exogenous events that provided new opportunities and allies for Moroccan women.

As can be detected from the above, we will demonstrate that effecting gender change, especially in a context such as that of a Muslim kingdom, requires multiple initiatives in many arenas because gender as an institution is found at the intersections of all aspects of society—state, family, economy, culture, ethnicity, race, religion, psychological assumptions and schemas. It especially operates through political and economic practices (formal and informal) and the marshalling of resources. Gender is not simply a policy or collection of policies; it is an institution with its own logic that requires and provides resources, affirms informal and formal practices across interlocking structures, affirms assumptions and codes, and requires maintenance and/or new initiatives. Thus any gender study from an institutional framework requires an analysis of both structure and agency at multiple intersections (taking note of feedback loops) in a country's gendered social formation, ideology, and cultural norms. Such a study also requires attention to resources and discursive attributes.

Through our institutional analysis we are aware that, on occasion, an independent variable is influenced by other variables through feedback loops and other mechanisms and we discuss this phenomenon where it occurs. We recognize, however, that while this methodology is accepted by institutional analysts, it is an anathema for some other theoretical approaches. In the study of politics, we believe that the institutional approach best captures the politics of individuals, parties, and non-profit organizations. As we demonstrate in this study, political actors, especially Moroccan female gender activists, must respond to backlash activities and threats and to counter movements following their initiation of strategies to improve the status of women in Morocco. These gender activists regroup, convene, deliberate, and respond to the responses to their actions. Thus gender campaigns are interactive in a way that is best captured by investigating feedback loops and other mechanisms utilized within an institutionalist framework.

To explore such an institution systematically is no easy task. Thus, while our argument above lacks parsimony, it does offer specific components of the institution of gender, including independent variables that can be studied to elucidate the dependent variable of institutional gender change. We are aware that some scholars argue that the notion of linear, independent variables influencing the dependent variable does not allow for feedback loops or for the interactive influences of some variables with the dependent variable. Consequently throughout this project we strive to show when such phenomena occur.

Further, other researchers argue that the reliance by actors on common practices and standard operating procedures helps institutions acquire a path dependency by which alternative options are excluded, as practices become reified and new decisions are taken in light of existing practices. We strive to identify where such occurrences were salient in the Moroccan case study that we present, and also where such path dependency collapses. We do this within the context of our study's main focus, which analyzes how gender as an institution in Morocco has evolved and changed.

In this study we argue that institutional theorizing itself can be improved by including the perspectives of feminist theorizing. For example, were we simply to have utilized an institutionalist framework to understand the agency of Moroccan women gender activists, we likely would have analyzed who took action, what resources they had, and where in Moroccan structures of decision making they were able to access and influence policy makers or become policy makers themselves. Our feminist theoretical framework, however, reminds us that women experience the world differently from men and forces us to circle back and ask how in a society that forbade women from even walking alone in public, Moroccan gender activists believed that they could attend meetings on their own and participate in the policy making realm as equals to men. How did Moroccan women come to believe they could take action in the political sphere? An institutional theoretical frame does not prevent us from asking such a question; rather, institutional theorizing does not require that we attend to such a question. Through feminist theorizing, such questions become foundational for understanding how women gender activists can create change in a society that does not guarantee individual rights regardless of sex. Feminist theorizing creates a more nuanced, "thick," and enriched study of agency than might otherwise be the case.

Institutionalist and Feminist Theorizing

Both institutional and feminist theorizing, like gender activism, have advanced steadily, especially in the last three decades. In scholarly circles, both institutionalism and feminism emerged as alternatives to the study of politics dominated by competing behavioralist and pluralist approaches, or as critiques of structural analyses that did not give sufficient attention to the evolution of structures or account for gendered power differentials.

The modern debates about which methodological practices best capture insights into the politics, economics, social, and cultural activities of the world have been carried on since Enlightenment scientists challenged the Christian Church's and ancient philosophers' explanations of social phenomenon. However within recent theorizing in the post-World War II period, positivists who utilized a behavioralist methodology in the discipline of political science, usually constructed large numerical data sets mainly on the characteristics of men and of male activities in social leadership positions including those outside of the government's administrative structures. Like natural scientists, social science behavioralists sought to discover correlations among variables that could be replicated in other studies. Political scientists utilizing the behavioralist approach offered predictions based on their research. Having discovered correlations, a good behavioralist then offered a theory, based on his or her research, of why a predicted correlation occurred.

Behavioralists brought society's human actors into methodological and political considerations in reaction to the formal legalist approaches employed during the 1940s that had compared constitutions and formal laws across countries. Pluralists also offered an important alternative to formal legalism. Pluralists focused on analyzing competing interest groups, rival political parties, or bureaucratic competition and turf wars within an administration.[3] In response to the approaches offered by behavioralists and pluralists, institutionalists like Karen Orren, Stephen Skowronek, Peter Hall, Kathleen Thelen, Sven Steinmo, Theda Skocpol, Peter Evans, and Dietrich Rueschemeyer brought the state itself, as well as state linked institutions, back into the focus of those who studied politics. These New Institutionalists began analyzing how institutional procedures and the often constrained agency of actors influenced politics and policy making.[4]

By the sixties and seventies, however, even among behavioralists who used a rational choice calculus of cost-benefit analysis by individuals and then aggregated those individual choices to discover trends, movements, and policies, there were many who came to understand the need to move beyond just the numbers on the curve and resulting theories. These scholars began to look at the institutional and structural constraints and opportunities for individuals pursuing their individual preferences.

Additionally, structural theorists who traced their lineage back through Locke, Hegel, Marx, Engels, etc. questioned the development and evolution of the structures through which they viewed the world. As March and Olsen asserted in their classic 1984 article, structural and other theorists became increasingly aware that the state and the activities it engages in are not exclusively subordinate to the context of social class structures.[5] Political scientists in the late 1970s throughout the 1980s and 1990s also were informed by political anthropology, sociology, economics, psychology, and linguistics, and these means of inquiry expanded their methodological approaches to the study of political questions.

This is not the place to attempt a definitive intellectual history of the forerunners to institutional analysis. What is important to note is that world events and phenomena influenced methodological approaches to the study of politics and society even as these world events influenced domestic policies in countries such as Morocco and elsewhere. Thus, in the late 1980s and 1990s, with the failure of neoliberal markets to create sustainable economic development in many late industrializing countries, investigations of institutional approaches were given a boost because markets (often imposed), by themselves, rarely took root in their new settings or functioned as intended. Attention shifted, therefore, from calculations of what results derived from injecting a certain amount of foreign exchange into an economy or what benefits resulted for a country's indebtedness from limiting government spending.

Researchers and practitioners began asking what norms, procedures, and policy programs could prevent corruption and manipulation by state actors in order to guarantee individuals their right to gains and losses in the market. Stated differently, development analysts began to ask how institutions could be reformed to support economic liberalization. As even economists began to tout the need for institutional reforms, many political scientists, who had been aware of the institutional debates in other disciplines as well as in their own, now joined their colleagues who sought new insights through observation of both formal and informal rules, resources, practices, and preference formation. Additionally, these political scientists began looking for the links between state actors and those outside the state to identify power networks, routines, hegemonies, and the psychological schemas that were foundational to action.[6]

Similarly, the activism of women in demanding change in the status of women globally and also in their domestic arenas during the post-World War II decades gave feminist theorizing and data collection on women a boost. Initial calls, like those by Ester Boserup in 1970, focused on the collection of data on women, the need to analyze women's activities, and the need to pay attention to the consequences of the international sexual division of labor.[7] Over the next decades, feminist theorizing soon exploded into many schools with multiple foci.

Institutionalists also found they were adopting many emphases in their analyses even as they attempted to identify an institutionalist approach in reaction to the behavioralist or pluralist paradigms. When one reads the feminist and institutional literatures of the last thirty years, however, there are few intersections of theorizing that have taken hold between these two theoretical frameworks, despite their proponents' reactive research agendas against earlier schools of thought.

Yet institutionalist approaches must be partnered with feminist research practices because feminist theorizing can offer institutionalists some of the same improvements that it offers other mainstream theorizing and feminist theorists can benefit from utilizing a mainstream, theoretical framework that will provide both an audience and a recognized methodology to help gain acceptance for the findings of feminist research. Further, as we demonstrate in this study, an institutional analysis of gender helps us locate the levers for change to improve the status of women. In the sections below, after we discuss key insights of institutionalist research drawn from diverse approaches to institutionalist theorizing, we then discuss seven core concerns of feminist theorizing.

In addition to drawing upon both methodologies, we pursue three important goals. The first is to analyze the complicated set of components that comprise a gender institution and to investigate the ways in which salient independent variables have effected change in Morocco's institution of gender since the 1980s. Second, we take up the important challenge of feminist theorists to base our research on the lived experiences of North African gender activists in Morocco. Third, unlike case studies of Western democracies, we seek to understand how group power dynamics within institutions are mediated by a country's exceptionally strong executive, such as are found in many late industrializing states. Thus, we believe our work contributes an important study of institutional theorizing and feminist theorizing in a setting that operates by different norms, procedures, and dynamics than many of those found in the West.

Some Core Concerns of Institutional Theorizing

Before launching a discussion of the core variables found commonly in most institutionalist approaches to the study of politics, it is important to identify what we mean by institutionalist methodologies. Definitions of institutional analysis vary, and ways of thinking about and clustering various approaches within various institutional methodological approaches also differ.[8] Below, as examples, we offer a few alternative understandings and definitions of institutionalism derived from prominent scholarly works.

James March and Johan P. Olsen explored what the new institutionalism was not, as well as what it encompassed. They noted that the new institutionalism is far from coherent or consistent, and they offered an understanding of institutions that they acknowledged comprises a focus on formal institutional definition but has utility for a more general view of institutions. For March and Olsen, the framework of an institution is best understood by analyzing the interdependence between relatively autonomous and complex social and political institutions. Actors do not mutually follow consistent ideas, take symbolic actions, or pursue goals, and despite actors' motives or the social context of politics, institutions themselves play a role in decision making, in accordance with time considerations, the historical and experiential knowledge of actors, and the resources of both endogenous and exogenous phenomena.[9] March and Olsen, however, believed that the complexity of recognizing institutions prevented the use of institutions as a theory or a critique of theory. Rather, they believed that the investigation of institutions merely produced an argument that "the organization of political life makes a difference."[10]

Alternatively, Peter Hall argued that institutionalism had proven to be the most fruitful framework of analysis in the social sciences in decades. Hall understood institutions as "regularized sets of practices with a rule-like quality" which "structure the behavior of political and economic actors."[11]

Wolfgang Streeck and Kathleen Thelen, however, defined institutions as "building blocks of social order . . . that represent socially sanctioned, that is, collectively enforced expectations" that "involve mutually related rights and obligations for actors."[12] Coming from an international politics perspective, after years of studying institutions, the role of ideas, and world politics, Robert Keohane noted that institutions "reflect power realities, institutionalize distributional inequalities, tend to freeze the status quo, generate distinctive symbolism, and create bureaucracies with standard operating procedures and some power base of their own."[13] Further, Keohane noted that to truly understand institutions, one needs to focus on how "power and legitimacy concerns interact."[14]

By 2009, Hall observed that second generation studies were examining how institutions change, despite the definition given by the editors (James Mahoney and Kathleen Thelen) of the volume in which his work appeared as "relatively enduring features of political and social life (rules, norms, procedures) that structure behavior and that cannot be changed easily or instantaneously."[15]

Another major tenet among institutionalist theorists is that state institutions and civil society institutions mediate power conflicts among contesting groups. Largely oriented toward the use of the case study and comparative studies, Orren, Skowronek, and those who write within their tradition, focus on the state as a mediating institution in a changing environment.[16] However, other American political development authors also analyze how civil society institutions mediate conflicts among groups. Both groups include scholars who see the state as an independent variable and also as a dependent variable.

Skowronek and Orren additionally investigated the role of ideas and agency, not just the interests that are mediated among contending groups. Peter Evans, Dietrich Rueschemeyer, and Theda Skocpol, the authors of *Bringing the State Back In*, argued in the mid 1980s against exclusive behavorialist and neo market attempts to explain winners and losers without focusing on how states mediate interests and ideas, as well as help to shape the strategies of, and outcomes for, various groups of actors.[17]

Later institutionalists who theorized about the interaction of formal and informal norms, networks and policies, as well as the practices that affect both citizens and the state, acknowledged that institutional theorizing is diverse.

Kathleen Thelen and Sven Steinmo (1992), for example, observed that "institutionalists are interested in the whole range of state and societal institutions that shape how political actors define their interests and structure their relations of power to other groups."[18]

In economics, Nobel Prize winner Douglass North's work is almost synonymous with institutional theorizing. For North, analyzing the institution of property rights is key to understanding economics, politics and the security of citizens. In North's institutional analyses, the state plays a central role in creating the formal rules for establishing and guaranteeing the property rights of its citizens, which is the central institution of every country. Property rights include the conditions for physical ownership of property, the costs of labor, information, and technology. According to North, in return for creating and maintaining property rights, the state demands revenue from its citizens. But North argues that informal norms and networks constrain the operation of formal institutions and that together these formal and informal influences create the framework for a country's institutions. Further, these informal networks and norms may either increase or decrease the efficiency of the dynamics of the political economy that rational choice experts often try to model. Thus, one of the core concerns of institutionalists like North, is the interaction of formal and informal norms, networks, policies, and practices that affect both rational actors as citizens and rational actors in the state.

Both structure and agency are stressed differentially in diverse institutional approaches. For many (though not all) economists, individual actors have not only bounded rationality but also bounded agency in the market of politics and the economics. For many institutionalists in political science or sociology, structures, as well as agency, are critically important to analyzing competing groups and the state that mediates the interests and ideas of citizens. For example, as Thelan and Steinmo explain when explicating the work of Paul DiMaggio and Walter Powell, actors are rule-following satisficers, not simply rational actor maximizers. Thus the study of institutions and their rules and norms as they are *practiced* within social structures is key to understanding politics and governance.[19]Actors carry psychological schema of experiential or learned lessons in their heads that inform decisions every bit as much as do the norms and rules of the systems they confront. Thus, agency must be understood from the perspective of the schema of the individuals who initiate actions and events, especially those who chose to advocate to change existing norms and rules within the structures of social institutions.

How institutions evolve is a core question of most institutional approaches in the last decade. This focus requires analyses of several time periods if one studies a single case in detail as we do in this study of gender change in Morocco. Additionally it requires a focus on procedural change and its context, as well as the rise and fall of influential groups and/or actors, and the resources and legitimacy of those actors and their organizational bases. Thus, state and civil society institutions of rule making and rule following must be analyzed over time and in relation to multiple groups.

Additionally, there are scholars who study institutional barriers to change and others who study the path dependency of institutions, such as Paul Pierson and Theda Skocpol, but still acknowledge the possibilities for institutional change. These scholars analyze the informal and formal norms and rules within an institution that provide organizations with a historical path and a forward trajectory. Pierson is particularly concerned with how paths not taken are largely (though not absolutely) unavailable later, as actors within institutions adopt standard operating procedures and practices that foreclose returning to earlier decision points. Thus actors, at any given point in time, make decisions based on known routines and options—of of their time—and each institutional decision lays the foundation for decisions yet to come. Additionally, among lead actors, who have material interests to defend, there are other motivations to resist institutional change.

Ideas can influence tendencies away from institutional stasis and determinism. Discursive institutional analysis seeks to understand the power of ideas and discourse as key to understanding institutional change and the knowledge bearers who are necessary to promoting ideas leading to change. Vivien Schmidt argues that discursive analysis must be taken seriously if one hopes to understand why institutions persist or change.[20] Additionally, citing B. Rothstein, Schmidt further contends that institutions should not be viewed "as neutral structures of incentives or (worse) immutable products of culture."[21] Rather institutions are "better understood as carriers of ideas or 'collective memories'" so that ideas and discourse about them can assist in changing institutions whose performance is evaluated in light of such discourse.[22]

In a related approach, studies of the success or failure of interest group activity have been explained cogently by utilizing an institutional analysis.[23] Many institutional scholars have argued that "knowledge bearers" are key to the leadership needed to change institutions because these actors change the discourse, legitimize changing the institutional agenda, and mobilize through appeals to interests, values, and ideas.

Exogenous shocks, not just internal discourse, argue other institutional theorists, also explain much institutional change. When comparing institutional dynamics across countries, exogenous shocks yield insight into policy choices and the success or failure of those policies, as such shocks frequently demand a reevaluation of the status quo. Katzenstein's work on foreign economic policy of advanced industrial countries focused on the exogenous economic shocks in the international political economy and the differences in the "'policy networks' linking state and society to explain the divergent responses of different states to the international economic shocks."[24] Especially when studying small state actors—like Morocco—in a global world, the impact of exogenous events offers important understandings of the review of procedural and policy issues and can prompt a re-evaluation of existing procedures, processes, and policies.

To analyze core concerns of institutionalist theorizing as they apply to the Moroccan case offers a robust understanding of gender change within an institutionalist theoretical frame. But because we believe that an institutional analysis, like other mainstream analyses, can benefit from being informed by feminist theorizing, below we identify seven core concerns found in feminist theorizing that we will overlay in our institutional analysis throughout this project.

Seven Core Concerns of Feminist Theorizing

From the 1970s, when feminist theorizing began to gain widespread attention, until the end of the twentieth century, feminist scholars not only offered a path that provided independent variables for the dependent variables that were being researched, but also offered a framework for methodology and additional scholarly language to express an author's findings. Below, we summarize seven core concerns of the feminist scholarship approach stressed by authors since the 1970s.

1. Account for women as well as men as subjects of study. Additionally, while the subset of women must be studied, women are not homogenous.

As Driscoll and McFarland noted, "Feminist work starts from assumptions about the importance and validity of women's experiences."[25] Giving a voice to women was the important starting point for feminist theorizing. But also noting that not all women are the same, and all women need voice was an important lesson learned by feminist theorists. According to Lugones and Spelman, "it is only possible for a woman who does not feel highly vulnerable with respect to other parts of her identity, e.g., race, class, ethnicity, religion, etc., to conceive of her voice simply or essentially as a "woman's voice."[26] Thus the adage became do not simply "add women and stir" but recognize the differing experiences of women on the basis of age, culture, sexuality, and the other categories noted above. A major goal of this concern was to begin to gather data on the many women who previously had been ignored in favor of describing some universal man. As Sandra Harding noted, "myriads of women living in elaborate historical complexes of class, race and culture" were to be the focus of feminist research designs.[27]

2. Investigate the nature of women's various forms of agency.

Women initiate strategies, movements, and policies. They are not simply recipients of the intersections of sex, race, class, age, religion, and sexuality, and the gender rules, norms, and practices imposed by men. Women are not merely victims of structural or intentional processes; they are not passive. As a researcher studies how changing circumstances affect women, he or she must also study how women respond to their changing circumstances. If a researcher studies state modernization and the re-institutionalization of state subunits and practices, feminist theorists argue that the researcher must study the responses of women to state modernization, not only how they are affected. Feminist theorists further argue that not just women's coping strategies should be studied, but how women actively respond to policy and social changes in their environment.

Even differentiating the agency of women during various periods of opportunities and costs, however, does not provide enough disaggregation of women's agency for many researchers. Schuler, for example, argued that three levels of empowerment needed analysis to understand women's abilities to strategize and respond to changing political, economic, and social formations. For Schuler, the first level is the personal level at which a woman must understand and confront her challenges. Level two explores whether or not a woman experiences group identification with other women concerning an identified challenge. Level three is the mobilization level in which skills and resources are translated "into action to produce the desired change."[28] At level three Schuler is interested in how women organize with one another, an important component for many feminists and one that this project will include in addition to analyzing the first two levels. But this study also investigates women's alliances with men, which proves to be important in the Moroccan case.

3. Researchers must produce something that benefits the group(s) being studied.

The demand that researchers benefit those they study tracked with those in feminist circles, such as Mary Margaret Fonow and Judith Cook who argued that "the aim of feminist research is liberation."[29] To accomplish such a goal likely meant that research design itself needed to be completed in consultation with those being studied. Hence feminist theorists suggested making modifications in the field to accommodate those being studied. Clearly, this goal flies in the face of any pristine claim of disinterested research and risks being dismissed by some mainstream theorists for that reason.

Few social science scholars today claim objectivity, yet collaboration with one's target population is highly problematic for social science scholarly activity. Many feminist theorists such as Susan Bordo, Sandra Harding, Helen Longino, and Lynn Hankinson Nelson, however, have written eloquently and cogently about alternative feminist epistemologies and their relations to objectivity, modes of interpretation, and experience.[30] According to such scholars, owning and advertising one's biases demystifies the claim of objectivity, which is difficult to achieve in any case, and allows readers to examine a study with reduced innocence. Further, celebrating the bridges formed between researchers and the women studied is applauded. Fonow and Cook argue, for example, that it is possible to celebrate the women being studied even as the author does not shy from critically evaluating the strategies, goals, and activities of the subject women.[31]

Some feminist theorists contend that not only should the research design be completed in collaboration with the studied population, its findings should be checked against the perceptions of those in the studied population. The process of checking is thought to benefit the studied population and to make certain that the researchers do not publish something based on their own misunderstandings. Feminist scholars are particularly sensitive to the horrific socially constructed errors concerning women historically and physiologically that came from supposedly objective studies grounded in biology and other natural sciences. Reviewing the data with the studied population does not mean the researcher must alter his or her results, but it does suggest that the researcher publicize where those studied and he or she differed in their interpretation of phenomena or the impact of events.

4. Offer the voices and language of those being studied.

The researcher must make those women who are studied visible and so use their language. Thus, sanitized, disciplinary jargon with neat supporting tables are often foregone in favor of, or accompanied by, pithy language from the researched population. As Devault argued, most researchers have been trained in men's language which reflects male experiences.[32] Yet the production of consciousness, including the political consciousness which may, in turn, be translated into political action, is linked to language categories. To secure quotable language requires purposeful questioning. Opie, however, has raised and discussed at least three problems with utilizing the language of those studied:[33] What are the criteria for selecting quotations? When and how should interview extracts be included in reported findings? What part should the researcher play in interpreting quotations?

Additionally, many feminist theorists argue that researchers should seek out and publicize the voices of the most marginalized women. Studying these women does not simply include and empower them, but also serves to de-center traditional templates that might force the experiences of marginalized women into premade frameworks. Additionally, in a departure from mainstream methodologists, feminist theorists argue that researchers should privilege the outliers, not focus on those in the middle of the statistical curve. In turn, though, some feminist theorists worry that publicizing individual voices should not be done exclusive of identifying under what conditions women's voices are representative of groups of women. Bordo argued, for example, that if too many studies focused on individual voices, we might "obscure the trans historical hierarchical patterns" that we also seek to uncover.[34] Thus women must be analyzed so that they better understand that while they have agency, they are not solely responsible for their own oppression and that a woman's individual circumstance is often a reflection of the circumstances of other women.

5. Contextualize, historicize, and periodize any study and also situate the researcher with regard to the population studied.

Women's realities are always changing, so feminist research should not be a-historical. Women must be studied in the midst of evolving structural and cultural norms of a community as that community interacts with changing national and international social formations. Mohanty, for example, has argued that Western women researchers tend to homogenize women from late industrializing countries. To guard against this, Mohanty argues that a goal of the feminist research project should be to formulate "autonomous, geographically, historically, and culturally grounded feminist concerns and strategies."[35] Further, as Gayatri Chakravorty Spivak and Alfred Arteaga worry, one should be careful of "rival ethnicities (that) compete for institutional precedence or academic turf" as well as the problems of one person speaking for a group.[36]

A related approach argues that the researcher should acknowledge him or herself and self-situate in relation to the proposed project. Thus, researchers are asked to provide information about themselves to the populations being studied and to the readers to whom they present their findings. Such information, which appears disjunctive and out of place in mainstream research, allows the feminist researcher to offer a version of what is called "standpoint feminism" in which contributing factors to the perspectives of any researcher are put on the table. This effort recognizes that women's realities are different and their economic, cultural, and other views also likely differ.

6. Dissolve the private/public distinction.

It is true that women have fought to leave their culturally allocated private, domestic realms to take up satisfying work and participate in societal decision making in the public sector (including in academe). But more importantly, feminist researchers have demonstrated the lack of distinctiveness between the private and public. In 1987 the prestigious Berkshire Conference held at Wellesley College took the theme, "Beyond the Public/Private Dichotomy: Reassessing Women's Place in History." Many scholars at that conference demonstrated that once the domestic sexual division of labor undertaken at the local and household levels is understood as critical to the resource mobilization and political economy of communities, nations, and interstate activity, the distinction between public and private activity collapses. For example, Maria de los Angeles Crummett explored how the needs of Latin American women in rural households lead women to migrate to urban areas in greater numbers than did men. This challenged the established theoretical patterns of "push-pull" that focused on male migration, and prompted de los Angeles to warn that national policies starting from the premise of male perceptions of push and pull will be doomed to fail.[37]

Additionally, research such as that by Truong has demonstrated how sex workers formerly of the private sector have been incorporated into the public tourism and development industries in the Philippines and Thailand.[38] Cynthia Enloe has analyzed the roles that private and personal activities of prostitution have played in national security arrangements among states.[39] Furthermore, feminist scholarship has shown that impact of the International Monetary Fund

(IMF) programs in late industrializing economies led to a new focus on the informal and secondary sectors of the market that previously were viewed as too close to the household to hold much significance. The public political repercussions that resulted from the personal struggles of women seeking strategies to cope with IMF hardship coupled with the actions of men seeking the same collapsed the domestic private and public spheres.[40] In light of such events, economist Janet Seiz has argued for utilizing a bargaining framework for understanding relations in the market place, the workplace, and within the household, as all these realms bear similarities.[41]

7. Conduct interdisciplinary global research.

Feminist scholars have argued for holistic approaches to studying the intersections of race, class, and gender globally. They believe that it is important to shift attention from Western male interactions and this can best be done by creating an awareness of women's interactions globally, for some by employing an interdisciplinary lens. This approach, however, is resisted by those who argue that disciplinary boundaries must be maintained, especially as the professional perils of working outside the boundaries of traditional disciplines is well known. But if we hope to give women voice, we must learn something from our anthropologist colleagues. If we are to study political movements, we must adopt some insights and aspects of research design from our sociology colleagues. To avoid gross generalizations our work must be situated historically. To understand the nature of power as it is politically contested we must learn from our political science colleagues. And to understand economic forces we need some insights from our economics colleagues. Likewise religion, culture (especially ethnicity and kinship) as well as literature and scholarship have proven to be important shapers of historical events and institutions. Whether or not we are willing to acknowledge our interdisciplinary debts, our research designs must reflect such holistic understandings or they will be flawed. Yet, we also must struggle with how much can be explored within any given study. In this study, we have chosen to focus on one case study as it evolves over time, largely due to the complexities noted above, but also because of our interest in utilizing both institutional and feminist theory frameworks.

Bridging the Work of Institutionalists and Feminists

In light of the decades of work on institutions and gender and some of the core ideas described above, one would expect some feminist theorists to utilize the lens of institutionalists and vice versa. Surprisingly, that took a long time to occur, but two recent scholarly books on gender and institutions have advanced the enterprise. First, Georgina Waylen's *Engendering Transitions: Women's Mobilization, Institutions, and Gender Outcomes* appeared in 2007. More recently in

2011, Mona Lena Krook and Fiona Mackay's edited volume appeared, *Gender, Politics and Institutions: Towards a Feminist Institutionalism.*[42]

Waylen's work asks "under what circumstances can transitions to democracy result in positive gender outcomes?"[43] Using case material from eight countries, Waylen finds that there is no determinate independent variable that promotes positive gender outcomes during democratic transitions. She can identify trends, however. Her methodology does not simply investigate the role of women's movements but rather also investigates actors and institutions. As a feminist researcher, Waylen is careful to note that the assumptions of women's homogeneity "must be taken apart to show how women are differentiated."[44] She argues for the dissolution of the private and public, noting "the sexual division of labour within the household differentially affects men and women's access to the public sphere."[45] Waylen's main question, what can be done to achieve higher levels of women's participation in public office, serves the needs of the women she researched. When considering the gendering of political institutions, Waylen utilizes a methodology that investigates the gendering of 1) political parties, 2) constitutions, 3) electoral systems, and 4) women's machinery in the national bureaucracy. Through political parties she also explores the role of ideology. The four institutions that she defines and on which she focuses provide the opportunity for her to explore the role of civil society organizations as they interface with various state agencies.

There can be no doubt that Waylen has combined a feminist approach with an institutionalist approach. She has chosen a focus on women and she has situated herself in the research project. She is looking at the evolution of four distinct political institutions. Her conclusions focus on the conditions under which women advance politically. By incorporating both a feminist and an institutionalist approach, Waylen offers a rich account of the four institutions that she analyzes in the political realm. This study builds on Waylen's work but investigates its subject from a higher level of institutional abstraction.

Another important recent effort is Mona Lena Krook's and Fiona Mackay's edited volume, *Gender, Politics and Institutions: Towards a Feminist Institutionalism.* Writing in 2011, Krook and Mackay note that "there has been little dialogue between mainstream new institutional scholars and institutionally oriented, feminist political scientists."[46] They then trace the advancement of feminist and institutional scholarship moving through the periods when feminists viewed states as uniformly patriarchal (citing work by Kathy Ferguson and Anne Witz and Mike Savage) to those (R.W. Connell and Sylvia Walby and Sophie Watson) who analyze feminist engagements within the state and in opposition to the state, thus rejecting the notion of a monolithic state in favor of one that theoretically allows for change in gender relations.

Krook and Mackay also document the shift from feminist scholarship focused on the individual woman or a group of women actors to an institutional analysis that seeks to find the underlying structures of socially constructed gender relations. They observe that recent work focuses on how power relations are gendered through institutional processes, practices, and rules. Moreover, recent scholars have investigated electoral systems, political parties, and the interactions of male and female legislators and gender activists with regard to policy making and legal arrangements. Fewer have investigated the informal rules and norms that shape formal institutions. Still others have investigated gendered political discourse and its consequences for women. Thus Krook and Mackay note that "theorizing institutions in their multiple forms, as well as recognizing their gendered dimensions, presents considerable challenges."[47]

In the conclusion to Krook's and Mackay's important edited volume, Fiona Mackay asserts that "there is no detailed consensus in response to the question what is Feminist Institutionalism?" But Mackay identifies four themes common to both institutional and feminist theorists that arose from the case studies in the book:

1. Equal status should be given to informal and formal institutions and special attention given to their interactions.
2. Institutional creation, maintenance, and evolution require attention to agency as well as structure. However, better understandings of agency are necessary. Despite path dependency tendencies, understanding that institutions may both change and simultaneously create ways to endure must be acknowledged. Multiple small changes may provide a tipping point for significant change. Better concepts of change must be developed.
3. The relative roles of structure and agency must be developed. Political opportunity structures may arise but how one explains the agency of those who act at that moment must be questioned.
4. The role of ideas is key, even in the practice of assigning definitions. Who determines definitions is key to a gendered understanding of power.

Mackay then argues that any research agenda hoping to utilize the insights from both feminist and institutional scholars will map out the contours of their subject matter through those four key themes and offers a call for research.

But as we will demonstrate in this study, whether one utilizes the Krook, MacKay approach or endeavors to include even broader concerns that we have derived from the institutional and feminist literatures, creating a research design that captures all concerns is not easily accomplished. We believe that Morocco is an important North African case that provides both challenges and promise in the endeavor to apply a feminist, institutionalist framework, in order to understand the possibilities for gender change. While we acknowledge we are adding to the ranks of those who have already begun to query the intersections of institutional and feminist theorizing, we believe that a thick analysis of a single case that begs for an explanation, as does the Moroccan case, has merit and also may serve as a model for others who seek to investigate the changing institution of gender in other national settings.

In our study of Morocco, we consider structure and agency, time and resources, endogenous and exogenous factors, mobilization of ideas, interests, and values, as well as the role of discourse. We situate ourselves in relation to our subject matter and we rely on the voices and insights of the women we study. We do this to help men and women like ourselves learn something from the successful efforts of Moroccan women activists who accomplished both major and minor changes in their country's gender institution during the period of 1980 through 2010.

Notes

1. The phrase "From Burka to Boardroom: Gender on the Agenda" is used in an Economist Intelligence Unit (EIU) report that offers an overview of events 1946 to 2006. *Celebrating 60 Years . . . with a glimpse of the future* (London: Economist Intelligence Unit, Ltd, 2006), 7.

2. Wolfgang Streeck and Kathleen Thelen, *Beyond Continuity: Institutional Change in Advanced Political Economies* (Oxford: Oxford University Press, 2005).

3. For a detailed account of the evolution of methodological and theoretical approaches to the study of states and politics, see Stephen D. Krasner, "Approaches to the State: Alternative Conceptions and Historical Dynamics," *Comparative Politics* 16, no. 2 (January 1984), 223-246.

4. Krasner, "Approaches."

5. James G. March and Johan P. Olsen, "The New Institutionalism: Organizational Factors in Political Life," *American Political Science Review* 78, no. 3 (September 1984), 735.

6. Similarly, scholars who studied advanced industrial countries responded to the attacks on labor by Thatcher, Reagan, and Kohl, by analyzing the institutions of Western countries and studying the "varieties of capitalism."

7. Ester Boserup, *The Conditions of Agricultural Growth: The Economics of Agrarian Change Under Population Pressure* (Chicago: Aldine, 1965) and *Women's Role in Economic Development* (London: George Allen and Unwin, 1970).

8. For examples of alternative frameworks for clustering institutional methodologies, see Kathleen Thelen and Sven Steinmo, "Historical Institutionalism in Comparative Politics," in *Structuring Politics: Historical Institutionalism in Comparative Analysis*, ed. Sven Steinmo, Kathleen Thelen, and Frank Longstreth (Cambridge: Cambridge University Press, 1992); Sue E.S. Crawford and Elinor Ostrom, "A Grammar of Institutions," *American Political Science Review* 89, no. 3 (September 1995), 582-600; Paul DiMaggio, "The New Institutionalism: Avenues of Collaboration," *Journal of Institutional and Theoretical Economics* 154, no. 4 (December 1998), 696-705; Claus Offe, "Institutions' Role in the Distribution and Control of Social Power" (paper presented at the "Crafting and Operating Institutions" conference at Yale University, New Haven, April 11-13, 2003).

9. March and Olsen, "The New Institutionalism," 738-744.

10. March and Olsen, "The New Institutionalism," 747.

11. Peter Hall, "Historical Institutionalism in Rationalist and Sociological Perspective" in *Explaining Institutional Change: Ambiguity, Agency, Power*, ed. James Mahoney and Kathleen Thelen (Cambridge and New York: Cambridge University Press, 2009).

12. Streeck and Thelen, *Beyond Continuity*.

13. Robert Keohane, "Theory Talk #9: Robert Keohane on Institutions and the Need for Innovation in the Field," Theory Talks 2008, www.theory-talks.org/2008/05/theory-talk-9.html (accessed February 24, 2013).

14. Keohane, "Theory Talk #9."

15. James Mahoney and Kathleen Thelen, eds., *Explaining Institutional Change: Ambiguity, Agency, Power* (Cambridge and New York: Cambridge University Press, 2009), 4.

16. Stephan Skowronek, *Building a New American State* (Cambridge: Cambridge University Press, 1982); Karen Orren and Stephen Skowronek, "Regimes and Regime Building: Review of Literature on from the 1940s," *Political Science Quarterly* 113 (Winter 1998-99), 689-702/.

17. Peter B. Evans, Dietrich Rueschemeyer, and Theda Skocpol, *Bring the State Back In* (Cambridge and New York: Cambridge University Press, 1985).

18. Thelen and Steinmo, "Historical Institutionalism," 2.

19. Thelen and Steinmo, "Historical Institutionalism," 8.

20. Vivien Schmidt, "Discursive Institutionalism: The Explanatory Power of Ideas and Discourse," *Annual Review of Political Science* 11 (2008), 303-326.

21. B. Rothstein, *Social Traps and the Problem of Trust* (Cambridge: Cambridge University Press, 2005), quoted in Schmidt, "Discursive Institutionalism," 318.

22. Schmidt, "Discursive Institutionalism."

23. On Kenneth A. Shepsle's work see Thelen and Steinmo, "Historical Institutionalism," 5.

24. Stephen Katzenstein, *Between Power and Plenty* (Madison: University of Wisconsin, 1978), quoted in Thelen and Steinmo, "Historical Institutionalism," 6.

25. Kathleen Driscoll and Joan McFarland, "The Impact of a Feminist Perspective on Research Methodologies: Social Sciences," in *The Effects of Feminist Approaches on Research Methodologies*, ed. Winnie Tomm (Waterloo, Ontario: Wilfrid Laurier University Press, 1989).

26. Maria C. Lugones and Elizabeth V. Spelman, "Have We Got a Theory for You! Feminist Theory, Cultural Imperialism and the Demand for 'the Woman's Voice,'" in *Women and Values: Readings in Recent Feminist Philosophy*, ed. Marilyn Pearsall (Belmont: Wadsworth, 1986).

27. Sandra Harding, "Introduction: Is There a Feminist Method?" in *Feminism and Methodology*, ed. Sandra Harding (Bloomington and Indianapolis: Indiana University Press, 1987).

28. Margaret Schuler, ed., *Empowerment and the Law*, (Washington DC: OEF International, 1986).

29. Mary Margaret Fonow and Judith Cook, eds., *Beyond Methodology: Feminist Research as Lived Research* (Bloomington: Indiana University Press, 1991).

30. See Susan Bordo, *The Flight to Objectivity: Essays on Cartesianism and Culture* (Albany: SUNY Press, 1987); Sandra Harding, *The Science Question in Feminism* (Ithaca: Cornell University Press, 1986); Helen Longino, *Science as Social Knowledge* (Princeton: Princeton University Press, 1990); Lynn Hankinson Nelson, *Who Knows: From Quine to a Feminist Empiricism* (Philadelphia: Temple University Press, 1990).

31. Fonow and Cook, *Beyond Methodology*.

32. Marjorie Devault, "Talking and Listening from Women's Standpoint: Feminist Strategies for Interviewing and Analysis," *Social Problems* 37, no. 1 (Feb. 1990), 96-110.

33. Anne Opie, "Qualitative Research: Appropriation of the 'Other' and Empowerment," *Feminist Review*, no. 40 (Spring 1992): 52-69.

34. Bordo, *The Flight to Objectivity*.

35. Chandra Talpade Mohanty, "Under Western Eyes: Feminist Scholarship and Colonial Discourses" in *Third World Women and the Politics of Feminism*, ed. Chandra Talpade Mohanty, Ann Russo, and Lourdes Torres (Bloomington: Indiana University Press, 1991), 51-80.

36. See Donna Landry and Gerald Maclean, eds. "Introduction: Reading Spivak," *The Spivak Reader: Selected Works of Gayatri Chakravorty Spivak* (London and New York: Routledge, 1996), 1-14.

37. María de los Ángeles-Crummett, "Rural Women and Migration in Latin America," in *Rural Women and State Policy*, ed. Carmen Diana Deere and Magdalena León (Boulder, CO: Westview Press, 1987).

38. Thanh-Dam Truong, *Sex, Money, and Morality: Prostitution and Tourism in Southeast Asia* (London: Zed Press, 1990).

39. Cynthia Enloe, *The Morning After: Sexual Politics at the End of the Cold* War (Berkeley and Los Angeles: University of California Press, 1993).

40. See Eve Sandberg and Amber Ault, "Our Policies, Their Consequences: Zambian Women's Lives Under Structural Adjustment," in *Feminist Frontiers IV: Rethinking Sex, Gender and Society*, ed. Laurel Richardson, Verta Taylor, and Nancy Whittier (New York: McGraw-Hill 1997), 493-496.

41. Janet Seiz, "The Bargaining Approach and Feminist Methodology," *Review of Radical Political Economics* 23, nos. 1- 2 (1991), 22-29.

42. Mona Lena Krook and Fiona Mackay, eds., *Gender, Politics and Institutions: Towards a Feminist Institutionalism* (London and New York: Palgrave Macmillan, 2011).

43. Georgina Waylen, *Engendering Transitions Women's Mobilization, Institutions, and Gender Outcomes* (Oxford: Oxford University Press, 2007), 4.

44. Waylen, *Engendering Transitions,* 4.

45. Waylen, *Engendering Transitions*, 5.

46. Krook and Mackay, *Gender, Politics and Institutions,* 1.

47. Krook and Mackay, *Gender, Politics and Institutions,* 7.

Chapter Two
Creating Morocco's Post-Independence Gender Institution

One might anticipate conquest by a foreign power would change the institutions of a country like nothing else. A powerful foreign power would be expected to impose strong central authority on the territory it invaded and effectively impose new practices. France's first Resident General governed Morocco between 1912 and 1925; others succeeded him until Morocco achieved independence from France in 1956. Spain had captured only a few northern enclaves and Moroccan ports, so it was the French colonial officials who had the power to effect change across its protectorate, the bulk of Moroccan territory.

Therefore, one might expect that progressive changes in the post-world war era of Morocco's gender practices would be attributed to the introduction of new gender initiatives by the French. Historically, however, it was not the French conquest but rather the Moroccan leaders who resisted French colonialism, including political activists, King Mohamed V, and Morocco's Islamic leaders, who initiated widespread changes to Morocco's gender practices and fashioned the gender institution within Morocco following the country's independence.

During the French protectorate (1912-1956), Morocco's nationalist political party leaders rejected the French authorities' policies, including those concerning Moroccan women. The nationalists argued for greater changes for women as part of their program of modernization for their country. Moroccan King Mohammed V's worldview, especially when it came to his daughter and her life possibilities, also encouraged changes in Morocco's gender institutions. Most of all, Morocco's religious leaders placed their stamp upon post-independence Morocco's gender institution.

French Colonialism and Moroccan Gender Issues

The French did not conquer a unified nation of Moroccans, nor were they particularly interested in attempting to unify Morocco, because it was far less strategic for French interests than, for example, Algeria, which many French officials hoped to incorporate into France itself. The French (and their Spanish allies who captured some coastal parts and small cities of the country) were mainly interested in maintaining their status in Morocco, not expending resources to unify it.

The goal of governance under French rule without unifying the country was challenged when resistance to both Sultan Yusef and the French colonials resulted in an uprising led by Berber leader Abd el-Krim, who hoped to create an independent Berber state in the Rif Mountains. France and Spain joined together to defeat the resistance in 1925, then moved the country's capital to Rabat where it was more protected from rebellious Arabs and Berbers and from Morocco's anti-Western Islamic leaders. The French militarily pacified the resisters and, hoping to avoid further resistance, moved to validate the Berbers' right to self government locally and guarantee the independence of their customary tribunals. The French also recognized that pockets of independence across Morocco weakened the Sultan's claim to governing a unified Morocco under his rule.

The Berber decree of 1930, which guaranteed Berber tribal independence from the Sultan and most central government officials, so alarmed Arab Islamic nationalists that, as Clifford Geertz noted, committees to save the Berbers as Islamic citizens and preserve a unified Morocco under an Arab Muslim Sultan were established outside Morocco.[1] Additionally, Arab Islamists across the Middle East included prayers for the reincorporation of Berbers into Morocco's Arab fold in their Friday worship.[2] These decrees were especially important in assisting Moroccans studying in France who later would become national party activists, such as Mohammed al-Fassi, Ahmed Balafrej, and Mohammed El-Ouezzani, to come together to work on behalf of Moroccan nationalism.[3]

The Berber decrees, with their recognition of Berber family courts and legitimation of the treatment of Berber women, became an important and strategic issue for Morocco's new political party leaders. Moroccan national debates now included the matter of the control of customary family laws by competing Berber and Islamic judicial councils.

Prior to the French invasion, Moroccan gender customs were disparate, depending on clan, tribe, religion, and exposure to ideas outside of a given region.[4] But not only gender practices in Morocco lacked uniformity, Morocco's political formation itself lacked uniformity. Some scholars have explained the political formation of pre-colonial Morocco as competing federated tribes of varying degrees of strength resisting incorporation into a national state that was controlled by the Sultan and the makhzen (central government bureaucrats and court favorites) around the Sultan.[5] During the pre-colonial period, in response to this resistance, the Sultan created a zawia, a religious institution, to represent him as a religious authority and to introduce Islamic traditions into daily life to undermine traditional tribal practices while offering the Sultanate and Islam as unifying symbols.[6] It should be noted, however, that tribal practices varied from tribe to tribe. Moreover, sometimes an intermediary political leader emerged from one tribe and managed to impose his leadership across a small region, uniting congruent tribes to oppose the (central) Sultan or other power rivals. When the French arrived, they looked for such regional leaders to support, thereby deepening the fissures in Morocco's body politic. Thus, no strong central authority managed Morocco's politics, economics, or customary practices, including gender practices, prior to independence.

One powerful resource for Morocco's monarch when dealing with resistant clans has always been that he traces his lineage to Mohamed the Prophet and is given the title, "Commander of the Faithful." Even politically rebellious Berber clans and others historically have recognized the King's religious authority, if not his political claims. Although Berbers and Arabs are linguistically differentiated (but not all Berber's speak the same dialect), they have all undergone Islamic conquest to differing degrees, depending on geography and historic factors, and those living within Morocco's borders generally remained outside the reach of the Ottoman empire. Thus, in their early battles for independence, Morocco's King and Moroccan nationalist political party leaders found common cause in promoting an Islamic-based Moroccan government against which French practices could be rejected and in which linguistically different Berbers could be subsumed. It should also be noted that when the nationalist party Istiqlal was formed in late 1943 and delivered its independence manifesto to the French on January 11, 1944, the Sultan was a supportive ally, despite the hopes by some of Istiqlal's younger, more militant leaders for a post-colonial party-based political system with little role for any King. Even though the King, his makhzen, and the nationalist party leaders shared common independence goals, the French were able to drive wedges between the King and the leadership and the rank and file of Morocco's new independence political parties.

In gender issues, as with other matters, new ideas clashed with the traditional practices as young Moroccans who mostly lived in households that practiced traditional and religious customs came into contact with Europeans, especially European women as they lived their daily lives with relative independence. Elite Moroccan youth encountered debates about equality and human rights while acquiring French education, thus a small subsector of Morocco's elites developed new views concerning the unveiling of women, the practice of arranged marriages, the education of women, the nature of women's work, etc. But these new ideas also came from communications among Arab intellectuals resisting colonialism across the Middle East. Arab nationalists sought modernization for their citizens as well as independence for their states.

French disinterest in a united Morocco or in modernizing the country was evident in the way that the French allowed four legal structures to simultaneously exist in Morocco during the period of the French Protectorate. These included the French legal structure in which French administrators and justices governed; the Islamic legal structure in which Islamic religious leaders governed through Sharifian courts; the Berber legal structures in which Berber customary laws were enforced through tribal authorities; and a Jewish legal system in which Jewish religious leaders imposed their traditional customs and practices on women.[7] While the French argued this reflected enlightened indirect rule, nationalists saw such practices as promoting a "divide and conquer" program designed to weaken Morocco's king and nationalist leaders. Notably, French attitudes toward independent Jewish determinations changed when the Nazis and their collaborators of Vichy, France, launched anti-Jewish policies across North

Africa. Some Moroccan nationalist politicians aligned themselves with the Nazis' attacks on Moroccan Jews, but the Sultan provided Jews with protection, arguing that the Moroccan Jewish community would be protected in accordance with Islamic dictates to protect minority religions within an Islamic community.

At the time of the French occupation, Morocco's gender practices were an amalgam of different customs, procedures, and power differentials among men and women according to whether the practitioners were rural, urban, educated, Berber, Arab, Jewish, or whether their affairs were overseen by a French court or another judicial body. Some commonalities for women across Morocco did exist, however. Moroccans by and large lived at that time in a pre-industrial country in which clan and kinship played an important role in both urban and rural communities.

For most individuals living in a pre-industrial society anywhere and during any time period, the most important resources are their kinship and clan ties. Kinship has obligations, but it also promises support in times of need. To fully understand the patriarchal institutions that mainly constrain women, though also some men, it is important to understand pre-industrial kinship obligations, especially as they are juxtaposed to oppressive relations within an industrial society.

For example, theorists ranging from Vladimir Lenin to Paulo Freire have argued that individual learning that leads to recognition of one's place in society, one's sense of self relative to others, is an important prerequisite to action and rebellion. Individual empowerment continues through the process of conscientization as one learns through both reflection and action. Parpart, Rai, and Staudt have argued that Freire's work was an important source for expanding the concept of "empowerment of the marginalized" by social activists in Southern countries in the 1990s, especially by women.[8] Empowerment of the marginalized in an oppressive situation is constrained in different ways in different contexts as Parpart, Rai, and Staudt note.

However, the Morocco case demonstrates that people oppressed in pre-industrial kinship relations differ in important ways from those undergoing conscientization of class and labor in an industrial or semi-industrial setting. In a class/labor situation, one's allies are those with whom one is most familiar, individuals in one's family and community. The enemy (owner or manager) generally (though of course not always) is of another family, clan, or community.

A woman who might yearn for a different set of choices than those dictated by the customs proscribed by her family and clan in a pre-industrial setting fears being ostracized from kin, one's social safety net, and from the people with whom an individual's life, love, and fate are most entwined. Such fear is a powerful deterrent to challenging the household patriarchal system. In the pre-industrial setting, one's closest natural allies are the targets of one's activism if one attempts to rebel. That most women in pre-industrial communities lack the agency to rebel should not be surprising.

In pre-industrial, colonial Morocco, traditional practices for families (whether Arab, Berber, or Jewish) included differential power relations among men and women. Women's roles and rights (where any rights existed) were always secondary to those of men in all three societies. Individual agency by women was mostly forbidden. Agency, the strategic actions of the participants in any institution, was recognized as being a male prerogative. Most women could not move about or take on tasks that a father, brother, husband, or son did not permit. In colonial Morocco, each woman was the property of some male during every period of her life. Islamic and Jewish laws, as well as Berber practices, sustained this lack of political decision making agency for women.

In addition to agency, the discursive activities that theorists have come to recognize are so important to the evolution or maintenance of an institution were also beyond the reach of most women during Morocco's colonial period. The ability to speak and write on a wide variety of subjects and to put forward ideas, to offer context, and take part in national dialogues were beyond the abilities of most Moroccan women. The educational goals for the majority of Moroccan women did not allow them to develop the skill sets necessary for undertaking effective discursive activities.

Women's lack of discursive activities and conscientization were not the only elements preventing solidarity over gender practices among women at the subaltern level during this period. Public scrutiny discouraged crossing lines between social groups such as clan, Arab, Berber, Jew, and French colonial, to examine situations and contexts for gender experience. Solidarity across the lines of clan, religion, and nationality was difficult to imagine, let alone achieve, even for men; for women it appeared quite impossible. A woman would have little hope of finding solidarity from others if she hoped to confront the father, brother, and husband in her own home, particularly when those fathers, husbands, and brothers helped to provide food and shelter.

Just as agency and discursive activities were curtailed for Moroccan women prior to independence, so too was their ability to engage with and challenge or change the rules through the informal and formal practices that supported discriminatory gender institutional practices. Decision making practices that yielded rule making for the members of communities were reserved for men, remaining generally beyond Moroccan women's reach. While the rare woman managed to move the boundaries that confined most women, she often did so with a supportive father, husband, or brother. Should her trespass of boundaries be challenged, the judicial courts and the court of public opinion in every community would find against her.

Finally, resources and allies were difficult for Moroccan women to obtain. According to Islamic law, a man's inheritance far outstripped anything allowed to a woman. According to most Berber tribal laws, a woman herself is inherited as part of a man's estate by other men. As Mounira Charrad reminds us, Berber practices permit a man who inherits a woman to claim her previous bride price and also to give her away to another man of his choice in return for a bride price or other agreement.[9] However if a woman is repudiated or widowed and has no means by which to support herself, her male kinsmen are obligated to provide some support according to both Islamic and Berber practices. But this support, often meager, will hardly allow her enough to accrue resources. Moreover, since few Moroccan women engaged in business and political activities, most lacked valuable assets with which to negotiate with Moroccan men. Thus, it was difficult for Moroccan women to secure allies on the basis of trading resources or on the basis of claiming resources.

We can see then that, although Moroccan women were constrained by the differing particulars of their various communities, until they were able to achieve some agency, undertake discursive activities, engage with the formal and informal means for changing societal rules, and have access to resources and allies, women in all Moroccan communities could little influence the gender practices that constrained them and appeared to be timeless. Under French administration, Moroccan women did not even face common constraints. It would be post-independence Morocco that would create an institution of gender for Moroccan women with commonalities in the areas of agency, discursive activities, formal and informal means for changing social, political and economic rules, and also availability of resources.

The means by which Moroccan women, over time, succeeded in achieving some power in these four arenas informs our understanding of how they were able to alter Morocco's gender institution. To appreciate the stunning accomplishments of those who came to be Morocco's women leaders striving to alter Morocco's gender institution in the 1980s, it is instructive to investigate, if only briefly, the context from which their work emerged. This includes the impact of the struggle for Moroccan independence from the French colonial government, because the nationalist struggle helped expand Moroccan women's access, activities, resources, and agency.

Yet we must be careful in such an endeavor. Postcolonial scholars such as Aijaz Ahmad and Ella Shohat urge us to guard against using the colonial period of any country as the primary marker of time when analyzing change in late industrializing countries that were occupied by colonial powers.[10] This is good advice and in the Moroccan case, our account of the lack of national unity before, during, and for a period after colonialism is in keeping with this caveat. So, too is our account of how colonization was differentially experienced by Moroccan women and men. But in the Morocco case, the struggle against French colonialism by Moroccan nationalists did assist in bringing issues of gender and gender institutional practices into Morocco's national political debates. As independence was debated, it offered an important opportunity for women and men to rethink their positions on gender practices in their communities. For many, it was French practices during the colonial period that helped spark a re-examination of the role of women in Morocco.

Acquiring a modern education in which rational debate, problem solving, and understanding the history that has produced the social formation in which one lives plays an important role in providing the skill sets necessary for discursive activities. Initially, the first schools created by the French leadership for Moroccan women were Berber schools designed to teach and maintain traditional handicrafts that, the French believed, would offer economic advancement to a woman and simultaneously reinforce traditional customs so as not to disrupt Moroccan "traditional society" with demands for nationalism and modernization.[11] These schools also included lessons on hygiene. But despite the wishes of the French teachers and French officials, Berber women students soon asked for instruction in handicrafts with European designs, not simply traditional patterns.[12] French schools did not expand their curricular offerings for women until the mid 1940s, when some Moroccan families and the royal court began demanding a more modern curriculum for girl students.[13]

What Moroccan women were to be taught became a politicized question within the fabric of Morocco's struggle for independence against the French. The debate saw educated Moroccan women taking part by publishing in nationalist papers using pseudonyms to hide their sex.[14] Other educated Moroccan women joined independence parties and even tried to influence the trade unions with which they or their family members were affiliated to support improved working conditions for Moroccan women.

Morocco's Sultan, Mohamed V, was a known supporter of new gender practices for women. Yet the Monarch's actions were laced with contradictions. On the one hand, the Monarch had two wives and forty-one concubines.[15] He liked expensive cars and sent his sons to French schools, but not his daughters. His fondness for having women at his disposal was evident when France forced the Sultan into exile in 1953 with his two wives and one concubine, but later allowed 26 more women to join him in exile "with all honors due to his rank."[16]

Yet the Sultan's own daughter was offered to the public as being an independent woman who thought for herself. Lalla (Lady) Aisha never wore a veil; she posited that women were free to wear them but they also had the right to take them off.[17] At age 16, in 1946, her father, the Sultan, arranged for her to stand without a veil to offer a public speech on the rights of women, which had been written for the Princess to present. She also was allowed to be seen in public wearing a bathing suit, a shocking event for many Moroccans. Following her first historic speech, Aisha soon was making many speeches to urge female emancipation on topics that she decided to support. Lalla Aisha was educated by French governesses, and by age twenty-five she wore lipstick and blue jeans and listened to the American pop star, Frankie Avalon.[18] Additionally, she drove her own car.[19]

Such demonstrations of modernity and female freedom were used prior to independence by the French Resident General to whip up anger against the Sultan and to justify the Sultan's exile in the eyes of Islamic and Berber Moroccans who supported traditional notions of modesty for women. But it is reported that in 1956, when the Sultan returned to his country (as King Mohammed V) to govern an independent Morocco, he was greeted by hundreds of unveiled women who demanded the right to vote, improved national education, and the right to join unions. The story of how these remarkable women came together to make such a political statement is one of many Moroccan women's stories about which little is known. Yet these women were but a fraction of the tens of thousands of Moroccans who greeted their King and what moved most Moroccans in their greetings was independence from the French.

What is known is that women who were active in Morocco's early political parties in the 1940s began to create women's branches of their parties. Sisters of Purity was the first and most famous. During the movement for independence, issues of nationalism were the priority of all party members but many women activists for independence hoped that following independence, women's issues would also be taken up by their party leaders as part of any new national agenda. As we discuss in later chapters of this study, this did not happen and it took until the 1970s for leading party women to initiate efforts to bring women's issues onto party agendas in the hope that they could be brought to national attention.

A critical milestone cited in almost every work on gender issues in Morocco notes that Malika al-Fassi, a relative of an important male leader of Istiqlal, was included in the signing of Istiqlal's Manifesto of Independence from France. The gesture was seen as political symbolism, as a concrete demonstration of the intent of Istiqlal to allow women to participate in the public sphere, and because Malika al-Fassi had earned the right through her own independence resistance. But as it would later be noted, even this emphasis on women's participation still focused on independence, not on changing gender practices. Additionally, the much cited and important work of Zakya Daoud, who published on the late colonial period in the early 1990s, noted that women activists were vitally involved in the independence movement and often took great risks in carrying everything from weapons, cash resources, and communications throughout French occupied Morocco.[20] Independence, not gender change, was the critical issue for all Moroccans during the period of the French Protectorate.

In the 1940s, in addition to advocating for more education and the removal of the veil, some women dared to argue in public that their husbands needed to treat their wives better.[21] These women had the support of male allies who argued for nationalism and modernity and against French colonial practices. Additionally, the advocacy of Arab women in other countries encouraged Moroccan male allies to support change in gender practices and to allow for brave Moroccan women to advocate publicly.

One of the most famous role models for Arab women across the Middle East and North Africa who organized to remove many of the restrictions of traditional and religious gender practices was Egyptian women's advocate, Huda Shaarawi. Shaarawi was born in 1879 and spent time as a child in a harem.[22] She was the daughter of a wealthy provincial administrator, however, and so had been educated at home like many Egyptian women of her family's standing.[23] She resisted an arranged marriage but under pressure acquiesced.[24] Over time, with a supportive husband who organized for nationalism, she devoted her energies to setting up public lectures and discussions of interest to women so they could leave their homes and come together to share perspectives and learn from one another. She successfully found financial backing from Egypt's princesses to establish a women's welfare society to provide a social safety net for poor women. In 1910 Shaarawi opened a girls' school with a curriculum constructed of many of the academic subjects that boys studied, not just skills thought to be needed by young women.[25]

In Egypt, many women left their homes and their harems to demonstrate publicly against British colonialism, and Shaarawi was one of the leaders of the 1919 Egyptian women's demonstration against British rule.[26] Egypt obtained independence from Britain (though Britain retained the right to maintain British troops in Egypt through 1956) in 1922, the same year Shaarawi's husband died. Like other Egyptian women who had allied with nationalist men to argue for independence and women's rights, Shaarawi had to have been disappointed with Egypt's new constitution, which denied women the right to vote as well as with the male nationalist allies who largely ignored the concerns of women once men were assigned roles in the new government.[27]

Shaarawi's most famous action occurred at this time in a Cairo Railway station. In 1923, Shaarawi attended an international women's conference, returned to Egypt and stunned those who came to meet her (as well as everyone else in the Cairo train station) by removing her veil. Some of the women who had come to greet her were moved to take off their veils as well in a public display of defiance and solidarity. Together with other Egyptian women, Shaarawi founded the Egyptian Feminist Union and served as its President, advocating for reforms in the gender practices that constrained women. In 1927, these Egyptian women reformers founded a secondary school for girls. The Egyptian women advocated domestically and networked internationally at conferences. The All-Arab Federation of Women was founded by Shaarawi in 1944, and she was active in this organization until her death in 1947.

Shaarawi was working in a tradition begun by Egyptian women writers who previously had advocated for change through journalism and salons. Margot Badran's account of pre-colonial Egyptian women's education, their writing, and their publications during the colonial period offers important insight as to how women, especially those in the fields of education and health, began analyzing and questioning their restraints in the late 1860s.[28]

However much Shaarawi's actions served as a role model for Arab women across the Middle East and North Africa, Moroccan women's experience of French colonialism did not mirror that of Egyptian women who labored under British colonialism, and not even all Moroccan women experienced French colonization in the same way. The work of Edward Said, Leila Abouzeid, and Salah Moukhlis reminds us that women in Morocco differentially experienced colonialism and also that colonialism was only one institution that oppressed women in Morocco and elsewhere.[29] Jonathan Wyrtzen's research demonstrates that the conditions of different groups of Moroccan women varied and were not easily categorized during the French Protectorate. For example, Wyrtzen reports that Berber women who lived mainly in rural areas were often unveiled and their husbands tended to be monogamous, while Arab women, who tended to live in cities, had to have their modesty safeguarded and so wore the veil. The husbands of those women commonly had several wives.[30] Yet like their Islamic counterparts, Berber women lacked adequate inheritance rights, rarely enjoyed property rights, had no or little say in arranged marriages. There was no established minimum age for marriage and different communities practiced child marriage at different ages. The commonality for Moroccan women was that none had the right to divorce; however, their husbands could easily renounce them. Generally, women in Morocco experienced the constraints of patriarchy differently according to their clan, tribe, and family's political affiliation.

Moreover, in addition to learning about women in other countries advocating to improve the status of women, global events promoted hope for nationalists and the many Moroccan women who saw their struggle tied to the nationalist struggle and believed that independence would usher in a new era for women. For example, the Atlantic Charter (August 1941) promulgated by Roosevelt and Churchill offered new means by which Morocco's elites claimed rights to self governance and practices of political modernization, with its pronouncement of respect for the right of people to choose their own form of government and its support for the principle that people have the right to live out their lives in freedom from want and fear. It also allowed women to claim they should have the right to live without fear of others or fear of what others think.

Another source of argument for improving the status of women in Morocco were the individually remarkable women in Morocco's past who had worked to advance women and who themselves had achieved a high degree of education. The oft noted historical example in the eleventh century was Fatima Al Fihria who founded a university, Al Karawayin, in the imperial city of Fez.

The leadership of Morocco's independence political party (Istiqlal) is reported to have argued not only for the country's independence but also to have taken up the call for empowering Moroccan women in the face of French efforts to keep women in traditional roles. But as I.W. Zartman has argued, Morocco's nationalists "were unable to generate power within the colonial system" so the advancement of the status of women made little progress during French occupation.[31]

Additionally, Zartman's account of this period reports that in the end, in order to prevent the French from dividing the nationalist activists, the nationalists had to "override divergent interests" and focus primarily on independence from France as their primary goal even as the movement was rooted in specific social groups through its appeal to those groups.[32] Zartman notes the nationalist movement drew from Berber military forces, workers, students, the unemployed, new middle class intellectuals, youth, civil servants, the makhzen, the bourgeoisie, and from those who had been deported or forced into exile. Zartman also argues that when the French deposed Morocco's sultan, they in effect crowned him as the major resister to French rule. When that symbolic view was coupled with the Sultan's Moroccan dynastic credentials, his religious role as a descendent of Mohamed, and his gestures to be a modernizing monarch, the sultan was assured support among the vast majority of Moroccans, many who related directly to their king and not to any independence party leadership.[33]

Thus with hindsight, we can see that women's issues may have been important to Moroccan women and to some of their male allies, but as the post-colonial period demonstrates, for many, these issues were raised as a strategy for confronting the French. The bloody attacks by French colonialists and their French government and military allies against the Moroccan independence activists and innocent citizens made independence the foremost concern of all Moroccans. For the minority who dreamed about an independent Moroccan state and considered issues of gender, sadly, once independence was achieved, Moroccan women and their male allies would be deeply disappointed.

By the time the disgraced French collaborator government was defeated along with its Nazi backers, the post-World War II Moroccan royal family, in selected breaks with Morocco's traditional gender roles, was allowing a few royal women the opportunity to travel to Europe, obtain a European education, and speak in public politically. Though their numbers were few, the symbolism of their activities was important for the young women who hoped for changes in their lives or at least in the lives of their daughters. Unfortunately, permitting these activities for Royals, along with allowing royal women to establish charity foundations, regardless of the fine work accomplished by these foundations, was about all that Mohammed V's administration would accomplish for women. There were occasional visits by royal women to international conferences for women, and although undoubtedly individuals such as Princess Aisha truly desired change for all Moroccans, little was accomplished.

After World War II and with the death of Roosevelt, it took until 1956 before Morocco achieved its independence from France. During this time, great mistrust deepened among the factions of the independence activists and between the activists and those at court with King Mohammed V, especially his son, Prince Moulay Hassan. While Moroccans debated the role of the political parties and the role of the monarchy as candidates campaigned for the country's first announced local elections, the Monarchy cancelled the elections and seized power for itself in May 1960 in the week prior to the scheduled election. King Mohamed V declared himself to be Morocco's Prime Minister and staffed his cabinet with supporters of the royal family. He appointed Prince Moulay Hassan as Morocco's Vice President.

When Mohammed V died the following year, in February 1961, Prince Hassan ascended to the throne. Morocco's post-independence years, like those during the French protectorate, included bitter, violent clashes by the police and military who now reported to King Hassan as they battled Morocco's legal democratic political activists. Issues of gender were hardly raised. The personal security of activists and the political stakes for the country—of political structure and economic policies—took precedence. But gender, like politics and economics, is all pervasive and affects the daily lives of all peoples, even if there are those who do not recognize the critical impact of gender practices. Moroccan activists were a product of their time and reacted to the vicious oppression waged against them by King Hassan. Gender practices to Moroccans in the

1950s through the beginning of the 1970s seemed to be of secondary importance to the struggle with their King for democracy and human rights. Yet while gender issues garnered little urgency during this period, Morocco's institution of gender was being crafted.

To understand the gender practices and the institution of gender that emerged in Morocco after independence, we turn now to the four arenas of a gender institution that we identified in Chapter One. We identify the independent variables relevant to Morocco in each of these four components that comprise Morocco's gender institution, which Moroccan women activists would confront in the 1980s as they began to find the means by which to influence the gender institution that they abhorred. As Marvine Howe so aptly described the status of women in Morocco at this time, "On the eve of independence, women were practically invisible."[34]

Morocco's Gender Institution

The Agency of Moroccan Women

Agency for Moroccan women was largely dependent on father, husband, brother, and later, son. In the years after independence, elderly women rarely left the house. Younger women left their houses to walk to visit friends, to shop, and in some instances go to work. All women were expected to be in their homes with their family at the end of the day and to assist in providing the evening meal. Moroccan women did not have freedom of movement to travel about the city at night unless they were in the company of their father, husbands, or brother. Older women who were divorced by their husbands had to return to their original family households.

Agency for women in the public sphere came only in families of left party leaders and democrats calling for change who allowed their female relatives to attend meetings. In these cases, agency for women rarely took the form of women arguing strategy, but rather consisted of women going to the meetings and participating in the rallies or activities determined by their male relatives in conversation with other men in their organizations. When Hassan II's police attacked the activists, however, they did not ignore the women, but captured them along with men and kept them in prisons without trial for decades. Istiqlal, in which a women's sub-organization had been organized, offered one of the few venues where women could talk politics, but largely with other women, mostly taking direction from Istiqlal's male membership. The Moroccan women displayed personal bravery for the democratic cause, demonstrating their agency capacity, but that did not make them full participants when strategies or tactics were debated.

However, as we discuss below, women's agency slowly began to expand and allowed women to have social contact with others on the way to work or school and afterwards when shopping or eating in a restaurant.

The Changing Rules (Informal and Formal), Structures of Action, and Paths Within Institutions That, In Part, Constitute Morocco's Gender Institution

After independence was achieved, women were excluded from structures and venues where government decisions were made that would affect all Moroccans, including women. King Hassan, like his father Mohamed V, allowed royal women to operate foundations for charitable work, but not to take part in government decision-making. There were women, however, who due to their performance in their educational institutions were employed as civil servants in the multitude of new state agencies that the new independence government had to create but for which there were not many qualified candidates. Even they were not assigned to important decision-making positions.

Education and its institutions were the focus of attention by Moroccan women who hoped to improve the status of women in Moroccan society. In independent Morocco as new schools opened across the country, Moroccan girls were enrolled at twice their numbers during the colonial period.[35] This meant that a new generation of Moroccan women came of age walking with their friends unveiled through the streets of mostly urban Moroccan cities to and from school. It was an easy step from that activity to stop to do some shopping for their mothers or themselves on their way home. These informal outings expanded the public space in which Moroccan women became accustomed to functioning and Moroccan men became accustomed to seeing women. Educating women had been a publicly declared goal of both the nationalist political party activists and King Mohammed V during the independence movement, and, while the independence male leadership did little to advance women's progress in many realms, they did support educational initiatives targeting women.

In Morocco, as in any other country in the world, education is empowering. Young Moroccan women began to assume that they would find jobs outside the home, that their school work would be put to good use, and just perhaps they would secure important resources for the family household. Instead Moroccan women were mainly encouraged to pursue careers in what were viewed as arenas suitable for women, working as nurses, receptionists, etc.[36] Even such a prominent woman in the independence movement as Malika al-Fassi, the only woman to sign Istiqlal's Declaration of Independence presented to the French in January 1944, was not offered a job in the independent Moroccan government.

Malika al-Fassi had carried out organizational work and published articles on women in the late 1930s under pseudonyms. Like other women, Malika al-Fassi had risked her life for the movement, first along with her husband as an early organizer, then carrying sensitive communications to areas where Istiqlal men dared not travel in order to keep the branches of the movement in contact with one another.[37] None of those activities won her a position in the post-independence government.

The number of women who lost their lives in the independence movement, at rallies, for organizational activities, or from the brutality of the prisons, is not known. Only anecdotal accounts offer witness that women, like men, gave their lives for the cause. After independence, Malika al-Fassi was relegated to a sphere thought appropriate for women. Married to Mohamed al-Fassi, the Istiqlal leader who became Minister of Education, she continued to teach at literacy centers in various Moroccan villages that she had helped to found under the protectorate and additionally she helped to found an association dedicated to improving literacy.[38] She did not, however, abandon her commitment to improving the lives of Moroccan women, those with disabilities, or those who suffered from poverty. In 1960, before many nonprofit organizations existed in Morocco, Malika al-Fassi co-founded Equality, or al-Moussat, which assisted orphans, people with disabilities, people in economic need and those with chronic illness.[39]

The major institution that would affect Moroccan women would not be the country's educational institutions, but rather the judiciary acting in accordance with Morocco's Islamic codes. Following independence, Mohamed V sought to unify the judicial system under control by the Palace. This new system was to reflect Islamic practices; the King claimed his legitimacy from Islam and many Islamic leaders also had been nationalist leaders. The new system was to establish a national system of law and undermine any local Berber customs that the French had promoted in hopes of keeping the nation divided.

To lead the effort to unify Morocco's judiciary code based on Islam, King Mohammed V chose Allal al-Fassi who was both a nationalist leader (a leader within the party Istiqlal) and also a nationally recognized religious figure in Morocco. Malika Zeghal's scholarship helps us to understand the choice of Allal al-Fassi by Mohammed V, and also al-Fassi's decision to create a judicial code based more on orthodox Islam than on Moroccan reformist notions of Islamic practices, including the reforms for women that he himself at times had proposed. Zeghal's work demonstrates that Morocco's religious leaders during the colonial period did not have the standing that Islamic leaders had in other Arab countries because Morocco's Islamic leaders arose from charisma and activism, rather than through the ranks of an organized single center of national religious learning that existed in other Islamic countries. Additionally, there were various Islamic tendencies in colonial Morocco, so the religious community did not speak with one voice.

One leading figure in Morocco had attended a major center of Islamic learning, had been a nationalist militant, had been born into a well known urban family, and had published on both independence and Islam in national venues. That individual was Allal al-Fassi. Like the King, al-Fassi had been exiled and so had earned respect in many quarters. Many saw him as a charismatic leader who could claim national power. Some were not surprised, even if they were disappointed, when the King chose not to include al-Fassi in the first post-independence government, but instead chose a Berber cleric from the Istiqlal party for the role of Minister of Religious Affairs, which many had thought al-Fassi would secure if he were not Morocco's first Prime Minister.[40] This choice appeared to have secondary effects beyond keeping a major national rival at bay. It seemed to be a demonstration that the King would not oppose Berbers, but he would rule in accordance with Islamic practices and that there were other leading religious and national leaders besides al-Fassi who could serve the nation. This is not to suggest that Berber practices were not within the practices of Islam, they were. But rather different regions of Berber communities incorporated different local customs and integrated them with the practice of Islam, yielding religious practices that were known as different by Moroccans of regions.

Of central importance to this study and to the post-independence institution of gender in Morocco was the King's decision to task al-Fassi with the presidency of the commission that in 1957 and 1958 codified shari'a law in Morocco. In that process, according to Zeghal, the intensity of anti-colonial ideas took precedence over issues of equality for women.[41] Because the French Berber Decree of 1930 and modernizing reforms were seen as efforts to weaken Islamic practice, al-Fassi and his committee of ten men opted for an orthodox interpretation of Islamic law and claimed it should be extended to the entire legal system, not just the legal doctrines governing family practices.[42] The throne accepted the commission's recommendations on family practice and that became an arena jealously guarded by the Islamic religious leaders in Morocco. The Palace, however, retained control of mosques and religious endowments, rather than give it to an independent religious body, and national laws were vested in the parliament, although the Palace acted according to its own rules as the King retained much political power.[43]

In light of the King's need to keep Islamic community support even as the monarchy tried to limit the power of the political parties, it is easy to see how Mohammed V might have been willing to sacrifice principles of women's equality in return for the ability to govern a newly united nation of Morocco. Zakia Salime's summation is fitting—the code of family law was the means by which "the monarchy inscribed the meanings of national identity and state sovereignty" as well as "affirmed the national unity of the Arabs and Amazigh (Berber) populations."[44] Daniel Zisenwine, however, argues that Istiqlal and its leaders, such as al-Fassi as well as other independence figures, never indicated that they would deviate from Moroccan social norms even during the independence struggle; party members merely reached out to various constituencies that were making their voices and concerns heard and the King reached out to all sectors of Moroccan society.[45]

The struggle over how Morocco's schools might be modernized to move beyond a religious curriculum also may have inclined the Monarch to allow the Islamic community control of at least family matters. For example, the University of Rabat was founded in 1957 and it adopted a secular curriculum. Schools nationally adopted a Moroccan-centric curriculum. In these two decisions, the Islamic religious leaders were seen to have suffered a setback to their goals.

What is clear in the post independence period is that women's rights were restricted in accordance with orthodox Islamic practices as the centralizing monarchy and its rivals fought other battles. The Islamic practices toward women codified in the family legal code included formal and informal practices and became part of the fabric of Morocco's gender institution.

The 297 articles of the Moudawana (family code of law) that al-Fassi and his colleagues released over 1957 to 1958 demonstrate that the structures of action for women were limited and that the male commissioners who proscribed the boundaries of women's lives were rooted in Morocco's Maliki Islamic law. Even al-Fassi, who in publications in 1952 had argued at least for the reform of polygamy, did not include such a reform in the product of the post-independence commission.[46] Laurie Brand and Mounira Charrad each provide excellent itemizations of the boundaries that the national code of family law of Morocco's gender institution set for women.[47] A few illustrative examples are: Women always have male tutors. A woman may not enter into a marriage contract on her own. Girls the age of 15 may be married off (this was considered a modern approach as orthodox Islam noted the onset of puberty was the minimum requirement for girls to marry).[48] Marriage was a private act and so not subject to national administration.[49] A man could divorce a woman simply by renouncing her according to Maliki law and if the repudiation was witnessed by two individuals who wrote it up for the courts, it would be upheld so that the husband could give the wife some compensation and then legally divorce her.[50] Additionally, a man could take more than one wife if he treated them justly. When a man died, a male heir would receive twice as much as a female heir.[51] Women and children were barred from certain work to protect them.[52] In general, except for traveling to and from work or school, women were not to be viewed in public places where they were not escorted by a male relative or family designated friend. It would have been a shameful act in most households for a woman to leave her house to go out on her own to a meeting.

Yet women's formal avenues for women's activities improved in the new independent state. As Laurie Brand has noted, every post colonial constitution in Morocco grants women the right to vote and states that women are equal to men despite the judicial status of Moroccan women as minors—a status that requires them to have a male tutor for every aspect of their lives.[53] In Morocco's gender institution following independence, no women were elected to office, and few worked in policy decision making positions within the government, but it would be in this arena, over time, particularly during the reign of Mohamed VI and the beginning of the twenty-first century, that the electoral arena and government agencies would offer greater opportunities for Moroccan women.

In the post independence era in the informal sector of not for profits (or in non governmental organizations as they are known in most of the world), a small number of Moroccan women began to play a role. But the sector itself was small and no organizations existed that exclusively took on the task of advancing the status of women in Morocco. Moroccan women were not yet seen to be legitimate if they organized on their own behalf rather than for others in need. Nor did there exist any means by which women were consulted by the Palace or the political elite when it came to women's affairs.

In short, the institutional, formal contours of Morocco's gender institution was created and regulated by Moroccan men. Only in informal and personal arenas where a female student or woman insisted on extending her freedom of movement to shop, eat in restaurants (before sundown), and be seen in appropriate public places did the informal spheres of women expand.

Discursive Initiatives

While Moroccan women may not have advocated for their own rights in Morocco's post-independence era, they were learning discursive skills within Morocco's student organizations, trade unions, and political parties, where they developed their own ideas, presentation skills (mainly for other women), and abilities to reflect and strategize across many arenas.

A natural arena for discursive initiatives is through journalism, but in Morocco, media outlets were controlled by the Palace and few women were journalists; Aicha Mekki (Rqia Fetha) is one of the notable exceptions. The work of women like Malika al-Fassi, who had offered an alternative logic on the status of women during the colonial period, faced hostile opposition in the post independence era from religious leaders and their followers should she or others write to reform the role of women that was now claimed as a representation of Maliki law and tradition. As Zakia Iraqui-Sinaceur and Moha Ennaji have noted, even during the colonial period, Malika al-Fassi had to write under a pseudonym while her work was published in the pages of the *Morocco Magazine*. Additionally, her arguments for women's education included general nationalistic appeals, such as the claim that educating women would yield good service to an independent Morocco and to a woman's family.[54]

Violence and repression were constant weapons used against democrats and modernizers, including women. The amazing story of young Touria Chaoui is a case in point. She was born to a father who was an actor and an anti-French activist, a path that she too followed.[55] Her father had her educated abroad and supported her fascination with airplanes by using his connections to help her gain admittance into flight school. Despite many deliberately nasty obstacles placed in her path, Touria Chaoui became the first Moroccan female pilot when she passed her exams at age sixteen. But she and her father fled Morocco when they were informed that the French planned to eliminate them. On the eve of independence, they returned to Morocco. Touria was shot at point blank range as she drove a car with her brother in it. The assassin also murdered several Istiqlal leaders in this way. To speak out or to model a modern democratic Morocco was a dangerous endeavor. During the reigns of both Mohammed V and (especially) his son Hassan II, the Moroccan national police and military adopted the same tactics of repression, torture, and murder against Moroccan democrats as the French had implemented during the colonial period.

Thus in the post-independence period the only real venue for women to explore their role and strategize with other women in a discursive give and take was in the women's associate organizations to political parties. After the 1957-1958 codification of Morocco's family law with its imposition of a minor status on all Moroccan women and its support by the male leaders of Istiqlal, some women became so disillusioned that they withdrew from politics completely.[56] Others joined the new party that was formed in September 1959 by leaders who had left Istiqlal in January 1959 and now formed a coalition for independence leaders as well as trade unionists and leftist dissidents from smaller parties. The National Union of Popular Forces (UNFP) promised to take up "left" and "modern" issues within Morocco. However, the UNFP too would splinter in 1975 and its rebels would form the Socialist Union of Popular Forces (USFP), a left of center party.

The decade after independence was a period when few statistics were kept on women's status in Morocco—or in any other country around the globe. Such attention to the differences in male and female activities would not take place until after the United Nations Women Conference in Mexico in 1975 and after authors like Esther Boserup wrote eloquently in the 1970s to demonstrate the need for development strategies that differentiated between men and women as well as the need for the collection of data by sex. Thus, the knowledge of facts that is so important to the discursive activities of those who advocate for reform was unavailable to women or to their male allies during the first decade following Morocco's independence.

In the decade after Morocco's independence, the discursive practices necessary to build an alternative logic and agenda and to knowledgeably persuade Moroccans of the need to reform the status of Moroccan women were all but invisible. These practices were undermined by both repression and by neglect on the part of Morocco's national male leaders.

Resources

As noted above, post independent Morocco was a divided society in which the monarch tried to unify the country under his thumb. Three linguistic groups of Berbers who had resisted or collaborated with the French occupation to differing degrees coexisted side by side with those culturally Arab Moroccans who differed on the form of political economy that should be instituted in an independent Morocco, as well as on what Morocco's foreign policies should be and to what extent Morocco's religious leaders should set rules for Moroccan citizens. In addition to these linguistic, cultural, ethnic, and ideological differences, Moroccans were also deeply divided by class. At the end of the colonial period,

Morocco was primarily reliant on agricultural exports for its income. A Moroccan affluent rural elite had developed over time while most of the country was composed of rural poor. As Gregory White notes, after independence, the Palace controlled the most important economic conglomerate in the country, the Omnium Nord Africain (ONA), which oversaw the mining and exports of phosphates, copper, and iron, and the makhzen close to the throne sought personal gain for their agricultural and business operations through their connections with the Royals.[57] Tourism also provided Moroccans with income and jobs. Like their rural counterparts, Morocco's urban residents included both a small affluent class and a larger class with few resources. However, a woman's class background did not necessarily predict her male family's disposition toward the range of women's activities it would permit her to undertake.

Of great importance to a woman's resources were the views of her male relatives, especially her father and husband. Class and income came into play in the cases when a father or husband wished to underwrite the financial costs of an education for his daughter or wife and her transportation to educational or other activities. Since Moroccan women legally were minors, very few had access to their own resources. When they did, in keeping with the times in which they lived, if they were moved to make a social contribution they might use their assets to help other women directly. One such example is Lalla Radia.

Lalla Radia lacked a formal education, but her wealthy Fez family had seen to it that she received a religious education appropriate for a woman. Her family also supported the nationalist cause. Radia came to know Malika al-Fassi and helped to financially support a secondary school for girls that Malika al-Fassi helped staff. Jouhara Filali Baba offers an account of an event on the eve of Morocco's independence in which Lalla Radia was honored by five prominent Fez women with excellent education by a public reading of a letter of gratitude and a small contribution to the Lalla Radia's educational initiatives.[58]

As previously noted, race, class, and ethnicity are not predictors of resources for Moroccan women, as most are dependent on Moroccan males for their spending allowance. Slowly, Moroccan women after independence would come to have some discretionary income through the contribution to family income that resulted from their employment. But it would not be until the late 1970s (and more effectively in the 1980s and 1990s) that activist Moroccan women would find resources external to Morocco from which they could draw to pursue their advocacy of an improved status for Moroccan women.

In the late 1950s and throughout the 1960s international donors and international organizations had little interest in the status of women; they were concerned instead with the development of a population and of the financial fortunes of national governments. Mostly they focused on the development of the universal man. During this time there were few international norms that galvanized women globally or pressured their governments to enact gender reforms. Women's rights were noted in some international charters as were covenants of human rights, but neither the East nor the West were much concerned with matters of human rights during the Cold War. The intensity of the bipolar conflict between the super powers and their allies eclipsed other possible movements during this period. Nor did any external events regionally or internationally shock the Moroccan system and force it to re-evaluate its gender practices.

Finally, the possible resource of political alliances with male leaders in the political parties, in the person of the King, in religious or trade organizations, or with those around the throne, was rarely available to Moroccan women. As noted above, few Moroccan independence leaders were interested in "the woman question" once independence had been wrested from France.

A Gender Institution in Morocco

In the four arenas where it is possible to discern the specifics that comprise an institution of gender and where change must occur to improve the status of women—women's agency, informal and formal routines and organizational pathways of decision making, discursive activities, and resources—Moroccan women lived a boundaried life with little leverage to effect gender change. How Moroccan women did effect changes in Morocco's gender institution and how increasing numbers of women came to participate in every aspect of Moroccan life is the subject of the following chapters.

Notes

1. Geertz is quoted in Mounira Charrad, *States and Women's Rights: The Making of Postcolonial Tunisia, Algeria, and Morocco* (Berkeley: University of California Press, 2001), 142.

2. Geertz is quoted in Charrad, *States and Women's Rights,* 142.

3. See Jonathan Wyrtzen, *Constructing Morocco: The Colonial Struggle to Define the Nation, 1912-1956.* Georgetown University Ph.D. Dissertation, April 15, 2009, 160-161 for an account of the summer of 1930 and after, when Chakib Arslan, a Lebanese Druz, *Amir,* poet and journalist who was based in Geneva, arranged for the Moroccan students studying in France to travel across Europe to publicize the negative impact on Moroccan nationalism that resulted from France's Berber decree. Wyrtzen's account also reports that Arslan publicized Moroccan issues through his journalism, which reached readers in Europe and Middle Eastern countries, especially those in Egypt. Thus while some sought to oppose the Berber decrees by unifying Morocco under the Sultan, other forms of resistance helped future political party leaders hone their public speaking skills prior to their returning to Morocco and playing leading roles in Morocco's political party organizational structures that agitated for independence.

4. Charrad, *States and Women's Rights,* 141-142.

5. See, for example, Brahim Fillali, "Morocco: On Pre-Colonial Morocco" ex-CLER (Morocco), published in Morocco on 11 October 2005, translated by Pat Murtagh, Canada, 2008, and edited by Michael Schmidt, South Africa, 2008. Posted by *tahriricn* August 5, 2008. http://tahriricn.wordpress.com/2013/03/01/morocco-on-pre-colonial-morocco/.

6. Fillali, "Morocco."

7. Wyrtzen, *Constructing* Morocco, 284.

8. Jane L. Parpart, Shirin M. Rai, and Kathleen Staudt, eds., *Rethinking Empowerment: Gender and Development in a Global/Local World*, Routledge/Warwick Studies in Globalization, 3 (London and New York: Routledge, 2002), 5.

9. Charrad, *States and Women's Rights*, 47.

10. Aijaz Ahmad, "The Politics of Literary Postcoloniality" *Race and Class* 36, no. 3 (1995), 1-20; Ella Shohat, "Notes on the "Post-Colonial" *Social Text* 10, no. 31/32 (1992), 99-113.

11. Wyrtzen, *Constructing Morocco,* 290-291.

12. Wyrtzen, *Constructing Morocco,* 295.

13. Wyrtzen, *Constructing Morocco*, 302-304.

14. Wyrtzen, *Constructing Morocco,* 304.

15. "Matters of Principle," *Time Magazine*, September 14, 1953.

16. "Matters of Principle," *Time Magazine*.

17. "The Women," *Time Magazine,* January 23, 1956.

18. "The Women," *Time Magazine*.

19. Marvine Howe, *Morocco: The Islamist Awakening and Other Challenges* (Oxford: Oxford University Press, 2005), 77.

20. Zakya Daoud, *Féminisme et Politique au Maghreb* (Casablanca: Éditions Eddif, 1993).

21. "The Women," *Time Magazine*. This entire account is based on *Time Magazine* reporting.

22. Women's Islamic Initiative in Spirituality and Equality, "Muslim Women: Past and Present: Huda Shaaeawi,"
http://www.wisemuslimwomen.org/muslimwomen/bio/huda_shaarawi/ (last modified 2013; accessed April 24, 2014).

23. Huda Shaarawi, *Harem Years: The Memoirs of an Egyptian Feminist 1879-1924*. Translated and edited by Margot Badran with an introduction by Margot Badran (New York: Feminist Press at the City University of New York, 1987).

24. Shaarawi, *Harem Years.*

25. Women's Islamic Initiative, "Muslim Women Past and Present."

26. Margot Badran, *Feminism in Islam: Secular and Religious Convergences* (Oxford: Oneworld Publications, 2009), 23-24.

27. Badran, *Feminism in Islam*, 23-24.

28. Badran, *Feminism in Islam,* 19-23.

29. Leila Abouzeid, *Year of the Elephant: A Moroccan Women's Journey Toward Independence*. Translator, Barbara Parmenter (Austin, TX: Center for Middle Eastern Studies, The University of Texas at Austin, 1989).

30 Wyrtzen, *Constructing Morocco*. Wyrtzen relies on an Algerian document that compares the legal status of the Kbayle tribe women in Algeria with Berber women in Morocco.

31. I. William Zartman, "Political Pluralism in Morocco" in I. William Zartman, ed. *Man, State, and Society in the Contemporary Maghrib* (New York: Praeger Publishers, 1973), 246.

32. Zartman, "Political Pluralism in Morocco," 246.

33. Zartman, "Political Pluralism in Morocco," 245-246.

34. Howe, *Morocco,* 146.

35. Howe, *Morocco,* 149-150.

36. Howe, *Morocco,* 150.

37. Osire Glacier, *Political Women in Morocco Then and Now.* Translator, Valérie Martin (Trenton: Red Sea Press, 2013), 99.

38. Glacier, *Political Women in Morocco Then and Now,* 100.

39. Glacier, *Political Women in Morocco Then and Now,* 100.

40. Malika Zeghal, *Islamism in Morocco: Religion, Authoritarianism, and Electoral Politics.* Translator, George Holoch (Princeton: Markus Weiner Publishers, 2008), 27.

41. Zeghal, *Islamism in Morocco,* 33.

42. Zeghal, *Islamism in Morocco,* 33.

43. Zeghal, *Islamism in Morocco,* 34.

44. Zakia Salime, *Between Feminism and Islam: Human Rights and Sharia Law in Morocco* (Minneapolis, University of Minnesota Press, 2011), 3.

45. Daniel Zisenwine, *The Emergence of Nationalist Politics in Morocco* (London: I.B. Taurus Publishers, 2010), 102-103.

46. Malika Zeghal, *Islamism in Morocco: Religion, Authoritarianism, and Electoral Politics* (London: I. B. Taurus Publishers, 2010), 33.

47. Laurie Brand, *Women, the State, and Political Liberalization: Middle Eastern and North Africans Experiences* (New York: Columbia University Press, 1998); Charrad, *States and Women's Rights.*

48. Charrad, *States and Women's Rights,* 163.

49. Charrad, *States and Women's Rights,* 164.

50. Charrad, *States and Women's Rights the Making of Postcolonial Tunisia, Algeria, and Morocco,* 165.

51. Charrad, *States and Women's Rights,* 165-166.

52. Brand, *Women, the State, and Political Liberalization,* 57-58.

53. Brand, *Women, the State, and Political Liberalization,* 57.

54. Zakia Iraqui-Sinaceur and Moha Ennaji, " 'Al Fatat' On Young Women's Education," in *Women Writing Africa: The Northern Region,* ed. Fatima Sadiqi, Amira Nowaira, Azza El Kholy, and Moha Ennaji, (New York, Feminist Press at the City University of New York, 2009), 144-146.

55. Glacier, *Political Women in Morocco,* 109-112.

56. Fatima Bouabdelli, "Habiba Guessoussa: An Opening Speech," in *Women Writing Africa,* ed. Sadiqi, Nowaira, El Kholy, and Ennaji, 173-175.

57. Gregory White, *A Comparative Political Economy of Tunisia and Morocco* (Albany: SUNY Press, 2001).

58. Jouhara Filali Baba, "To Lalla Radia, Our Eternal Lighthouse," in *Women Writing Africa,* ed. Sadiqi, Nowaira, El Kholy, and Ennaji, 191-192. The five women who signed the letter of gratitude were Zhor Lhiyania, Farima Ali Mernissi, Hiba Elbaqali, Aziza Kerzaai, and Fatima Bourqadia.

Chapter Three
The Agency of Moroccan Women

How Moroccan women expanded their country's social spaces for women's activities and created linkages to organize and improve the status of women in their country deserves careful analysis. It deserves both uncovering the context that can be captured from scholarly investigations but also it demands that the narratives of individual pioneer Moroccan woman who stretched the boundaries for all Moroccan women should be told. In this chapter, we cannot hope to present the narratives of all the brave and smart Moroccan women who contributed to improving the status of women in their country. But we can, based on interviews of a handful of select women activists, offer an understanding of how, despite the odds, these women called forth their agency and began their public, political activities that would, in time, create opportunities for Moroccan women and bring women into public positions in most sectors of Moroccan society. Presenting such material allows us to better understand how Morocco's gender institution evolved. It also allows us to understand the conditions for evoking effective agency by women living in an authoritarian, patriarchal system and how the claimed agency by some women promoted the expansion of freedoms for many Moroccan women.

As discussed in the previous chapter, during the resistance years for Moroccan independence of 1953-1956, some Moroccan women broke the barriers of talking with men other than male family members as they carried hidden arms and brought messages from one resistance cell to another. But following the country's independence, most returned to the confines of caring for their families and interacting only with the men in their immediate families. Even Fatima Monsour who finally secured, after much effort and many challenges in the late 1970s (as documented in the research of Alison Baker), a Carte de Rèsistant, rarely granted to any woman, returned to her traditional duties in the decade after independence.[1] How then, did Moroccan women manage to move themselves out of their houses and into the meeting rooms where politics and women's issues could be debated and advanced?

Fatima Sadiqi and Moha Ennaji argue that the traditional public/private distinction in early feminist thinking clearly applied to the Moroccan context largely due to Moroccan Islamic practices.[2] Sadiqi and Ennaji observed, for example, that in the post-independence setting, Moroccan women could enter the public space of the street but could not linger there. They also noted that men rarely entered the women's sphere where food was cooked and clothes were cleaned and the basic needs for everyday life were attended to. As Sadiqi and Ennaji would argue as late as 2006, for some Moroccan women, the division between male public space and domestic private space was still so delineated that the "only public spaces accessible to women in some places are the hammãm (public bath) and the siyyid (the tomb of a dead saint)" during the limited hours allocated for women to enter.[3] But Sadiqi and Ennaji also note that many women's access to public space began changing in the 1960s when industrialization pulled poor women to the factories as well as to domestic work in other Moroccans' or foreigners' houses. However, women from upper and middle income families who had been educated after independence were expected to be expert at running the home and rearing children and so most were not claiming much space in public work settings.[4] For those urban middle or upper class women who did take jobs in the public sphere, they still fulfilled their domestic duties because their "housework valorizes them" in the eyes of their families.[5] And for all Moroccan women, should they walk alone or with other women at night on the street, they certainly would be thought to be prostitutes and deserving of any harassment or violence they might encounter.

Sadiqi and Ennaji echo others in saying that when leftist male leaders promoted greater mobility for women, as well as other reforms, they often did so as part of the greater Islamic modernization project that these leaders espoused for their country.[6] Additionally, as we will learn from some of the women who pioneered working in Morocco's public space to improve the status of Moroccan women, male support—be it a father or brother or male teacher—was critical to the ability of these women to believe that they could enter the public space and that they organize for political issues, including those of concern to women.

Activating Agency: The Narratives of Some Prominent Moroccan Women Activists

As noted in the Introduction, to understand the changes in Morocco's gender institution, and all the sub organizations and institutions that it comprises, requires an understanding of both structure and agency. Before we can explore how issues were chosen and what lessons were applied during their advocacy for improving the status of Moroccan women, we must first understand how Moroccan women created a space for themselves in which to promote legislation and programs to advance the status of women. We first must understand how some Moroccan women began to place themselves in public spaces where they could organize and strategize and learn important lessons for strategic action. Thus, we now turn to some of these women for their accounts of how they came to be active politically in a public space that was beyond the reach of many other Moroccan women who remained constrained in the private spaces of their home and families.

As noted above, we could not interview all early Moroccan activists and some whom we wanted to interview, whom many readers as well as these two authors would want to learn from and learn about, chose not to respond to our requests or inquiries. Also because we were constrained by space, we selected only a handful of women whose narratives could serve as representative of active women in leadership roles. We are grateful to those women who responded to our inquiries and who believed that future generations, as well as women living in other settings today, should understand how Moroccan women found the agency to begin their political journeys.

Below we offer an account of how each of the women activists interviewed found her way into political spaces and additionally we offer some insight into each woman's path in the public sphere of political life. No doubt, by the time this book is published, many of these women will have shifted positions and moved on to meet new challenges. But because we are interested mainly in their early years, we focus on how, in their own minds, they were permitted to enter into political activism. In later chapters in this book we will return to consider the work and organizations developed by these women, but first we offer their own stories and their own interpretation of their entry into the political world.

Nezha Alaoui

Nezha Alaoui remembers that she first became active and involved when she was a university student in Morocco at about the age of eighteen. The main issue that motivated her and others who began to engage publically in politics was the Palestinian question.[7]

Alaoui recalled that the university was already a place for students to express themselves politically: many Moroccans on the campuses in the late 1960s and early 1970s were influenced by the events of 1968 in France and specifically in Paris. The French student strikes correlated with the start up of an energized left in Morocco both on Morocco's campuses and among older Moroccan intellectuals who leaned left.[8]

However, Alaoui was from a family that was not left leaning but rather conservative. This made it difficult for her to feel comfortable in participating in left politics both due to the ideological framework and also due to the fact that a conservative family would be less likely to encourage a daughter to engage publicly in politics. Alaoui credits her brother for helping her to become involved in left campus politics. Alaoui's brother was both active politically himself, and also willing to offer her the kind of support she needed to become involved. As Alaoui noted, "This mattered a lot. My involvement was easier because of my brother since I was from a conservative family."[9]

Alaoui noted that on the campuses, competing leftist political groups with a range of perspectives were growing in the early 1970s. One group, "the 23rd of March" was a group on the left that adopted Marxist Leninist views. Another called itself "Force" and came out of the Communist Party (CP) in Morocco. So for Moroccan students attending a university who were becoming aware of politics in general and their own connections to politics in the world, there was a leftist presence on their campus that challenged them to think and act.[10]

It would not be until 1983 that Nezha Alaoui would join with other women to prioritize their concerns about issues concerning women and begin to challenge the national discourse on men and women and build the infrastructure upon which to press for improvements in the lives of Moroccan women. But her exposure as a university student and her subsequent political activities laid the groundwork for Alaoui and other women like her to understand how to organize and plan and strategize for advancing political concerns. Ten years later in the 1980s, Alaoui and other like-minded women organized a new national discourse about women in Morocco through their publication of the magazine *March 8th* famously edited by Latifa Jbabdi, a bright, brave woman who had spent time in Morocco's prisons for her political beliefs. *March 8th* published articles by women and men on the need to improve Moroccan women's status and on the realities of their everyday lives.[11] Later, the *March 8th* women created a civil society legal entity, the Union de l'Action Fèminine (UAF), and launched a million signature campaign with the help of other women's organizations and women's sections of political parties to push for national reforms that benefitted Moroccan women. Alaoui was a President of the UAF and a member of the L'Union Socialiste des Forces Populaires (USFP), a left of center political party. Her work for the UAF continued into the twenty-first century.

Ghizlan Benachir

Ghizlan Benachir served as the President of Joussour (Bridges), an important national Moroccan women's non-governmental organization (NGO), as a member of the political party, the L'Union Socialiste des Forces Populaires (USFP), and she was elected as a municipal official from Suisse district of Rabat. In many ways Ghizlan Benachir had advantages that other Moroccan women did not have and she is the first to say so. But Benachir, like other Moroccan women, still had to find within herself the strength and energy to undertake and sustain the important work that she has accomplished.

Ghizlan Benachir characterizes her family as a family of "political militants" so she grew up with parents and relatives speaking about patriotism and nationalism in her home.[12] Yet she notes that she had cousins who also matured in this atmosphere but chose not to follow a political path. Benachir's comparison to her cousins is telling because, in fact, her uncle was an activist in the L'Union Socialiste des Forces Populaires (USFP) and he was an important male figure who was supportive of her entry into politics and political activism.[13] Benachir notes that she did not choose her party—it was her family's party in which she became active. But it was a party that was a good fit for her personally so there was no need for her to seek another party with which to affiliate.[14]

Benachir was lucky in another way. At about age eighteen she was studying in France, and she was located mainly in Paris and Montpelier. While abroad in a setting where there was more space for women politically, she became active in the Union of Moroccan Students. Also as an educated woman, Benachir recalled that, over the years, she was able to read some of the theoretical work on women and so was influenced by the work of Fatima Mernissi and other prominent feminist authors in Morocco and elsewhere. Benachir noted that she was always drawn to the question of women because as a woman she has witnessed the problems women face and she knew such issues from personal experience.[15]

When Benachir later began to organize for women's issues she chose to do so as a member and leader of Joussour. Joussour's mission was to build a bridge among women that facilitated collaboration. Joussour drew its membership from women in any political party, from women in non-governmental organizations (NGOs), and from non party-affiliated women. Its board consisted of women active from a variety of parties and NGOs and varying political perspectives.[16] In 2003, Joussour was one of the major women's organizations that was invited to participate as an organizational member of the Palace's Consultative Committee for amending the Moudawana, Morocco's legal code for men, women, and families.

Zahra Chaggaf

For Zahra Chaggaf, politics was always a part of her family's atmosphere. She came from a family active in Saharan politics. It affected the men in her family and the women, too. She had two brothers who served in parliament. She had a sister-in-law who also was active politically.

Chaggaf was a member of the Democratic Union which merged with two other parties to form the Movement Populaire (MP). She stepped forward when her party was looking for women to run for parliament in response to the changing times. Chaggaf said she had "spent twenty years getting ready by working in the men's campaigns."[17] When there was an opening for women, her husband encouraged her to step forward and she did, winning a seat in parliament. Chaggaf explained that the opening came largely because the new King, Mohammed VI, "sent signals and messages that he wanted changes. Political parties knew they had to respond to the request from the top."[18]

Chaggaf was also influenced by what women could achieve in the political sphere in other countries. She traveled to Scandinavia and was impressed with the example of the role of women politically there. She took part in international exchanges and learned more about women's activities elsewhere. As the head of the Association of Women for the Popular Movement she toured the country to encourage other women who had shown leadership qualities to get involved in politics and run for political office.[19]

As a member of the executive board of the Movement Populaire party, Chaggaf noted that "I express my views openly with all freedom. I come from a society in the South where women have strong personalities. We wear five meters of cloth to cover our heads, but we are not afraid to open our mouths."[20]

Meluda Hazib

Meluda Hazib became involved with women's issues at quite a young age. When she was thirteen or fourteen she volunteered for a community service organization, received training, and then went around her neighborhood teaching women how to care for their children properly on a daily basis. She remembered that "she felt even at a young age that there was inequality among people and between men and women."[21]

Hazib also began working at an early age; she began teaching at age fifteen. For a young woman to join an organization and walk the streets of her neighborhood, and to engage with other women in their houses and then begin to teach at such an early age, raises questions for anyone who has studied how many Moroccan women were restricted in their homes and kept themselves from public places. But Hazib said her father was an influential person in her upbringing. He had a strong personality and he continually encouraged her to be strong and to be active. She credits her father as being influential in that he not only encouraged her to undertake responsibility and improve herself, but she also modeled her behavior after him so as to grow and become a strong person.[22]

Hazib also found an interest in reading about Arab women and the Arab world. Her activism, however, has generally been through her political party that was founded in 1982 with the objective of promoting the rural areas. Hazib said that through the actions of women in the party and some of their male allies, they have managed to make the party attentive to the issues of women. However, her party is a small party [National Democratic Party (PND)] and its main focus has been on improving the lives of those in rural areas, both men and women.[23]

In 2002, when Morocco instituted its national women's slate, Meluda Hazib was chosen to lead her party's women's slate. As a smart, well educated, politically experienced leader who also had successfully run her own business (a tourism business), Meluda Hazib was often sought after by the media to comment on parliamentary issues and on women's issues. An effective public speaker, Hazib established a national reputation beyond that of her party for her effective work and insightful commentary. In the 2007 elections, Hazib's party did not garner enough votes to return her to parliament as an elected MP.

But in a later chapter we will return to analyze the work of Meluda Hazib who was a successful businesswoman, then a member of parliament, and then selected as a councilor or adviser to a parliamentary caucus of several parties that entered Moroccan politics at a key moment in the country's history.

Amina Ouchelh

Amina Ouchelh was a former President of the women's section of the Socialist Union of Popular Forces (USFP). Ouchelh was elected to local political office and then served as an adviser to the Speaker of Morocco's parliament from 1998 to 2002. For the 2002 national Moroccan elections, her party placed her on the national women's slate and Amina Ouchelh was elected as a Member of Parliament and served in Morocco's National Assembly between 2002 and 2007. Amina Ouchelh also was one of a number of women who founded a coordinating committee for the collaboration of women across political parties.

Amina Ouchelh recalls that she became immersed in politics during her student years. As a student in the lycee, she benefitted from the nationalist movement that had built an Arabic curriculum that was Arab centered. During that period, the Director of her school and all the teachers were quite politicized. It was the 1960s, and everyone around her was interested in politics.[24]

Additionally, Ouchelh came from a family active in politics. Her father was active in the Istiqlal Party (Party of Independence). Even though Istiqlal was a conservative party, her father was alert to the concerns of women because Istiqlal women would come to see him in the evening at home in order to speak with him about issues of concern to them and their families. One of her father's responsibilities was to promote cultural activities in Sale. So his activism was one element that caught Ouchelh's attention and engaged her politically.[25]

In addition to her father, Ouchelh's brother made a strong impression on her. Her brother was an activist but he had joined a party other than that of his father.[26] Ouchelh's brother joined the USFP, a leftist party some of whose founding leaders had split from Istiqlal.

By the time Amina Ouchelh attended the university in Fez, her brother was an important figure helping her to negotiate student activities. The early 1970s was a significant period in Moroccan politics and, along with other students, Ouchelh spent hours discussing issues and problems and looking for solutions. It was during this period that she found the answers to many of her questions and then hoped to help to implement them.

As a young student she remembers that one of the very first books that she read was by Gamal Abd El Nasser. Later, she also read Régis Debray's work on Che Guevara. She was encouraged to read broadly, but Ouchelh remembers that the attention given to women's issues during discussions of politics in the early years was minimal. In fact, she recalled, "prior to the 1970s, there was a particular way of thinking, especially on the left of the political spectrum in Morocco. This thinking argued that when improvements came for the average citizens, all citizens including the status of women would improve."[27] When the USFP was founded as a new left party, many women joined the party to fight to improve the lives of all Moroccan citizens.

But then in the 1970s,"we began to realize that this (improving the lives of all citizens generally would improve the lives of women) was not the case. Other societies that were more developed still had big gaps between men and women. So we concluded that women needed parallel strategies for development to those devised for society generally, which we came to see was meant for men."[28]

In 1975, the USFP members had conversations about a women's sector. The USFP activist Badia Skalli and other women were pushing to establish a women's section of the party. [Badia Skalli was a founder of the USFP and in

1976 she ran for a local public office but was defeated. Then, Skalli ran for a parliamentary seat and she was again defeated. It wasn't until 1993 that Badia Skalli won a seat in Parliament and was only one of two women (with Latifa Bennani Smiress of Istiqlal) members of Parliament, the first two ever elected. Both within the USFP and outside in the wider world, conversations about women's rights were taking place.

Ouchelh noted that sometime after the United Nations 1975 Mexican conference on women, the USFP drafted the first statement on the current status of women in Morocco. This report included a wide range of recommendations, including those from women outside of the USFP. By 1977, a USFP's women's section had bylaws and was very organized. It had outreach to all parts of the country through its branches all over. It was a formal structure. It began to discuss and press for the reform of the Moudawana. It began to consider what reforms could be made.[29]

Amina Ouchelh was active in the women's section of the USFP. Along with the other USFP women she helped to lobby for a formal women's section in the party. However she remembers that this was difficult not because women's issues were not important but because "during the 'Iron Period' our party was the most targeted. Our party members were jailed, tortured, and there were trials. Some went into exile. There were major obstacles to being in our party and to raising the issues of women first" before other party concerns. "Each attack by the government meant we had to defend a party member and so these were times when we had to trade away our concerns for raising women's issues in order to support those individuals we knew in our party."[30]

The women in Ouchelh's women's section had all been active in the party first. They were party women. They each had responsibilities as political party woman. She recalls,"At the time, not too many women were in the decision making circles, so we were asking how could we integrate women into all of the party and political life?"[31]

By 1977, Ouchelh was elected to the National Secretariat of the USFP. She was in charge of coordinating issues related to women. When she traveled outside Morocco, she came to know the works of Freida Brown, a Russian woman. She also traveled to Syria where people were discussing Brown's work and this further encouraged Ouchelh to read Brown's writings. Over the years, Ouchelh took part in many exchanges and learned from others through both conversation and by being introduced to new authors, especially those who were writing on women's issues. Ouchelh was elected to the central committee of USFP in 1984 and served for over twenty years.[32]

Looking back, Ouchelh noted,"in the 1960s and 1970s, political studies was not allowed. You would never have students majoring in a subject like political science. It was unheard of. The government would not allow it and parents would not risk their children. No one publicly had anything to do with anything called politics." But things began to change for her party and for politics in Morocco in the late 1990s.[33]

In 1992, King Hassan II asked parliament to form a government. Negotiations between the USFP and Istiqlal took place. Then there were negotiations between the palace and the two parties. In 1993, the first set of reforms to the Moudawana occurred. King Hassan II invited women from political parties and from NGOs to send him a memo of the changes they were hoping for. Ouchelh recalled, "Although the King made only some minor changes to the Moudawana, we were ecstatic. The significance of any change to the Moudawana must be understood. By some it was argued that Moudawana was like a sacred text and could never be changed. But by making even minor changes, the King—and we—broke the taboo on change. This opened the way for discussions on what changes could be proposed next, not whether or not we could change the Moudawana."[34]

In 1994, King Hassan II granted amnesty to Moroccan political prisoners. He allowed many people living in exile to return to Morocco. Many USFP members returned. In 1996, King Hassan II suggested constitutional reforms. For the first time USFP members chose to vote for and support the reforms. "In the past our party always voted no on reforms" because we did not think the reforms went far enough toward establishing democracy. This new support for reforms was a key change during a critical period."[35]

"For 40 years we had been in opposition. In 1997, people could begin to see change. We could participate in politics. In 1998, Abdul-Rahman Al-Youssoufi became Morocco's Prime Minister. He was the president of the USFP party! This was a huge breakthrough."[36] In contemplating these changes, Ouchelh offered, "I remember that King Hassan II gave a speech and he said, 'Morocco is close to having a heart attack.' He knew that we needed to make changes."[37]

In 1996, a popular referendum had replaced Morocco's unicameral legislature with a bicameral legislature in which the lower house was popularly elected. In August 1997, the laws and procedures for the election of both houses was announced and later, the date (November 14) of the 1997 elections also was announced. 3300 candidates including 69 women competed for 325 parliamentary seats. Only two women were elected to Morocco's Parliament in 1997 and both came from the USFP party which won 57 parliamentary seats, the most of any party. In 1997, the USFP was able to elect one of the women into the national parliament, Badia Skalli (from Casablanca). Skalli was joined in the parliament by Amina Lamrini of the Party of Progress and Socialism (PPS) (from Rabat).

Regarding women's affairs, Ouchelh recalled that the latter part of the 1970s and early 1980s was a time of activism for women globally. The first United Nations international women's conference was held in Mexico in 1975. The years 1976-1985 were designated as the UN International Decade for Women. In 1979, the UN General Assembly adopted the Convention on the Elimination of All Forms of Discrimination Against Women (CEDAW). In 1980, the second UN conference on women was held in Copenhagen and resulted in calls for women's rights to property, child custody, inheritance, etc. Preparatory meetings took place by women's groups across countries as they readied themselves for the 1985 third UN Conference on Women in Nairobi, Kenya. Ouchelh noted that a lot of women from Africa, the Arab states, and Europe attended these conferences and shared information.[38]

Ouchelh also noted that no one woman could make significant changes in Morocco or elsewhere. She and the other women in her party collaborated across political parties and with NGOs in Morocco from 1970s until the present. "I did not work alone; all my work is in circles and all my work is in collaboration with others." With regard to foreign issues such as Palestine and the Intifada, it was easier for the women from different political parties and from NGOs to collaborate. It was more difficult for the women to achieve consensus on their demands for changing the Moudawana. "We had more difficulty when we discussed changes to the Moudawana; the coordination would improve for a while and then there would be an interruption in coordination."[39]

Ouchelh was among the 34 women elected as Moroccan parliamentarians in 2002 with the assistance of a gender slate (discussed in a later chapter). She was also active in the advocacy movements to further revise the Moudawana that occurred in 2003.

Nouzha Skalli

Nouzha Skalli has been an elected municipal official (Casablanca), a member of Morocco's national parliament, a nationally and internationally known women's activist, and when we interviewed her, a Cabinet Minister in Morocco's government in which she served as the Minister of Social Development, Family, and Solidarity. She has also worked in the NGO sector to advance the status of women. Skalli has taken bold public steps for women's causes in Morocco, gaining national attention. Skalli's accomplishments have been unusual, but she did not achieve her public posts without pain, hard work, excellent skills, overcoming the jealousy of others, and determination. Skalli has a warm smile, a warm disposition, and a quick mind. While she is known to hold opinions, she does not look for quarrels. She looks for the path by which to achieve gains for her causes, especially gains for women.

Reflecting on her early years of becoming politically aware, Skalli recalled that "very early in my life I knew I was interested in politics. I was less than eighteen years old when I was drawn to discussions and wanted to understand things. For example, in high school I studied and made presentations about the Chinese Revolution. Since age nineteen I have been in a political party. First, I had chosen one party, but then I changed to another party. In Morocco, at that time, there were only about three or four political parties on the left fighting for democracy and human rights and change. I chose to join a party on the left that I thought was fighting for social justice."[40]

"I was impressed by the French student activities in May 1968. I was passionate and involved. And I made my choice that I was to be active politically for my whole life. I was determined that I would not give up; I would spend my life fighting for just causes."[41]

"I know many women, most women, when they marry or when they have children, they give up politics to focus on the family. I decided that I would be vigilant and not give up politics even when I married and had a family. So when I married I was still active politically and when I had children I was still active politically. It is important to be strong and committed because there are many problems in politics and society and there are many obstacles, but I was determined to work for women and for the improvement of my country throughout my lifetime. I was determined not to give up."[42]

Piecing together Skalli's background (as with the other women above) there is much information available from those who knew her at various times and from documents and reports and news clippings, as well as from the interviews we conducted. Nouzha Skalli was a devoted member of her party even as she was an advocate for women's rights, and other disenfranchised groups. A member of the political party, the Popular Party Socialist (PPS), Skalli had been appointed the head of the PPS's Women's Bureau. In Morocco, as in other postcolonial states, political parties organized youth, women, labor, and other subgroup bureaus. The parties claimed these bureaus provided them with informational input from their identified constituencies, but in fact, mostly these bureaus were tasked as outreach vehicles of mobilization to voters during election periods.

Skalli tried to make the PPS women's bureau both an important electoral player that could advance her party's electoral fortunes, but also use the legitimacy of the bureau to bring to party leaders issues of importance to improving the status of women. Skalli made the Women's Bureau position an active one even when campaigns were not underway.

In 1977, Skalli was one of eight women nation-wide to run for communal (municipal) office; she was the only one to succeed and win her election. She believed that her success stemmed not only from her work in the PPS, a smaller party than some of its rival parties, but also because men and women in her district neighborhoods knew her and knew that she was committed to helping them solve their local problems.[43] As anyone who has met Skalli would have to attest, and as her constituents must also have recognized, Nouzha Skalli is an intelligent, energetic woman, who, with the support of male allies within a political party, could place on the agenda many issues on which she campaigned. Skalli also managed her family and children while staying committed to her political ideals, thus she maintained the image of a proper urban, Muslim woman even as she convinced her constituents of the expanded role that a woman could play in the public sphere.

Although Skalli would not win all of her elections, the PPS would remain Skalli's political venue for many years. Over time, Skalli was approached by a woman from the next generation of her party's activists. PPS member Khadija Errebbah became convinced that the party's Women's Bureau was important, but that the PPS needed a second institutional center where women, together with the men who supported improving the status of women, could come together to talk and strategize.

Skalli and Errebbah worked hard together to secure the support of leaders in the party's districts in order to create an Equality Assembly within the party. Then they and their women and male allies in the PPS began to analyze and advocate for women's improvement nationally. But the PPS was a small party on Morocco's national scene, and while the party's leaders allowed the Equality Assembly to pursue its own activities, many in the leadership chose to focus on building the party nationally.[44]

In 1985, many women in post-colonial states and late industrializing countries were aware of the impending United Nations Conference on Women to be held in Africa. Women's organizations around the world were trying to push their governments to do more for women and government leaders were aware that they would be required to report to the United Nations and the world on the steps they had taken to improve women's status since the United Nations Convention for Women in Mexico in 1975. The UN reporting conference in Nairobi was scheduled for July 1985.

In Morocco, in 1985, a number of PPS women felt the time was right to found the first Moroccan women's political organization dedicated to advancing the status of Moroccan women. Earlier a number of these women had worked on the women's committee in the Association Morocaine des Droits de l'Homme (AMDH), a Moroccan human rights organization. Most of the women also were working on development and support projects for Moroccan women that were critically important for the women they targeted. But these centers and projects did not address the fundamental issues of Moroccan women's equality and women's rights.

Nouzha Skalli, Amina Lamrini, Malika Naciri, along with other bright, educated, politically active and articulate women founded the Association Dèmocratique des Femmes Marocaines (ADFM) in June 1985. Rachida Tahiri, would serve as a President of this organization and as its spokesperson. Later, the next generation leader, Khadija Errebbah, would become ADFM's Director and the organization would identify itself as a completely independent entity without special ties to any one political party.

Early on, the ADFM allowed the PPS women an independent venue from that of just working within the PPS. They could take advantage of the international platform that the upcoming international United Nations conference on women offered. They would be free to pursue the issues that the women increasingly believed the PPS would not vigorously pursue. They came from the PPS, but they founded an organization independent of the PPS. Yet on a personal level, many of the ADFM women kept their ties with colleagues and friends within the PPS and remained active as party members. Nouzha Skalli was one of these who straddled both worlds.

After a decade of working on Moroccan women's issues, in 1996 when the United Nations was holding hearings on the implementation of the Convention on the Elimination of Discrimination Against Women (CEDAW), it was the ADFM that sent its representatives to New York City to engage in this process. Nouzha Skalli of the ADFM presented an alternative report on the status of Moroccan women to the report that had been submitted by the Moroccan government when King Hassan II still reigned. The counter report represented a great deal of careful research and it cost the ADFM women scarce resources to get their representatives to New York. Additionally, it also took courage for Moroccan women, who were still facing stiff resistance at home in some quarters to their advocacy for women (as we discuss in later chapters), to internationally appear and offer an alternative logic to the one provided by their own government. But it also put pressure on Morocco's government administrators to do more for women or be embarrassed by the facts.

In 2002, Skalli ran for Parliament on her party's gender slate and earned a seat in the National Assembly as one of Morocco's MPs. The national gender slate that was established for the 2002 election contained the names of only women candidates in the top rungs of the slate. The regular slate contained the names of mostly male candidates with only a few exceptions. Skalli, like the overwhelming majority of women who won in the 2002 election, was elected on the new women's slate. But Skalli came to the parliament with the experience of having worked as an elected official at the local level and so understood the needs of her constituency and how a legislature might work. Additionally, she had been active engaging with women internationally about women's issues and their strategies in many other countries. She had high hopes of working hard and pushing for those issues that she cared about.

While in Parliament, Nouzha Skalli gained extended recognition across Morocco as an excellent spokesperson and someone engaged in the national dialogue on a range of issues. As an articulate, calm, bright woman, the media often sought Skalli out to comment on issues for the nightly news.

Then, astonishingly, when it came time to select candidates to run for parliament in the next parliamentary round of elections (2007) Skalli's male party leaders chose not to place her high on the list of candidates for the women's slate, but rather to choose other women less skilled and with less service to the party. Since Skalli was from a small party, if the party did not secure enough votes, then only its top candidate, or at most its second candidate, on the party's women's slate would be elected. Nouzha Skalli was listed at number three behind two women who were politically inexperienced and had not been party activists. The first woman on the list had only joined the party six months earlier. The second woman was chosen from outside of the party. Skalli was placed third where she would have little chance of succeeding and returning to parliament. All of the politically alert public in Morocco was abuzz; Skalli had been publicly humiliated by her male party leaders.

Several lines of reasoning were put forward to these authors by a range of political observers who tried to explain this puzzle. Perhaps these male party leaders were jealous. Perhaps they wanted Skalli to leave the party as she was always working to get things accomplished and they felt she was pushing their agenda in ways they might not want to take it. Perhaps they did not like that she had earned a national spotlight.

Women activists in other countries noticed as well. Nouzha Skalli had become one of a number of Moroccan women speakers on issues of importance to women as well as on more general Moroccan affairs in international circles. When asked why her party leaders made such a decision, Skalli responded, "If the party had talked to me and explained their reasons, I might have understood. But this was not the case." Skalli reflected that if she "had been placed number three behind other women in her party who had been activists and militants, she might have understood if it was said that the party needed to give others a turn. But this was not the case."[46]

Nouzha Skalli had to decide whether or not to leave her party and whether to sit out the election on the side lines. She had been publicly humiliated and many in her party smirked or whispered when she passed near them. Skalli withdrew from the electoral candidacy as the third person on the list and, so for the first time in eleven elections, she did not run for political office. But she decided that she would not withdraw from the party. So, she did not withdraw from the party or the party's politbureau on which she served. This was difficult because by not leaving the party, she had to live day to day with the political actors who looked at her askance and with the people who she knew talked about her, but did not come to talk to her.

But Skalli remembered the creed she had established for herself. "I had pledged when I began my political activism in my youth that my work was not just for me to advance. I knew I could still be useful and help others politically and fight for the right people to be elected. So I spent the campaign as a member of my party campaigning for some of the people that I believed deserved to be in parliament. And I lived every day with the disappointment I felt about my party's actions to me. But I was determined to continue to be politically active and advance the issues I felt strongly needed to be addressed in Morocco and also to advance the status of women. But it was a very hard time."[47]

Skalli campaigned energetically for those in her party whom she supported. She did not know what the future would hold when the election was concluded.

Then, following the conclusion of the 2007 elections, when Morocco's King Mohammed VI was choosing national political leaders to staff Morocco's cabinet, he reached over the male party leaders of the PPS, and instead selected Nouzha Skalli to serve in a cabinet position as the Minister of Social Development, Family, and Solidarity. There were few who could argue that the King might have found a better person when he chose to appoint a new minister to this position. And his choice of Skalli to serve at such a high level in such a critical position to women and their families was interpreted by many as a redemptive act by the King on behalf of Skalli. As importantly, such an appointment was a strong statement by the King as to what he considered important and to what he was paying attention.

Nouzha Skalli went on to serve with distinction as a cabinet member of Morocco. And when the elected women of the next parliament arrived in Rabat to start their terms, Skalli organized a reception for all the women from all parties to come and meet each other and talk.

Rachida Tahiri

Rachida Tahiri, along with Nouzha Skalli and others, was a founder (in 1985) of the nongovernmental organization, The Democratic Association for Moroccan Women, that was discussed above. The ADFM was an organization that largely focused on making political advances for Moroccan women. For a period, Tahiri served as ADFM's Director. She also served as a Deputy of the Progress and Development Party. Additionally, she served as a representative to the EU-Morocco Joint Parliamentary Commission.

Tahiri came of age during the 1960s when Moroccan women were disenfranchised under the status quo. She recalls that in Morocco, schools served as a central location in which students could organize politically. "In the 1970s, we organized like other students around the world in the schools. We asked for the voting age to be lowered, for students to be able legally to form organizations and associations. There was an anti-authoritarian student movement around the world and Moroccan students participated in it."[48]

Her own path into political activity came largely because "My father had struggled in the independence movement; so my family understood politics."[49] When she was about sixteen she became highly alert to political issues and debates. When she joined a party, it was the Party of Progress and Socialism (PPS), a leftist party. But PPS women, "like women in other parties, learned that the women's question was not front and center in the political parties."[50]

The women read the works of prominent women scholars in Morocco and from around the world and talked among themselves as well as with a few male allies about women's issues. But in their parties it was "believed that if we changed the general political and economic situation in Morocco, then the situation of the women would improve."[51]

"Then in 1985, after some years of thinking, we decided that women needed their own non governmental organization" that addressed politics important to women and we "should not try simply to work through the parties. We realized that we needed an organization that had a vision for women. So on June 1, 1985 we created our NGO for women."[52] And the ADFM became the first women's political non governmental organization for Moroccan women.

Over time, the women had moved from attending political party meetings with men present, to attending women's meetings, often with only women present. But, they could not easily travel alone. This was especially the case for international conventions. Tahiri recalled that the United Nations Conference on Women was set to be held in Nairobi Kenya, in Africa. Clearly it would be an important international conference on Women. However Tahiri noted, "only three or four women attended. They went through their parties because women in Morocco were not yet organized enough to go on their own."[53] Women in Morocco were not yet in the habit of connecting on their own or through their organizations with other women leaders around the world. And they were not used to taking the initiative to travel. The party leaders could receive invitations and could sponsor women to attend or the women in political parties could go to their leaders and ask for permission to represent the party at such international events.

While women activists were beginning to imagine an alternative situation and status for Moroccan women, Tahiri remembers, "from 1985 until about the time King Mohammed VI became king, when we talked about women's issues, people looked at us like we were crazy." Even those who hoped to be helpful advised the women to target less fortunate women by improving them through illiteracy programs, anti violence programs, etc.[54]

As Moroccan women activists debated their best route to making improvements for Moroccan women, Tahiri remembers that, "over time we came to see that the Moudawana was the fundamental, primordial issue affecting the status of women. This main text was the basis for discrimination against women in many areas: work, penal, education, political, social, etc. The text was important. It said that the wife had to be obedient and submissive to her husband. She had to not only accommodate her husband, but also her husband's family. Even if the new constitution said that women and men were equal, this text took priority and kept women in a status of second class citizens. We began to see that the language of the text *had* to be changed. But we did not know exactly how to change it."[55]

Activating Women's Political Agency in Morocco

The women above, many of the pioneers of Moroccan women's activism, came of age in the late 1960s and early 1970s. By analyzing the narratives that they have provided we can understand how these women were able to achieve the agency to participate in political action in a country and culture that largely frowned on such activities for women.

#1. A Mentor, a Male Mentor:

Each of these women can name a male—a father, brother, uncle, or teacher—who offered her the permission to engage in the political realm of political parties, organizing, and/or protests. Not only did this male figure offer permission, this male actively encouraged and supported his sister, daughter, niece, or student, to engage in the national politics of the time. The male supporter likely imagined that the young woman would take up activities to support the agenda that the male and his allies supported. Generally, the young women did this for some time. The male offered himself as a guide into the world of campus or party politics and as a protector of the woman's right to engage in the political arena. All of this was critical for a young woman who possessed an interest to become involved, but whose neighbors and non immediate family members might have criticized such activities by a woman.[56] Such a guide was also able to act as the mandatory escort needed to attend political meetings.

#2. A Household or Cohort Accustomed to and/or Valuing Political Activity:

Most of these Moroccan women activists came from a household in which politics was discussed at home. If they did not come from such a household, they found themselves surrounded by students and faculty who took politics seriously and discussed national problems and debated possible solutions. These women were not coming from homes whose family members all agreed that it was corrupt or worthless to engage in political activity. So on a daily basis, these women did not need to risk a family's wrath in order to engage their interests in the questions of the day.

For those who came from homes that had fought for independence less than a decade earlier, the talk about Morocco's future and its place in the world was considered to be what serious citizens talked about. If fathers, brothers and uncles were involved in political parties, they modeled political activism for the women at an early age.

For those women at the university, they were often surrounded by the debates and discussions of male students and faculty. Being privileged enough to attend university meant that they could take the next step and fully explore the topics of conversation that surrounded them.

#3. I am Not Alone; There are Others Who Value Political Activism:

These women were able to become part of a circle of family, friends, comrades, and colleagues, who believed it was a duty for Moroccans to improve their country. Being part of a reinforcing cohort offered emotional and intellectual support for the women's choices.

Once at the party headquarters or at the university, it was a short mental distance as well as a physical one to move from one meeting table to another meeting room for discussions when others were doing so as well. Once in the confines of these institutions, the women could move from room to room and discussion to discussion. The women could expand their relationships and seek to learn about new issues and strategies. They began to build their own networks within their parties and universities beyond those of their male mentors.

#4. These women Came of Age during an International Moment of Student Activism

These women, like millions globally, were affected by the historic times in which they were living and by the activities which they read about that were being undertaken by other students and older activists in their country as well as in other countries. While these women began with the support of male guides, permission givers, and encouragers, they soon learned that their actions had importance beyond their local setting; they were part of a movement larger than themselves during a historic moment in time when young people globally increasingly were politically active.

#5. The Politics of Brutality and Injustice was All Around Them during the early 1970s in Morocco under King Hassan II.

Especially in the early 1970s, King Hassan II was using the force of the state police and its military to attack, jail, and torture protestors. Injustice and human rights violations were on display for all to see. Hundreds attending a peaceful demonstration for increased pay for workers, better working conditions, or an expansion of democratic institutions in Morocco, for example, would suddenly be swooped down upon and grabbed by brutal state police and incarcerated and tortured – women as well as men. They also would be sexually abused.

When one's family, friends, and party members are so attacked, one cannot then just walk off and forget about them. Public pressure had to be initiated so these friends and family members were not forgotten. Especially among the young and hopeful, such actions required a political response.

Public reactions and continued demonstrations prompted the European Union (EU) officials to which King Hassan II had appealed for EU membership to note that human rights violations in Morocco precluded its membership (as well as the fact that Morocco was not a European country, its location being about nine miles from Spain across the Mediterranean Sea).

In 1965 King Hassan had issued a state of emergency following bitter riots in Casablanca mainly over living conditions but also due to a lack of democracy for individual Moroccans. This lack of democracy also marginalized any political participation by Morocco's political parties. Then, the King barely survived failed coup attempts in 1971 and 1972. Observers suggest that King Hassan was seeking some legitimacy when the King sent a letter to the executive committee of Istiqlal as well as to some other political parties to invite them to participate in a new government. But Allal al-Fassi, the leader of Istiqlal, wrote a letter of rejection in response and published the letter. He asked for free elections, not a government organized by the King. And in his letter, al-Fassi itemized the political grievances of many Moroccans regarding the King's politics of the previous decade.[57] Other party leaders also rejected the King's proposal.

King Hassan had begun to nationalize Moroccan businesses (mainly from former French colonists) and in a quest for legitimacy he accelerated this policy. Then, in 1974, King Hassan announced his intention of restoring some democratic processes and announced that local elections would be held in 1976 and new parliamentary elections would be held in 1977. He also granted amnesty to most of those arrested during protests and raids in 1971 and 1972.

Moroccan women activists were coming of age while their parties were focused on national politics. But despite the ongoing lack of democratization, by the mid 1970s, the women were pushing their male colleagues to include issues of concern to women as among the national issues that had to be addressed.

Then in 1975, the King announced the reintegration of the Western Sahara into Morocco proper and led a nationalist, patriotic "Green" march of about 350,000 Moroccans to the Saharan territory. The march was overwhelmingly supported by Moroccans of all political parties across the country.

Shifting from National to Women's Issues

Thus, even in a culture that shunned women's participation in politics, one can understand how it was possible for young politically alert women to be pulled into the politics of their time. These women were a product of the contexts of numbers one through five above: each had a male mentor; each grew up in a household or a cohort that valued political activity; each placed herself in a position where she continued to be surrounded by politically active Moroccans; each was alert to international events and felt her youth activities were part of a larger global phenomenon; each was politicized by witnessing injustice and lack of democratization in the politics in Morocco during the late 1960s and the 1970s.

If we shift the question from how these young women began to take agency in the public, political sphere and ask how the women began to focus on gender issues and take agency in this realm, we must rely on the information within their narratives.

In their readings of politics they read texts on the woman's question. In their own country as they learned about the human rights movements generally, they became acquainted with issues that they would claim as their own. Unions, Berber cultural groups, human rights groups all advocated better treatment for humans. Why not for women?

Moroccan women activists mostly gained agency with permission from some male supporter or ally and within their political parties and student organizations. But once Moroccan women activists began to ask for social justice for Moroccan women, they learned to look beyond their families, parties, and existing organizations. How they did this, and the forms and pathways that that Moroccan women created throughout the 1980s to address issues of social injustice for women is the subject of the next chapter.

Notes

1. Alison Baker, "History and Myth: Women's Stories of the Moroccan Resistance," *The Oral History Review* 22, no. 1 (Summer, 1995), 29-49.

2. Fatima Sadiqi, "The Image of Moroccan Women in Public Spheres," in *The Idea of the University* ed. Taieb Belghazi (Rabat: Publications de la Faculté des Lettres, 1997), 257-270, cited in Fatima Sadiqi and Moha Ennaji, "The Feminization of Public Space: Women's Activism, the Family Law, and Social Change in Morocco," *Journal of Middle East Women's Studies* 2, no. 2 (Spring 2006), 88. The observations attributed to Sadiqi in this paragraph are all derived from this source.

3. Sadiqi and Ennaji, "The Feminization of Public Space," 88.

4. Sadiqi and Ennaji, "The Feminization of Public Space," 89.

5. Sadiqi and Ennaji, "The Feminization of Public Space," 91.

6. Sadiqi and Ennaji, "The Feminization of Public Space," 97.

7. Nezha Alaoui, interview with author in Casablanca, Morocco, November 20, 2007.

8. Alaoui, interview with author, 2007.

9. Alaoui, interview with author, Casablanca, Morocco. The above paragraph is taken from interviews with Nezha Alaoui in 2007 and in Casablanca, Morocco, July 20, 2009.

10. Alaoui, interview with author. The above paragraph is taken from interviews with Nezha Alaoui in 2007 and 2009.

11. Alaoui, interview with author, 2009.

12. Ghizlan Benachir, interview with author, Rabat, Morocco, November 23, 2007.

13. Ghizlan Benachir, interview with author, Rabat, Morocco, July 21, 2009.

14. Benachir, interview with author, 2007.

15. Benachir, interviews with author, 2007 and 2009.

16. Benachir, interview with author, 2007.

17. Zahra Chaggaf, interview with author, Rabat Morocco, November 22, 2007.

18. Chaggaf, interview with author, 2007. The paragraph above is based on information provided by Chaggaf during this interview.

19. Chaggaf, interview with author, 2007.

20. Chaggaf, interview with author, 2007.

21. Meluda Hazib, interview with author, Rabat Morocco, November 29, 2007.

22. Hazib, interview with author, 2007. The paragraph above is based on information offered during during interview.

23. Hazib, interview with author, 2007.

24. Amina Ouchelh, interview with author, Rabat, Morocco, November 28, 2007. The information for this paragraph is taken from this interview.

25. Ouchelh, interview with author, 2007. The information for this paragraph is taken from this interview.

26. Ouchelh, interview with author, 2007.

27. Ouchelh, interview with author, 2007. The information for this paragraph is taken from this interview.

28. Ouchelh, interview with author, 2007. The information for this paragraph is taken from this interview.

29. Ouchelh, interview with author, 2007. The information for this paragraph is taken from this interview.

30. Ouchelh, interview with author, 2007. The information for this paragraph is taken from this interview.

31. Ouchelh, interview with author, 2007. The information for this paragraph is taken from this interview.

32. Ouchelh, interview with author, 2007. The information for this paragraph is taken from this interview.

33. Ouchelh, interview with author, 2007. The information for this paragraph is taken from this interview..

34. Ouchelh, interview with author, 2007. The information for this paragraph is taken from this interview.

35. Ouchelh, interview with author, 2007.

36. Ouchelh, interview with author, 2007.

37. Ouchelh, interview with author, 2007.

38. Ouchelh, interview with author, 2007.

39. Ouchelh, interview with author, 2007. The information for this paragraph is taken from this interview.

40. Nouzha Skalli, interview with author, Rabat Morocco, November 28, 2007. The information in this paragraph is taken from this interview.

41. Skalli, interview with author, Rabat Morocco, November 28, 2007. The information in this paragraph is taken from this interview.

42. Skalli, interview with author, 2007. The information in this paragraph is taken from this interview.

43. Nouzha Skalli, discussion with author, Rabat Morocco, November, 2002, NDI and ADFM campaign workshop for Moroccan women running for parliamentary seats.

44. Khadija Errebbah, interview with author, Casablanca, Morocco, July, 2009.

45. Skalli, interview with author, 2007. The information in this paragraph is taken from this interview.

46. Skalli, interview with author, 2007. The information in this paragraph is taken from this interview.

47. Skalli, interview with author, 2007. The information in this paragraph is taken from this interview.

48. Rachida Tahiri, interview with author, Rabat, Morocco, November 23, 2007.

49. Tahiri, interview with author, 2007.

50. Tahiri, interview with author, 2007.

51. Tahiri, interview with author, 2007.

52. Tahiri, interview with author, 2007. The information in this paragraph is taken from this interview.

53. Tahiri, interview with author, 2007. The information in this paragraph is taken from this interview.

54. Tahiri, interview with author, 2007. The information in this paragraph is taken from this interview.

55. Tahiri, interview with author, 2007. The information in this paragraph is taken from this interview.

56. This section does not attempt to explain why some individuals are attracted to acting in the political sphere while others might be more passionate about artistic initiatives. Rather it offers insight as to how those women with interest in politics, but facing social obstacles to participation, came to participate.

57. Malika Zeghal, *Islamism in Morocco: Religion, Authoritarianism, and Electoral Politics.* Translator, George Holoch (Princeton: Marcus Weiner Publishers, 2008), 73.

Chapter Four
Changing Rules and Paths within Institutions and the Creation of Discursive Initiatives to Alter Morocco's Gender Discourses

As demonstrated in chapter three, Moroccan women who would become leaders in the struggle for advancing the status of women in their country and changing Morocco's institution of gender did not gain their agency from the King's support, or from the staff and officers of international organizations coming to Morocco in the 1960s. Instead, Moroccan women gained their agency with the support of Moroccan male mentors (fathers, brothers, uncles, teachers, friends) who brought them into the (mostly left) political parties, study groups, and campus organizations that sought to create political space for organizing and also sought an informed analysis for understanding Morocco's political economy. These women cut their teeth learning political organizing and agenda setting on the campuses and in the high stakes arena of Moroccan public politics.

But while Moroccan women activists worked to support their parties and their male mentors, it became clear over time that most politically active Moroccan men would not engage with the issues of gender that concerned Moroccan women. Thus, some of the politically active women came to believe that they had to find ways to intervene in Morocco's national discourse to legitimize women's issues. These women began to search for discursive interventions that would bring gender issues to the attention of Morocco's political leadership.

During the 1970s and early 1980s Moroccan women academics, and also some journalists, had begun writing on the situation of Moroccan women. But the audience for these writings was small and, even among those familiar with the works, few tried to determine how to create new social and legal policies that would advance the status of Moroccan women.

Obviously, Moroccan women political activists were not aware of institutionalist theories that argued that one lever of change by which institutions (such as a gender institution) transform is by promoting discursive interventions in national dialogue, or that a second lever of change is to create new institutional structures circumventing veto points and/or other obstacles, or that creating new parallel institutional forms could legitimately advance the women's goals. However, in the early 1980s, Moroccan women activists concerned with gender issues and seeking to promote gender equity were looking for new strategies. Thus, although at the time they lacked proof that their actions would bring change, they nonetheless determined to raise consciousness concerning issues of gender among the members of their own groups and/or political parties by joining with other women of their party or group. They initiated women's divisions or caucuses within the existing frameworks of their organizations and most of these divisions or caucuses were for women only. Other women opened their caucuses and divisions to the male members of their organizations, though some only undertook such outreach to their male colleagues after the women had established themselves for a few years, conducting self education activities and lobbying male party activists concerning women's concerns. But despite women doing good work for their parties, it was clear that the mostly male party leadership would not give attention to issues that concerned the women as women.

In Morocco, the political party system was put in place in 1963 and party leaders were consumed with their performance and the advancement of their parties relative to other parties. Additionally, the "opposition" parties were focused on attempts to gain more power for party leaders and parliament relative to Morocco's monarch. Few, if any, male party leaders were concerned with women's issues. And the leaders of those parties that supported the monarchy (known as, les partis de l'administration) were unlikely to advance women's concerns unless orders to do so came from the Palace.

Three efforts to address women's issues were attempted in the 1970s. First, in 1972, King Hassan established a Royal Commission to prepare a draft on the feasibility of making changes to Morocco's family code; the commission never completed any work and no draft was offered. One can only guess at the political reaction to this effort and assume that the Monarch's decision, therefore, was to simply let the matter rest until a later, more propitious moment. Then in 1979, a few leaders of the political party, The Rassemblement National des Independants (RNI) submitted drafts to revise the family code. The RNI was one of the parties that supported the monarchy. Thus, both of these initiatives were supported by King Hassan and the second occurred following his 1977 initiative to take small steps to liberalize politics even while retaining the right to use repression.[1]

The Minister of Justice, however, turned the RNI's drafts over to leading Ulama and the only issue on which there was any change was that divorced women were given a food pension.[2] Political party leaders were remarkably lacking in taking up the cause of revising the family code. So the Monarchy tried again. In 1979, the King set up a royal commission of three magistrates to review the Moudawana or family code. This commission proposed a number of improvements for women. For example, the legal age for marriage in Morocco was to be raised for girls and boys. A husband could no longer prevent his wife from working if the work served the needs of the family. The grounds on which a woman could request a divorce would be broadened. But all of these proposals came to naught. The Ulama and their religious followers argued that the family code was a sacred text and therefore could not be modified.[3]

We cannot know for certain why King Hassan II raised such issues at the times that he did. We can only imagine that the King, who prided himself on reading works by Western policy strategists like the U.S.'s Henry Kissinger and who sought to engage as an international, not just a regional actor, was far more aware, than was the average Moroccan citizen, that throughout the 1970s, the United Nations and other international agencies such as the United Nations Dvelopment Programme (UNDP) and World Bank, were working to advance the status of women. As we discuss later in this chapter, when considering the context in which Moroccan women were advocating, the King faced many internal obstacles in the 1970s, including coups, riots, and protests. Thus, looking for support among his women subjects might have been a deliberate strategy to mitigate the opposition that the Monarchy faced during this period.

But while the Royal efforts at modest reform for women failed, between 1983 and 1986, three groups of Moroccan women determined to address the issues that concerned them. They created civil society organizations outside the framework of their political parties in order to advance the status of women in Morocco. They strategically chose when to organize and which particular issues they wanted to focus upon with a calculation regarding both the exogenous and endogenous factors affecting Morocco. Their discursive initiatives to impact the national discourse and influence national consciousness about gender issues were purposeful and ground breaking.

In 1983, an Arabic language monthly magazine named *8 Mars* (*March 8*), or *Thamania Mars*, was founded by Latifa Jbabdi, Aicha Lkhoumass, Khadija Amiti, Fatima Outaleb, and other women associated with the political party, the Union Socialistes des Forces Populaires (USFP). These women hoped to use the date of International Women's Day to catch the attention of those who wanted to read seriously about women's issues in Morocco.[4] They determined that promoting thought about their issues was a necessary preliminary step to political activism and they utilized a connection to exogenous events to make their initiative newsworthy.

As Loubna Skalli, a scholar on women's writing and globalization in the Arab world has noted, *8 Mars* was the only journal of its kind in the Arab world.[5] Latifa Jbabdi served as Editor of the new feminist publication from 1983 to 1995.[6] As founder Fatima Outaleb recalls, "We raised issues such as the family code, women's condition, women's status, the legal framework, and violence against women."[7] Indeed, *8 Mars* was initiated at a time when it had a real impact and was able to catch the attention of Morocco's political leadership. *8 Mars* was not the first feminist publication to write and question the role of women in Morocco; there were some earlier efforts during the independence period. But *8 Mars* would help to lay the groundwork of strategic Moroccan gender activities in the 1980s. As we discuss below, the publication would influence the endogenous political debate among Morocco's elite political actors and reactions to the journal would make the women rethink their strategies for how they should present their concerns.

The first Moroccan civil society organization founded explicitly to undertake political work on behalf of Moroccan women was the Democratic Association of Moroccan Women or ADFM. The ADFM was founded by Amina Lamrini, Nouzha Skalli, Malika Naciri, and other Party of Progress and Socialism (PPS) women activists in 1985 who wanted an organization that reached beyond their party to address Moroccan issues of gender. As noted in chapter three, the Party of Progress and Socialism was created in 1968 and included many members of the former Communist Party that was banned in 1960 because a Communist Party was perceived as a threat to Morocco's monarchy, even as communist parties were perceived as rivals to all monarchies.[8]

ADFM's founders had been active politically for over a decade and for many years they had been searching for ways to advocate for women. These women were from a small party, but they wanted to build on the new public debates about women that were taking place in Morocco and globally in order to organize politically across parties for the benefit of Moroccan women. Additionally, they founded their organization only about one month before the close of the United Nation's (UN) International Decade for Women and the related World Conference to Review and Appraise the Achievements of the UN Decade for Women (1975-1985) that was scheduled to be hosted in Nairobi, Kenya during June (15-26) 1985. The women of the ADFM clearly were aware that exogenous activities, such as those of the UN, could be harnessed for good purpose within Morocco's domestic political arena. The ADFM would play an important role in many future Moroccan women's initiatives and its leadership would find ways to shine a light on Moroccan women at important international and national junctures. However, in its early years, the ADFM was perceived by many as being closely associated with the PPS and this limited its appeal to women not affiliated with the PPS.

Realizing the importance of contributing to the national debate on issues, as well as undertaking political action, in 1986, the ADFM introduced its own women's political magazine, an Arab language publication called *Nissa' al-Maghrib*. The new publication was meant to direct the public's attention to the concerns of women and, ADFM's founders hoped, to create a "space for 'understanding and debating' the challenges facing women in a transitional society."[9]

Also in 1986, another group of Moroccan women organized to publish *Kalima*, a third women's journal in Morocco. *Kalima* was famous for moving beyond "modest" public topics to address issues that previously were considered private and rarely spoken about: abortion, sexuality, etc. *Kalima* directly addressed issues concerning relationships between men and women.[10] The name *Kalima*, often translated as "The Word," is derived from its reference to one of the five pillars of Islam, the "testimony of faith."[11] *Kalima*, however, was censored and banned, lasting only a little over two years.

Clearly, those who sought to advance the status of women in Morocco, while coming from different political camps, all recognized the importance of promoting debate about the possible alternative logics by which Moroccan women could live. The new feminist journals provided Moroccan gender activists with a vehicle to discursively challenge the existing norms of Moroccan gender roles. The new women's advocacy organization modeled the advocacy that women could undertake to improve the status of all Moroccan women. But these Moroccan women also sought to prioritize specific goals for achieving gender change in Morocco. Additionally, they spent time debating the strategies by which to achieve the changes that they sought.

One such venue for debating goals and strategies was the new women's organization that developed as an outgrowth of *8 Mars*. In 1987, many of the women who had founded *8 Mars* founded the civil society organization, the Union of Women Action (UAF) to work for the advancement of women's status in Morocco. About 50-60 women had been affiliated with *8 Mars*.[12] Some of these women also were affiliated with the political party USFP, some were affiliated with Arab nationalist parties, some came from other parties and some had not been party activists. By the late 1980s when the UAF began holding meetings, "thousands attended"... and the "rooms could not hold all the women."[13]

The UAF's success was based partially on the agency of its Moroccan women leaders and the strategies that they adopted to insert themselves into the national dialogue. Additionally, its success would come from women's activism and the politics of democratization found in the 1980s across Morocco through the new structures of civil society organizations that required the attention of policy makers. The UAF would find enormous success in 1992 when it led an effective national petition campaign to collect one million signatures requesting a change in the status of Moroccan women.

Thus, Moroccan women leaders of three civil society organizations—*Mars 8* founded in 1983 whose leaders then founded UAF in 1987, the AFDM founded in 1985, and *Kalima* founded in 1986—helped to put women's issues on the national agenda in Morocco and discursively altered Moroccan national debates to include the "question of women." Later in this study, we will return to consider the work of the women of *Mars 8*/UAF and ADFM in some detail, along with Moroccan women who, in 1995, founded another important organization—Joussour/Bridges.

What is clear, however, is that Moroccan women focused on: 1) discursively intervening in Morocco's national political dialogue to offer an alternative logic of gender and its institutional forms in Morocco, and 2) creating new spaces for political activity that had not previously existed in order to further their goals which had been stymied within traditional political organizations. The women's pioneer organizations we discuss in this chapter played critical roles in the restructuring of Morocco's gender institution in ways that bypassed the traditional routes and pathways for practicing politics in Morocco in the 1980s.

A number of other women's organizations would follow and also play constructive roles in altering the institution of gender in Morocco. For example, in February 1987, Istiqlal women formed their own organization, the Organization de la Femme de l'Istiqlalienne (OFI) which stood separate from their party. But these women anticipated that they could ally with their party activists when they needed to.[14] The Parti de l'Istiqlal (PI) had been the first party to create a women's bureau. Additionally, Istiqlal women were quick to note that women had, over time, been appointed to high positions in their party. In the 1982 Istiqlal Central Committee, women occupied 8 of 80 seats or 10 percent of the party's

Central Committee seats. Such an arrangement for a political party in the Arab world was highly unusual.[15]

Throughout the 1980s, creating an organization for women, not a women's organization for their party, tracked with the model that many politically active Moroccan women preferred. They joined an independent civil society organization for women, but they also maintained some links to their original political party base. The largely male party activists and the women in their women's organization interacted on the basis of the relationships which they had developed over previous decades. This interactive dynamic would, over time, become a resource for Moroccan women activists as we will discuss in chapter five.

The Morocco League for Women's Rights (LDDP) was founded in 1993 by Fouzia Assouli, Bouchra Abdou, Halima Bennaoui, and other women activists. By 2009, it reported 13,000 members across Morocco. The LDDP was founded as a secular organization for women's advocacy. At the time of its founding the debate in Morocco over women's rights had evolved into a debate over the interpretation of the role of women in the Koran. The LDDP afforded women who were secular a place to gather and offer their voices in the national debate. The LDDP allowed Moroccan women to frame their issues without always having to defend their position with reference to the Koran.

Additionally, another Moroccan women's advocacy organization was founded in 1995, Joussour (Bridges). Joussour was founded by Ghizlan Benachir, Ouaffa Hajji, and other women who felt they could work together and wanted a space outside that of any political party. Benachir noted that while the women were strong members of their political parties, "We did not have space in our parties. So we wanted to take action within a different framework. These were women who had ties to one another and worked with each other across party lines."[16] Like others before them, the founders of Bridges hoped to truly offer a cross-party and non-party venue for women who wanted to focus on improving the status of Moroccan women. Bridges could not easily be identified with any single party as its founders and its Board came from several parties. Additionally, these women, like those in the decade before them, recognized that they ultimately could not rely on their political party leadership to make issues of gender a top priority, no matter how sympathetic some of their party allies might have been. Thus, Moroccan women founded this new organization and hoped that women who did not want to be perceived as associated with just one party's position on gender would come together and determine their own position on gender.

Clearly the women who created these Moroccan non governmental organizations after years of trying to work within their party, campus, and study group structures were elite, educated women. In Morocco, to be an educated woman, is to be elite. And the early goals of these women (as we can see from their recognition that they needed first to found publications that addressed women's issues) was discursively to interrupt Morocco's ongoing political debates in order to inject issues of concern to women onto the national agenda so that Moroccan male leaders would have to take a stand on these issues.

Over time, we see that many women's organizations came to appear on Morocco's political horizon. The U.S. State Department reported that in 2001, Morocco had seventy-six women's organizations working "to advance women's rights."[17] But by analyzing the critical goals chosen and strategies undertaken by the leadership of the Moroccan Union de L'Action Feminine (UAF), the ADFM, and the leadership of Bridges/Joussour we can better understand how Morocco's gender institution, established through common practice(s) and by the post-independence family code (the Moudawana), discussed in chapter two, was reformed. First, however, it is important to provide some political, economic, and social background to the struggles of those in Morocco's civil society movement of the 1980s and 1990s, as civil society organizations formed and expanded across Morocco's landscape.

The Moroccan Political Context and the Emergence of Women's Civil Society Organizations

During the reign of Mohammed V and then his son Hassan II, the political contestation in Morocco would find its expression largely in the struggle between the political parties and the Monarchy. Each would mobilize its resources as best it could and the Monarchy, with its monopoly on the use of force and electoral manipulation, would trump the parties and then determine the contours within which the parties could contest one another and contest issues with Moroccan monarchs. The Monarchy also attempted to counter any growing influence of Islamists that might take away from the legitimacy and authority of the Monarchy. These contestations among Moroccan male leaders and their followers constituted Morocco's post-independence political framework. And it is through this prism that scholars have argued that Morocco's monarchy played off the left parties against the right clerics when it suited the Palace's interest. This framework began to change when Moroccan women began to advocate for a change in their status. To understand what it took for Moroccan women to alter Morocco's national dialogue and the "politics as usual" in their country, we offer below an analysis of the context into which Moroccan gender activists had to introduce their ideas and create their organizational structures. Because the greatest resistance to the women's campaigns would come from Morocco's religious communities, we first offer below an account of the politics of the religious communities in Morocco as well as the practices and beliefs of the political parties, especially with respect to the Monarchy.

The post-independence male religious community in Morocco can be understood, for our purposes, through the work of Malika Zeghal. Zeghal's analysis is structured in opposition to that put forth by the (earlier) work of Oliver Roy. First, Zeghal argues that the interpretation of splits within most Islamic communities as proposed by Oliver Roy did not hold in Morocco after the 1990s. Roy had proposed that Islamic activists could best be understood as composed of two groups. The Ulama, who were traditional religious practitioners and operated, according to Zeghal's interpretation of Roy, "in a closed and circular religious canon, anchored in transcendence" in which they and their texts are "unchanged" and "represent fixity, submission, and repetition."[18] In contrast, according to Zeghal's account of Roy, the modern Islamists often had no official religious status, could well have been educated in the West, had no problem integrating texts from many sources, were undisciplined by traditional religious leaders and their institutions, and the Islamists' aim was to challenge not only the state but also the state's traditional religious partners.[19] Zeghal argues, in contrast, that, in Morocco, Ulama were increasingly fluid in where they obtained their texts and how they conducted themselves. The real differences between Morocco's Ulama and the Islamists, according to Zeghal, concerned their "institutional arrangements."[20] For the purposes of this study, we find persuasive Zeghal's account that Moroccan religious activists differ in the kinds of their resources garnered through their institutional arrangements. In chapter five we note that King Hassan's minister who in the late 1980s and early 1990s attempted to coopt the Ulema offered them new institutional resources that his critics claim allowed the Islamist movement to grow stronger.

In the early independence years, religious leaders, largely the Ulama during this period, struggled with the Monarchy over who would control education – both its content and in what language it would be conducted (the Monarchy preferred French to Arabic) and whether or not there would be any central religious institutions. Zeghal demonstrates that the Ulama were not a homogenous group though they gathered together from time to time. The Ulama differed on their positions regarding the Monarchy, largely in relation to their individual relations with the King. When the Ulama were able to unite, the Monarchy sometimes lost battles to the Ulama, for example, early educational training was conducted in Arabic. This control by the Ulama over early education would have important implications for the institution of gender in Morocco because all primary school students were schooled and socialized to accept the family code or Moudawana. However, the Monarchy usually won important battles; for example, no formal national religious institution independent of the Monarchy was created. Thus, there was no religious center to compete with Morocco's Monarchy regarding legitimacy and rule. Moreover, as Zeghal explains, the particular vision of the state and religious institutions within Morocco's religious practices favored the position of the Monarchy.

In contrast to religious competition, the institution of political party contestation within Morocco was seen prior to independence when the Istiqlal Party organized against the French but was upstaged by the Monarchy in the struggle for political authority and independence. Three years after independence, with the goal of independence achieved, the competing ideological wings of Istiqlal fractured and with it went hopes for a united front vis à vis the King and also for a functioning political alternative to the monarchy. In 1959, Istiqlal's own Prime Minister left the party to its conservative wing and joined other, largely urban, political activists coming from the trade unions and campuses to form the National Union of Popular Forces (UNFP). UNFP leaders pledged to campaign to restrain royal authority, expand democracy and trade unionism, and enact economic reforms of redistribution. In the short term, UNFP campaigned for a new democratic constitution that would limit the monarch's powers.[21] But the UNFP itself had leaders with competing visions and strategies and also its support was localized in the urban areas.

The Monarchy was careful to court rural strongmen, especially those from among the religious Sherifian families. Redistribution of formerly French-owned land and business interests was strategically managed by the King. The left's threat of land reform also kept wealthy landowners supportive of the King.[22] As Joel Migdal might have anticipated through his theories of governance in late industrializing states, Morocco operated through a "triangle of accommodation" in which the King spoke of redistribution and proclaimed changes in land ownership, but government implementers failed to carry out the reforms in areas where wealthy landowners delivered rural support to the King.[23] Additionally, the Monarch attended to its ties within the military and police largely by purchasing their support. The King also encouraged the founding of a rural based, Berber affiliated political party, the Popular Movement (MP), and promptly awarded its leaders with numerous government ministries.[24]

Morocco's monarch was not unafraid to use the stick as well as the carrot, however. The King's Interior Minister did not hesitate to use violence against those who challenged the King. Thus, under Mohammed V but especially under King Hassan II, Morocco's political activists suffered horribly from repression, incarceration, and torture. It was taken as fact by most Moroccans that the 1965 assassination of opposition leader Mehdi Ben Barka, the UNPF leader exiled in Paris, was the work of Morocco's Interior Minister and secret service. Then, following an investigation, the French government concluded that Moroccan secret service individuals were, in fact, to blame.

Supporting an autocratic King were the Makhzen or royal advisers to the King that included family members and trusted advisors from leading Moroccan families, the political parties, and government agencies close to the king. The Ulama tied to the King were consulted on religious matters and the King clothed himself in mystical and ceremonial religious garb as befitting a privileged religious leader descended from the prophet Mohammed.

Since independence, Morocco's Islamic movement has taken many forms with many of Morocco's religious leaders advancing alternative visions of Moroccan society. Some religious leaders shun political parties and seek to create an Islamic society. Others work through political parties hoping to reform Moroccan society to their vision of an Islamic country. What is important to remember is that Islamic movements are active and have been influential throughout Morocco's post-independence history. Thus, women's civil society organizations have had to respond to religious leaders as well as to try to convince political party leaders, government officials, and Morocco's King, to adopt the goals and policies for Moroccan women espoused by Moroccan women gender activists. And as Zakia Salime's research reveals, and we discuss later in this chapter, the political advocacy of Moroccan women's activists who wanted to reform the Moudawana sparked, in return, attacks from women activists within religious parties and religious associations. Yet the Islamist women, while opposing most of the reforms of Morocco's gender activists, nevertheless used the issue of the inequality of women to push for changes within their own religious parties and associations.[25]

As noted above, from time to time, Morocco's monarch demonstrated support for advancing the status of Moroccan women. The King did not object in 1961, for example, when the only Moroccan trade union in existence at the time, the Union Marocaine du Travail (UMT) created the Union Progressiste des Femmes Marocaines (UPFM) and organized sections across Morocco to press for changes in women's labor and in the treatment of Moroccan women.[26] The union, however, never became an enduring force for women's advancement because, according to Laurie Brand, the union became "a victim of repression by management," incurred "a variety of political battles," and suffered from a "lack of upper level female cadres."[27] And as Sadiqi and Ennaji report, some observers believed that the union and the King recognized that relegating women to a subordinate organization distanced women from the centers of decision making and thus they were willing to allow subordinate women's organizations to exist, but not to expand.[28]

In various arenas King Hassan II offered mixed signals about the public role of women. For example, the King appointed his famous sister, who had given the public speech in 1947 without a veil, as Ambassador to Britain (1965-1969), Greece (1969-1970), and Italy (1970-1973). Also, in 1969, King Hassan founded the Union Nationale des Femmes Marocaines (UNFM) which was led by Moroccan women royalty who were charged with guiding any proposed changes for women through avenues that would accommodate Morocco's Islamic scholars.[29] It was problematic to propose any changes in the status of Moroccan women, however, because Morocco's family law was claimed to be unchangeable by those who wanted no transformation of women's status. It was argued that the Code reflected the will of the Imams and their religious authority and no political actions legitimately could modify it. Certainly the King's newly organized UNFM attempted no serious challenge to any of the code's prescripts during the 1970s.

As referenced by the women activists discussed in Chapter Three, the period of the 1960s and early 1970s had included acts of severe repression by the King against Left party leaders. Political leaders and Left activists "disappeared." During this period of repression, many women, especially those on the Left, were concerned with national freedoms and a concern for the disappeared. Women, too, were incarcerated. This was the period in which those who later founded women's organizations in Morocco came of age politically. Almost every party had a woman's bureau but its role was to mobilize women to support the goals of the party and elect its candidates, not to formulate national policies for women.

In the 1970s, a proposed national constitution (in 1972) that inscribed the power of the Palace vis-à-vis political parties, attempted coups against King

Hassan, and a nationalist upsurge in support of Morocco's claims to the Western Sahara (that were being challenged by neighboring states in their support for Western Saharan tribes), swamped any efforts Moroccan women might have considered regarding organizing for women's rights.

So although in 1975, the first United Nations Conference for Women (in Mexico) took place, Moroccan women were not focused on that first conference as they would focus on later UN conferences. The Mexico conference was to be followed every five years with reporting conferences, and every ten years with major conferences on women and their advancement. Each UN member state was to participate and report on the improvements for women within its country. Thus leaders of UN member states were incentivized to promote some changes for women within their states even if these were small changes.

The 1980s brought new exogenous and endogenous influences to the social context for the battle for the advancement of Moroccan women. In 1984, Moroccan scholar Fatima Mernissi published *Doing Daily Battle: Interviews with Moroccan Women*. Mernissi's publication coincided with an international effort to focus on the role of women and with a Moroccan political phase in which King Hassan II advocated that the advancement of women would yield positive gains for Morocco.[30] Mernissi was famous for her 1975 book on Moroccan women, *Beyond the Veil,* but her 1984 publication was published just as Moroccan women were beginning to organize themselves and strategize to advance women's rights.[31] Mernissi, like those who founded feminist publications in Morocco, was a discursive force for altering Morocco's political agenda and making male as well as female elites take notice of the status of Moroccan women.

Then in the 1980s, like other monarchs across the Middle East, King Hassan II sought to wrap himself in the garb of Islam reminding Moroccans that, through his lineage, he was the Commander of the Faithful, as well as the monarch of his country. This made it difficult for radical Islamists to try to elevate Islam over the State. And the King worked hard to make certain that Moroccans viewed the state and religion as two sides of the same coin. The dynamic for accomplishing this has been as Malika Zeghal observed, Morocco's monarchs "situated themselves as arbiters of the political game, above political actors, whom they divided in order to rule. They used the same strategy of division with religious actors."[32]

For the purpose of this study it is important to remember that in the 1980s, at various points, it appeared that King Hassan II might emphasize Islam at the cost of the goals for Moroccan women's human rights. Yet, King Hassan also seemed to offer some hope for advancing the status of Moroccan women. For some observers, however, the ability of King Hassan II to play off the rightist Islamic forces against Left political party leaders is the best means by which to analyze and understand the Moroccan political economy and its social/cultural formation. However, as we can see in this study, such an analysis ignores the agency of Moroccan women. Some, in an attempt to amend this analysis, put the women activists in the same "left" box as the political party leaders. This, too, however, fails to account for the fact that, in the 1980s, Moroccan women began to act independently of political parties and theirs was less of a "left" ideological position than it was a human rights struggle on behalf of all Moroccan women.

In the mid 1980s, King Hassan II initiated a political opening in response to both external and indigenous pressures and it was this period that saw the creation of Morocco's leading women's organizations. The 1980s liberalization has been attributed to several causes. First, the Monarchy's political repression of the 1960s through the 1970s had undermined the legitimacy of the Palace. Second, the very institutions and processes of Morocco's political economy were controlled largely by King Mohammed V and then King Hassan II's family and court advisors. This was increasingly resented throughout Morocco. The latter half of the1980s also saw international assistance organizations and some donor states begin to search for ways to advance democratic elections and the status of women globally and to look more favorably upon those leaders and countries working to improve conditions for women in their home states. This was especially true of the European Union to which Morocco applied for membership during the 1980s.

In the 1980s, an estimated 6500 landowners (mainly army and government officials, merchants and rural notables) owned 30% of Moroccan land and most of its modern sector.[33] The Moroccan population in 1982 was estimated at about twenty million and three hundred thousand so the compression of land ownership is a staggering statement about inequality in Morocco. While enriching the elite around the King, this arrangement obviously did not serve the average Moroccan. Morocco's citizenry grew restless. Additionally, while Morocco's territorial claims in the Western Sahara in the 1970s had provided a rallying point for its population to support the flag, the Monarchy, and to assert a common national Moroccan identity, the cost of the Western Sahara war diverted scarce resources from a citizenry aching for advancement. Further, Morocco's population increased in numbers and the country's economy failed to expand and keep pace. Periodic droughts also increased the hardship of most Moroccans.[34]

In Western international circles, during the 1980s, Hassan II appeared as a moderate leader and his foreign policies and worldview were appreciated by the United States and Morocco's European neighbors. However, despite Hassan's hopes for the good will of the West, when EU officials and business investors, looking for places in which to invest, compared Morocco's economic progress with that of other late industrializing countries, few investors invested in Morocco. Most foreign investors at the time were looking for relatively open markets in countries in which they invested; Morocco's economy, in contrast, was dominated by those close to the King and these select few enjoyed special economic privileges and did not have to compete in a free-market economic open playing field. Thus, King Hassan, who sought greater financial integration with the West, was said to have been motivated by the actions of Western investors coupled with the pressures within Morocco to begin to offer some changes in the lives of the average Moroccan, including Moroccan women.

In the 1980s, there also was an increase in international pressures targeting political changes through democratizing government procedures and supporting civil society organizations. Morocco, like other late industrializing countries, felt the international pressures. International donors increasingly viewed non-governmental organizations (NGOs) as effective vehicles by which to reach society and bypass government corruption and incompetency within aid-recipient states. The United Nations and the World Bank began including NGO leaders in their policy consultations and their programs in the 1970s. This effort accelerated in the late 1980s and early 1990s when good governance became an internationally recognized target that was linked to economic development.

In Morocco, the Crown was losing its legitimacy to govern as the country lagged in its economic development compared to other developing countries and also lagged in the freedoms that it granted its citizens. Lacking effective revenue streams and bleeding resources to military efforts in the Western Sahara, King Hassan had to enact International Monetary Fund structural adjustment programs whose policies of belt tightening added to the unpopularity of the government among Moroccans. Taxes were raised, civil servant salaries were frozen, public investment was slowed.[35] Riots in 1981 saw, in Gregory White's words, "crowds attacking upper-class privilege and Makhzen authority."[36] Police fired into the demonstrations, killing and wounding demonstrators. Elites and those advisors around the King, grew alarmed and began again to use events to arrest political opposition and trade union leaders.[37]

The King's political repression alarmed Morocco's increasingly educated citizenry even as that repression injured, imprisoned, or killed thousands of Morocco's most ardent democrats. Morocco came to be considered a tinderbox by some observers. Perhaps, permitting new civil society organizations to establish themselves and grow may have been seen by the Palace as the safest vehicle for social expression—if these organizations could be kept from real power. Moreover, perhaps these new forms of political organizing could offer yet another way to balance against both opposition political parties and religious leaders' organizations and their parties.

Moroccans began creating civil society organizations to advance their claims and to address the lack of a social safety net in Morocco. For example, in 1985, Mrs. Aicha Ech-Channa founded the Association Solidarite Feminine. This organization helped desperate single women and their children. Those women (and their children) who were raped, thrown from their homes, and labeled prostitutes, were aided by this new NGO that taught skills (mainly catering through the non governmental organization's own business enterprise), provided medical information and care, as well as sheltered these outcasts from violence. Ech-Chenna would observe years later, "Money is power. Money is independence… When I help a woman achieve a change in her income, there is a great change in that person's life and in her child's."[38] Thus, this civil society organization focused on service delivery and skill building in the catering sector, work that secured an income for the women and their children. However, Ech-Chenna, and others like her, did not attempt to upend politics or influence Moroccan policy making. They did, however, touch the lives and fortunes of thousands. They also modeled an alternative logic for responding to women and children in need. Additionally, by founding a service delivery NGO, they helped to legitimize the new civil society activism space. Theirs was important work, but clearly there was a need to address the rights of women in the face of those who would rape and discard them.

Other organizations sprang up that taught reading and writing, health care, or did other volunteer work to benefit women. These NGOs were formed by those who were motivated to bring changes to Morocco. King Hassan II tolerated the new NGOs that targeted development while keeping a close eye on those political organizations, parties, or movements that sought to shift decision making powers away from the King.

Democracy and better economic conditions were clearly desired by Moroccan citizens who increasingly had little to lose. Thus, despite the fact that King Hassan II continued to jail those who spoke against the regime, when the King raised the price of food in January 1984, riots broke out across Northern Moroccan cities. Diplomats in Morocco estimated sixty demonstrators were killed during the riots over increased food prices.[39] And the King's explanation for such riots was puzzling. Hassan II blamed the riots on Marxist-Leninists, Zionists, and Khomeinists which, as Stephen Hughes has noted, had to be considered "strange bedfellows indeed" though the King was vague on whether these groups collaborated.[40]

The growth of NGOs sprouted. Their leaders claimed to be of the people working at the grassroots and therefore democratic in nature. They demanded great changes. Then, in 1986 and 1987, the King again cracked down. Government officials jailed and repressed political party and trade union activists, many of whom were advocating for expanded democratic practices in Morocco with fewer Western foreign ties.

Then, in 1987, within a revived labor union movement, labor union women also began to organize to address labor issues as women, not just workers' issues. The Women's Labour Party was created by women active in the Popular Democratic Labour Association.[41] Needless to say, while these women were aware of the issues around the status of women in all forms, they were especially concerned with those of working women.

In the mid 1980s, women's status and women's affairs were gaining ground internationally as legitimate political concerns that had to be addressed. 1975 had been designated as the Year of the Woman by the United Nations and the decade that followed was designated as the United Nations International Decade for Women (1975-1985).[42] In 1985, women across Africa were particularly excited that the United Nations planned to hold an international conference on the status of women on the African continent. Preparations by each UN member country and by women's NGOs for the parallel civil society conference that was being held (in the same city) alongside the United Nations' official government conference, spurred action in women around the world. The purpose of the July 1985 conference held in Kenya was to appraise the progress made during the decade for women. Leticia R. Shahani, Secretary-General of the World Conference marking the end of the Decade, was quoted as saying that "the Decade has caused the invisible majority of humankind—the women—to be more visible on the global scene."[43]

It was within this domestic politically contested environment and within an internationally growing women's movement that Moroccan women began to found their own political non-governmental organizations/civic society organizations and advocate for improved changes in the lives of Moroccan women. As noted previously, the USFP women organized outside their party's structures to found the journal *Mars 8* in 1983 and they founded their politically oriented civil society organization the Union de l'Action Fèminine (UAF) in 1987. In 1985, the Association Democratique des Femmes Marocaines (ADFM) was the first Moroccan political organization for women and was founded after PPS women organized the ADFM as a civil society organization outside of their political party's structures. Joussour or Bridges was founded in 1995.

Utilizing Morocco's New Political Spaces to Gain Entry for Women Activists into Morocco's Political Processes

Morocco's women's civil society organization, ADFM, was created just in time to contribute to the international review on the status of women. For one of the founders of the ADFM, Nouzha Skalli, the ADFM was yet another effort to bring about changes for Moroccan women. As an active member of the communist affiliated political party, Popular Party Socialist, or PPS, Skalli had served as head of the PPS's Women's Bureau. But as we discussed in chapter three, after expanding the activism of the PPS's women's bureau, Skalli was looking for a venue outside her party. This was after an alternative to the women's bureau had been tried within the party. At the suggestion of a younger woman in the PPS, Skalli had backed a plan to create a space within the party not simply for women, but rather to create a subunit for women and men together, who were willing to address women's issues. PPS member Khadija Errebbah became convinced that the party's Women's Bureau was important, but that the PPS needed a second institutional center where women, together with the men who supported improving the status of women, could come together to talk and strategize.[44]

Khadija Errebbah had joined the PPS as a thirteen year old with the encouragement of some of her public school teachers and a cohort of school friends who had visited the PPS offices and learned from the political activists there.[45] Over the years, Errebbah had served as a PPS youth member of the regional bureau in Casablanca and on the PPS's national Central Committee. Eventually she came to believe that there were enough men in PPS to support women's causes and that a new structure in the party should be created. She brought her idea to Nouzha Skalli who agreed, but cautioned Errebbah not to start at the top when introducing a proposal for a new initiative.[46] Skalli's years of political work prompted her to suggest a strategy whereby they would first gather support for the proposal before forwarding it to the leadership.

Together, Errebbah and Skalli traveled to all sixteen of the party's regions to explain, advocate, and listen to what the members in the region might have to say about the proposal for a sub-caucus within the PPS that would be composed of both women and men with the purpose of advancing the status of women. Morocco was divided into sixteen political districts and the party's structure mirrored that of the country. The two women listened and learned from local leaders and the grassroots party members. By the time Khadija Errebbah and Nouzha Skalli brought the idea of an Equality Assembly for both women and men within the PPS to the leadership of the PPS, they could argue that they had grassroots party support across Morocco. Additionally, Errebbah and Skalli were able to respond with researched information and solutions to accommodate some of the concerns that they anticipated various party leaders might raise.

Skalli and Errebbah and other PPS women and their male allies began to analyze and advocate for women's improvement. But the PPS was a small party in Morocco and while the party's leaders allowed the Equality Assembly to pursue its own activities, many in the leadership chose to focus on building the party nationally. Having worked both within the PPS's women's bureau and now in the new Equality Assembly, a number of the PPS women came to believe that they could accomplish more outside the party. Even if they made progress within the PPS, if their goal was to seek change for women in Morocco, they needed a venue outside the PPS. These PPS women felt the time was right to found the first Moroccan women's civic organization to advance the status of Moroccan women.

Two years earlier, in 1983, many of these women had worked on the women's committee of the Association Morocaine des Droits de l"Homme (AMDH), a human rights organization.[47] Many of the PPS women were also working on development and support projects for women. These projects were essential for the women (and girls) that they targeted, but these centers and projects did not address the fundamental issues of Moroccan women's equality and women's rights.

Thus, in June 1985, Nouzha Skalli, Amina Lamrini, and Malika Naciri, along with other bright, educated, politically active PPS women founded the Association Dèmocratique des Femmes Marocaines (ADFM). As noted in chapter three, the ADFM would take advantage of the international platform that the upcoming United Nations conference offered. Additionally, by working through the ADFM, the women would be free to pursue the issues that the women increasingly had come to believe the PPS would not vigorously address. And by presenting themselves as members of the ADFM, the women were now able to make their own public statements without reflecting on their party, or having to clear their positions with their party.

On a personal level, many of the ADFM women kept their ties with male colleagues and female friends who remained within the PPS. But as the first political civil society organization for Moroccan women, the ADFM invited all Moroccan women to join them and it tried to lay the ground work for action in advocating for changes in the status of Moroccan women. Further, the ADFM began social activities to benefit women and their families. The ADFM leadership also reached out to labor unions, other political parties, and other women's organizations as these organizations developed across Morocco's political landscape.

As Rachida Tahiri explains the activities of the ADFM's early years:

> from 1985 until 1989 the organization undertook many kinds of activities. It began as a center where women could come and talk about their grievances and especially about violence against women. Today (2007) there are about 65-70 such centers around the country. But in those days we were the first. In the early years, we had programs for the centers where women could come and talk. We had illiteracy programs; we had female financial independence initiatives such as teaching women to knit. We had legal and health advice centers.[48]

Then, in 1989, four years after ADFM was founded, its board decided to focus on key political issues for women. As Tahiri reported:

> Other organizations were springing up to do work in specific areas and we did not need to try doing everything. So in 1989 we made a strategic decision to focus on human rights for women and anything to do with the international convention on the rights of women. We decided to strategically focus so we could have impact on the status of women. So we then went through a transition period. We could not just tell those women in our financial and health programs good bye. We began introducing those women to other organizations which were now developing and specializing in certain problems.[49]

For many Moroccans, one of the ADFM's most important successes was sending representatives to the United Nations presentations in 1996 when the UN was holding hearings on how countries were implementing the Convention for the Elimination of Discrimination Against Women (CEDAW). At those United Nations hearings, Nouzha Skalli, on behalf of the ADFM, presented an alternative report on the status of Moroccan women that differed from the report which had been submitted by the Moroccan government. Skalli's alternative country report represented a great deal of careful research. But making such a presentation, however, shocked some in Morocco even while it was liberating to others.

It cost the ADFM women scarce resources to get their representatives to New York. It also took courage for Moroccan women, who were told to shun public venues, to internationally appear and offer an alternative logic to the one provided by their own government, a government that was busy incarcerating and otherwise repressing dissent. But the actions of the ADFM women at the

United Nations' hearings put pressure on Morocco's government administrators to do more for women in the coming years or be embarrassed by the facts. And clearly the ADFM had demonstrated that through the creation of new civic associations, and the actions of its members, that new political pathways could be created to raise issues that Morocco's political establishment had neglected previously.

Two years after the ADFM was founded, PPS activist Khadija Errebbah joined the ADFM in 1987 and was soon in charge of the ADFM's youth committee and outreach initiatives. The ADFM women seemed poised to help lead the fight for women's equality in Morocco and many members would now emphasize their commitment to women's issues over those of the party. In fact, sixteen years later, in 2003, Errebbah, who by then had assumed the Presidency of the ADFM, would leave the PPS altogether. Errebbah and other ADFM women would devote themselves to conducting outreach to women's organizations across the country. With the ADFM's President no longer a member of the PPS, it created some distance between the organization's members and their original party allies.[50] However, other ADFM women maintained their ties to their political party even as they continued to work on women's affairs.

The ADFM women, however, were not the only ones in Morocco that formed new political structures outside of their parties in order to focus on their concerns for women. In 1985, many women in post-colonial states and late industrializing countries were aware of the impending United Nations Conference on Women to be held in Africa (Kenya). Women's organizations around the world were trying to push their governments to do more for women and government leaders were aware they would be required to report via the United Nations to the world on the steps they had taken to improve women's status.

In Morocco, the Union Socialiste des Forces Populaires (USFP) included activists who split from the trade union branch of the USNP and it was the USFP women who founded *Mars 8* in 1983. Then, in 1987, the USFP women who had founded the *8 Mars* feminist monthly magazine decided that they needed to take the next step. Their magazine had helped to raise Moroccan public consciousness concerning women's affairs but they had struggled to find the resources (without creating a formal organization) to print the magazine. The magazine's printing lapsed for periods of time. So in 1987, the USFP women associated with *8 Mars* founded L'Union de l'Action Féminine (UAF).

Latifa Jbabdi, who had served as the first Editor of *8 Mars* and who spent years in jail for her political advocacy of democratization in Morocco, was also a founding member of the UAF and its first President. Other prominent USFP women's activists like Nezha Alaoui also had worked on *8 Mars* and Zhor El Alaoui Mdaghri, Asmae Benadada, and many others then helped to found the UAF.

According to Alaoui:

> The March 8 paper wrote only about women's affairs, but it was written by both men and women. We had representatives in different cities who would re-

> port to us and write and also who would distribute the newspaper. From 1983-1987 the paper was the focus of our efforts. It was our central focus. In 1987 we realized that it was necessary to have a legal entity and a formal entity so we formed the UAF. From 1987 onwards, the newspaper was now a tool for our outreach on other activities and concerns. Each year we chose a topic to shine a light on, to highlight. Some of our topics were: illiteracy, divorce, violence against women, etc.[51]

But the UAF also had a political goal as well as general goals for social change for women. Alaoui reported, "A political aspect was embedded in our mission: support and advocate to place women representatives in decision making places in Morocco."[52] Like gender activists in other civil society organizations, UAF women leaders tried to promote national discussion on issues tied to specific issues that concerned grassroots women. But they also realized that change would largely come through the policy making process. Likely, the goal of promoting women in decision making venues also evolved from the lessons USFP women learned in 1983–according to accounts by a number of USFP women and by published accounts.

Like other political parties, the USFP had created a women's branch of the party. The USFP branch was created in 1975, the International Year of the Woman. USFP affiliated women were especially proud that an early prominent party leader (Abdullah Ibrahim) had, in 1973, argued for women's emancipation. Yet, by 1983, only ten years later, a number of USFP women came to believe that they needed to create another political structure outside the party for their advocacy for women. Not all the members of the USFP in 1983 were as willing as their earlier leader was to focus attention on the issues of women.

For some USFP women, bitter lessons following the events surrounding the local elections in Casablanca demonstrated this truth. In 1983, Badia Skalli ran for local office/municipal council in Casablanca and won. This was Skalli's third electoral attempt in a society where women running for office often were advised to return to their kitchens. In 1976, Badia Skalli (a founder of the party) had run for local office but been defeated. After running for Parliament and losing, she then ran again in Casablanca for the Municipal Council in the 1983 elections and won. Because two Socialist Party women had been elected to the same council, the USFP decided it would support Skalli for the Council President. When word of this proposal was received by the USFP rank and file men, they could not support such a policy. Out came all of their prejudices against women that many of them still held, including their versions of references to Mohammed's teachings which surprised some of these left party women.

Instead of supporting Skalli, the USFP party leadership supported a young man whom the women perceived as being much less qualified than Skalli for the post of President of the Council. This young man was appointed President and Skalli was given the post of Vice President. So it is no wonder that in 1983 many USFP women decided they needed a vehicle outside their party to raise issues related to women. The Casablanca election and its aftermath was not the sole reason that *8 Mars* was formed, but it no doubt contributed to some USFP women's decisions to support the journal. And later, as noted above, when the women realized the magazine could not stand on its own or accomplish all they had hoped, they founded their own women's civil society organization, the UAF.

While the UAF was a new organization in 1987, the women who founded it were longtime political activists. For example, Nezha Aloui, whose background we discussed in chapter three, came to her women's activism after years of student and party activism. Latifa Jbabdi began her political activism at the age of fourteen when she joined the Party of Liberation and Socialism and took part in the 1960s agitations for the democratization of Morocco. In 1977, Jababdi was condemned for threatening state security and imprisoned in one of Morocco's notorious and dangerous prisons. After two and a half years of imprisonment, Jbabdi was freed. Health problems from that ordeal remain with her throughout her life.

As a founder of *8 Mars* in 1983, Jbabdi ran for political office in 1984 but was not successful, running at a time when it was difficult for a woman to be elected. In 1987, she was a founder of L'Union de L'Action Feminine (UAF). Like other UAF members, Aloui and Jbabdi brought to the table the kind of commitment and insight that helped UAF Moroccan women identify effective goals and strategies.[53]

The UAF women had political goals as well as social and economic goals for advancing the status of Moroccan women. The organization's members learned they had to simultaneously focus on two sets of concerns: one was the struggle to maintain their basic service programs that aided women in need, and the second was to respond to outside events, forces, and challenges that required advocating for the rights of Moroccan women.[54] Their challenges were difficult, however, as Morocco's Family Code continued to stand as a barrier to improving the status of Moroccan women. And the women also encountered opposition from the conservative religious parties as well as from some socially conservative men and women within the left secular parties.

By 1989, however, the number of Moroccan women's organizations had increased to 29 associations.[55] During the 1980s, Moroccan gender activists created new political structures to coordinate across organizations with each women's group sending two representatives to the coordinating sessions. This practice was continued into the 1990s and also into the twenty-first century. These coordination meetings allowed Moroccan gender activists to identify priorities, research their concerns, establish goals and create talking points around those goals. A number of the women's groups rotated the two members who would attend each inter-organizational meeting, spreading the work and the leadership as well as ensuring that if one woman could not attend at the last minute, at least one woman from each group would be present at the coordination meetings.[56]

1989 saw the fall of the Berlin Wall and the success of democracy movements in Eastern Europe. Central African states, too, were holding national conferences demanding democracy and equality among ethnic groups. Democracy was in the air and women were vocal participants. In many new political settings, contending forces vied for the support of their country's women. Moroccan women, in the late 1980s and early 1990s, were writing, speaking, organizing and garnering international funds through donor agencies for their work to advance the status of Moroccan women.

Then, in 1990, King Hassan II established the Consultative Council for Human Rights (CCDH), signaling the changing times and giving hope to Moroccan women activists. A series of international conferences is credited with reinforcing the consciousness of women's civil society organizations in the Arab world according to the Arab Human Development Report 2005.[57] Among these were the 1992 Conference on Environment and Development in Rio de Janeiro, the 1993 World Conference on Human Rights in Vienna, the 1994 International Conference on Population and Development in Cairo, and the 1995 World Summit for Social Development in Copenhagen. But the 1995 Women's World Conference in Beijing was hugely influential as was Morocco's 1993 decision to become, albeit with reservations, a signatory to the United Nations Convention on the Elimination of All Forms of Discrimination Against Women (CEDAW). Moroccan women in their civil society organizations saw what was possible and recognized that they had created institutionalized interactions with one another, political parties, labor unions, and with women's centers and their program activists. All around them they could see women working for change.

Additionally, due to both exogenous pressures and the endogenous need for legitimacy on the part of the Monarchy, there was hope for increased support from the Monarchy for women's reforms and other democratic initiatives. King Hassan II was increasing his efforts, in light of the rapprochement between Eastern and Western Europe, to demonstrate that Morocco was a modernizing country and should be invited to join the European Union (which Moroccans can reach by a nine mile crossing to Spain).

On March 3, 1992 King Hassan II gave his annual throne address and announced that Morocco would enjoy democratic reforms via changes in the constitution.[58] Also as the King reached out for consultative sessions, Moroccan women working in their women's organizations now came to be viewed as legitimate voices speaking on behalf of Moroccan women. Their leaders now could work through the committees established by the Monarchy because these women leaders now represented an identifiable membership. Thus, because of all the years of work by Moroccan women activists, the women were viewed as legitimate leaders for their issues, and when the Palace determined that circumstances required women's participation, women leaders of civic organizations were the obvious choices to include in the national consultation process. The strategy of creating new civil society organizations, new pathways to raising important political questions for women, brought women to the decision making tables of established forms of decision making—those of the King's consultative committees.

Normatively, this inclusion in the decision making process was incredibly important because parliament was not the center of decision making in Morocco, the monarchy was. Having women among those working in consultation with the King allowed gender activists to sit at the table alongside, or sometimes in place of, Islamist participants whose views on women greatly differed from those of the gender activists. Yet the King could not act alone. Thus, Moroccan women had to continue to make inroads in educating Moroccans across the country, find allies in parliament, as well as choose which issues to raise to foster the King's inclination to support their causes.

The UAF women sought to find a way to further move Moroccan public opinion. They determined to take the lead in organizing their allies to demonstrate the breadth of their support. They determined to demonstrate the need for immediate and far reaching reform that focused on Morocco's family code. The Moudawana seemed to be an ever present obstacle to many of the aspirations of Moroccan women for gender equity. As they explained their strategy, "Our goal was to raise awareness, especially among rural women, that widespread poverty, illiteracy, and even domestic violence stemmed from the Moudawana... We believe being Muslim is our identity — but our religion should never prohibit us from coming out with progressive interpretations of Islamic laws."[59]

On March 7, 1992, just prior to International Women's Day, the Union de l'Action Feminine (UAF) launched a campaign to gather one million signatures of Moroccan citizens and so petition the government to change the Moudawana, the core family code that decreed Moroccan women must remain without full citizenship or human rights compared to Moroccan men and boys. For many observers, it was this petition campaign that jump-started Morocco's efforts to achieve gender equity. However, it would take over a decade and the efforts of thousands of women (and their male allies) and many organizations before any real change was accomplished.

The petitions targeted the Moudawana and the UAF women and their allies argued that it could be changed; it was *not* sacred as was the Koran. The Moudawana was a document written in the 1950s and, like secular law, it should be open to debate. The UAF's petition gathered momentum as other Moroccan women's groups, their associated political party allies, and their allies throughout largely urban middle and upper class Moroccan society collaborated to demand change. In fact, during this period when Moroccan women political activists were sensing that this was their time for change, more non profits sprang up across the country to work on issues that were of special concern to women.

But the Islamist resistance to the women's momentum was intense. Soon reports reached the UAF women that Moroccan fundamentalists had issued a fatwah (a religious ruling) against the women and their organization calling for the appropriate penalty in response to such an apostate attack on Islam... death.[60] The religious leaders did not shun encouraging violence against those who originated or signed the petition.[61] The fundamentalists also sought to position the Moroccan women's efforts as Western inspired attacks on authentic Moroccan and Arab values. They noted the close proximity of the launching of the campaign to International Women's Day and sought to tie the women to some of the Western programs detested across Morocco, such as International Monetary Fund and World Bank structural adjustment programs.

The nationalist and secular political parties, whom the women thought they could depend upon for support instead turned on the women and attempted to pressure them to halt the campaign and focus instead on the project of democratization and for parties' expanded participation in government. The Moudawana with its restraints on women, it seemed, was off limits for many of the men in Morocco's political parties (even as they argued for increased democracy and human rights in general). But for the UAF and their allies in other women's organizations, and among women not affiliated with any organizations but who felt the injustices of having men dictate the decisions they took in their lives, it was time to inject women into the national democratization debates. Democratization should not move forward ignoring the rights of women to participate in the public realm and to make their own decisions in the private realm.

The vehement and life threatening responses to Moroccan women activists by the Islamic leadership and the lack of support from the political parties stunned Morocco's gender activists and many observers abroad. Morocco's Islamic practices were certainly powerful; however, Morocco was viewed by many around the globe as a moderate Islamic nation.

King Hassan himself also was seen as a moderate, modernizing King by many outsiders. In 1989, King Hassan hosted the Casablanca summit which had "reintegrated Egypt into the Arab fold and endorsed a moderate Palestinian approach to the peace process."[62] Additionally, the King had promised democratization. Perhaps the King had made this promise in light of the disintegration of the Soviet Union and the rising forces of liberal economic democracies as well as pressures for democracy at home. But the King had made the promise. Additionally, the King looked toward the European Union for increased interaction and membership.

As part of his democratization program and in an attempt to find a pathway by which to engage the political parties in government, King Hassan announced he was permitting constitutional reform that would establish a new "Koutla government" in which Moroccan opposition political parties could participate together as a "ruling bloc" and would control the votes in parliament with their combined majority of parliamentarians.

Thus, in the early 1990s, political party leaders were concerned with their parties. But the women continued their work, going door to door and to the baths to collect one million signatures on their petitions to change the Moudawana. With a population of twenty-six million in 1992, this was quite a feat, and it was accomplished in a relatively short amount of time, between three and four months.

The million signature campaign represented the breadth of support for changing the Moudawana and the determination of Morocco's civil society women leaders.[63] To accomplish their task, the women's groups had created a coordinating council for all women's groups (al-Majlis al-Watani lil-Tansiq). As Fatima Harrak has so concisely put it, "the massive support for reform was stunning to all: the political parties, the religious scholars and the King."[64] And as Harrak's careful research highlights, the women had not petitioned the King. Rather their million signature petition was addressed to the Prime Minister, the head government official and so the women asked for their hearing in the political realm, not in the religious sphere.[65]

The backlash and the death threats from Islamists that accompanied the women's success stunned the women. Looking back at those events during an interview in 2001, three Moroccan women activist leaders, Latifa Jbabdi, Abdelillah Benkirane, and Leila Rhiwi, tried to explain the national climate at the time. Latifa Jbabdi recalled,"They went repeatedly to the most distant cities in Morocco, to many mosques, to incite violence against and the killing of all those who signed the campaign petition." [66] Abdelillah Benkirane recounted "There was an eminent Islamic scholar who said, 'In our religion, if somebody dares to counter the divine laws that we must interpret according to *Sharia*, they must be punished.' That is what they considered a fatwah. They made big media coverage of this. But there was never a fatwah." [67]

Questions about whether or not there was ever a fatwah continued for many years, though no one disputed the torrents of hate speech directed toward Morocco's women activists. And the possibility of a fatwah was chilling. Zakia Salime's research, published in 2013, definitively demonstrated that there was a fatwah issued in April 1992 (one month after the million signature petitions were launched) by al-Tajkani, an independent religious scholar active in the al-Islãh wa-l-tajdid (Reform and Renewal) movement.[68]

But the Moroccan women gender activists were not only threatened by the male religious community, they were also opposed by Moroccan women Islamists who were active in religious organizations and religious parties. In fact, Zakia Salime argues that much of the Islamist's response was the result of the Islamist women activists working within Islamic organizations and pushing the men to take a hard line against Moroccan women who wanted to reform the Moudawana.[69]

Salime's scholarship reveals that the work of the Moroccan gender activists in the 1980s who wanted to reform women's status in Morocco had required a response by the Islamist actors in Morocco. Thus, following the launch by Moroccan gender activists of the magazine *8 Mars* in 1983, the religious community launched the magazine, *Al Forkãne,* in 1984. *Al Forkãne* became an important Islamist magazine in which Moroccan Muslim identity in a changing world could be explored.

From Salime's work (which provides a powerful antidote to the lens offered by many authors of Morocco which focuses exclusively on male actors when discussing Morocco's religious community), we learn that in the 1980s while the Moroccan gender activists were making arguments about the inequalities of men and women and challenging patriarchal practices, Moroccan women Islamists were trying to counter expanding practices by Moroccan women to adopt European dress as well as counter Moroccan gender activists' arguments concerning women's inequalities.

Salime shows how throughout the 1980s, Islamist women worked to identify passages in the Koran that demonstrated that women should be role models for their families and that their work is equal to men's in demonstrating faith. Additionally, women have important responsibilities/duties because women must create a moral and religious household and so must reject Western corruption and instead mark themselves as authentic Muslim women through the practice of veiling.

The important discursive work conducted by women Islamists, however, legitimized women's work in the public sphere and thus freed them from being confined to the private sphere. The Islamist women embraced their new space in the public sphere even as they rejected Moroccan gender women activists who had fought to keep women from being confined to the private sphere. Because a proper Muslim woman of faith needed to model her faith in public as part of her duty to "invite others to follow the message" of Allah, a proper Muslim woman also needed to dress in a way that marked her as Muslim and to model her message in public.[70] A woman's emancipation did not come from turning away from religious practices, but rather from embracing Islam in public spheres.[71]

When the one million signature campaign first emerged, the Ulama leadership was largely silent. But the Islamist women jumped into action, organizing meetings and conferences to coordinate their response to the Moroccan gender activists. They also challenged the Ulama to respond, in some cases, to respond harshly, to the Moroccan women gender activists. These Islamist women put forward their view of a pious Moroccan woman that they had been developing since the 1980s when *8 Mars* first challenged them.[72]

Throughout 1992, Moroccan public debate of the women's question was consuming the public and eclipsing the other goals of King Hassan. King Hassan needed Moroccans to focus on the steps he was taking to democratize because Moroccan patience with the Monarchy was growing thin. In December 1990, riots had erupted in Fez, largely in response to harsh economic conditions but also, according to many observers, due to the secondary concern of the lack of democratic practices in the Kingdom. Then on February 4, 1991 between 300,000 and 500,000 demonstrators took to the streets in Rabat, Morocco's capital, to protest Morocco's participation in the Gulf War on the side of Saudi Arabia, the United States, and Kuwait.[73] This was reinforced by a national strike.

As Michael Willis has noted, King Hassan II was a monarch with good relations with Saudi Arabia and Kuwait, two countries that also were monarchies.[74] Further, Hassan was skeptical of Saddam Hussein's nationalism just as he had been skeptical of Gamal abd el Nasser's Egyptian nationalism previously. Morocco's Hassan II was an ally of NATO and the U.S. and he sent Moroccan troops to join the U.S. led coalition under George H.W. Bush and condemned Iraq's invasion of Kuwait. Hassan was not alone in this. Tunisia and Algeria, countries not seen as having particularly close links to the U.S., had done so as well—given that Iraq had invaded a neighboring country. But the person-on-the-street reaction in all three countries was overwhelmingly on the side of Saddam Hussein. This was true even among the religious communities which long had objected to Hussein's secular, military approach to governing.[75] Willis supports Yahia Zoubir's analysis that the average Moroccan was motivated by three considerations. First, when U.S. troops began arriving in the Gulf, Moroccans' "collective memories" of colonialism, during which period they had suffered from harsh rule, prompted them to oppose any rationalization for U.S. actions in the Middle East. Second, rich Gulf Arabs were not viewed kindly by Moroccans so their plight did not resonate with the Moroccan on the street. Finally, the opportunity to protest allowed an avenue for the expression of discontent for conditions in Morocco.[76]

Further, Willis argues that opposition parties were seizing on the events in the Gulf to link public policy determined by the King with lack of democracy in Morocco.[77] And the street protests saw the King alter his foreign policy, a first reversal of this kind, argues Willis. Fortunately, for King Hassan the Gulf war ended quickly as the Iraqi army crumbled and surrendered. But it is no wonder that the King wanted his citizens to focus on those steps he had taken to democratize. And he did not want further unrest due to Morocco's women's question. Thus, in a national broadcast on August 20, 1992, King Hassan intervened in the heated arguments about Moroccan women.

In his speech, King Hassan noted that Moroccan women faced many injustices but he also argued that the Moudawana was his responsibility, as only he had the authority to amend it. By proclaiming this, the King was asserting his primacy above the legislature and above the Ulama and suggesting that Moroccans needed their King. He indicated that he would rectify the situation.

Reflecting back on the King's speech, Leila Rhiwi recalled, "When in 1992, the King made his statement and recognized the injustices against women in this country, it was a moment for all women, for me and for everyone who was fighting for women's causes. It was a great victory."[78]

Following the King's speech, many Moroccan women activists hoped for major changes, even as the process of consultation took some time. In fact, the King kept his word and he met with various women leaders of Morocco's women organizations who advocated to improve the status of Moroccan women. But as Harrak reports, the King did not invite the UAF women.[79] He also met with academics and Ulama. King Hassan created a council that held twenty male and one female religious scholar and promised reforms would be forthcoming.[80] But when concluding the process, while some changes were made to Morocco's family code, it was nothing on the scale for which Morocco's gender activists had hoped.

The new version of the Moudawana curtailed a father's right to marry off a young woman without her consent. It did away with the need for male guardianship if a father died and the woman was of majority age (21). Husbands who sought to repudiate their wives now needed to secure approval from a judge. Likewise, a man needed to secure the permission of a judge to engage in polygamy. A mother could now have legal guardianship of her children.[81] Clearly these were important changes, but they fell far short of the aspirations of Moroccan women activists for change.

However, and most importantly for Moroccan women gender activists, despite their disappointment at only small changes being made to the Moudawana, Moroccan activist women successfully had changed the Moudawana for the first time in Moroccan history. Therefore the text could never again be called sacred, untouchable, or not changeable.[82] This was a huge victory.

Some believed that King Hassan II had had to intervene at a time when the country was torn over this national question of women because the tension had to end. The women's question was dividing families, erupting in places of work, and even appearing on the national news. Additionally, this debate had offered the Islamists a national platform from which they would contend for more power just before the democratic elections that the king was promising were to be held. According to others, the women's debate simply threatened to overshadow the political party and constitutional reforms which the King was presenting to the Moroccan people in the upcoming referendum on a new constitution. The new constitution was the King's showpiece legislation both domestically and internationally.

It followed, therefore, that when King Hassan II publicly asked both the women and the religious leaders to submit their concerns to the Royal cabinet the King defused the issue at hand in the short term "by adopting it himself and by establishing a committee that would have months to deliberate and decide upon recommendations."[83] A period of quiescence about the women's question followed as Moroccans waited to see what the King would decide.

For the purposes of this study, during this period, women's civil society organizations had shown their strength as institutionalized and organized entities within Morocco's polity. They had not worked through the parties, and in fact, they had learned that most party leaders would not join them on the front lines of pushing for an improvement in the status of Moroccan women. Rather, these women had created new political structures and new pathways for inserting themselves into the national policy making apparatus. They had altered the institution of who controlled decision making about Moroccan women and they altered the Moudawana itself.

During this period, many women activists retained ties to their parties as individuals but also sought a distance that allowed them the opportunity to take decisions their parties might not have approved or prioritized. The reactions, or lack of action, by many male party members in the face of the attacks against women activists made many women during this period reconsider the strategy of their personal relationship with their parties. After this episode, some of the women maintained their seniority and positions that they had worked so hard to earn within the parties. But others retreated from the political parties and determined to dedicate themselves to work primarily on issues of concern to women. The relations between women in civil society and their parties would continue, but it would be based on the strength of personal contacts and not a generalized belief in the work that the two kinds of social organizations could accomplish in tandem.

Additionally, Morocco's activist women realized that they would still need to keep fighting for change, but that as they did so, some Moroccans believed that they were rejecting Islam, which, of course most of these women did not believe they were doing. Most of these women believed they were merely bringing a modern interpretation of the practices of Islam to Morocco. Their predicament was complicated by the fact that when the Moudawana finally was reformed in 1993, the opposition Islamist women gathered in 1994 to talk and then create the Organization for the Renewal of Women's Awareness (ORWA) to offer women throughout Morocco an alternative logic and alternative practices to those espoused by the Moroccan gender activists. The Islamist women attempted to portray the activist women as lacking Muslim beliefs and values.

Having been attacked as not authentic Muslims and being too pro-West, Moroccan gender activists, especially the UAF women, were determined to analyze how Islam and women's rights were compatible. As Latifa Jbabdi explained, "We began taking classes and studying the Koran. We read the text from a woman's perspective and undertook a sort of 'taking back' of our Islamic heritage. We found many Koranic verses that stress equality and human rights. We realized that Islamic Sharia is based on a set of guiding principles, not on preconceived judgments…[and] we wanted to show people that the Moudawana was not so sacred like the Koran, but rather secular law that should be open to debate."[84] When they returned to debate the Islamists in the future, the women would have ready answers for what true Islam required and where it allowed for equality and human rights.

In addition to winning future intellectual debates, Moroccan gender activists realized that they needed legitimacy within their own country. Studying the Koran and demonstrating that they were not anti-Muslim, but rather they embraced their Muslim identity even as they sought to learn about progressive interpretations of the Koran, would help to protect them from charges that they were anti-religion or else Western puppets. The activist women hoped to present their claims for change within the legitimate framework of Moroccan values and politics. As Salime's research has demonstrated, the Islamist women and the women advocating to change the Moudawana were engaged in culture wars for intellectual hegemony. And the strategies by both sides would sharpen throughout the 1990s.

However, not all Moroccan women needed to find a way to harmonize women's rights and Islam. Some simply believed that women's rights were human rights within the context of democratization. As we shall explore in chapter five, secular approaches to securing women's rights also gained traction during the decade of the 1990s.

It was within this context in the mid 1990s that some Moroccan gender activists felt the time was ripe to create a new national women's organization that had never been affiliated with any political party and to which all women from any party—or those not active in parties—could come. The Morocco's women's advocacy organization, Joussour (Bridges), was founded in 1995 and has played an important role in the struggle for women's rights in Morocco ever since. It was founded by Ghizlan Benachir, Ouaffa Hajji, Latifa Jbabdi, and other women who felt they could work together and wanted a space that was clearly outside that of any of the political parties.

Benachir, who served as President of the Association of Joussour explained that Joussour was created in 1995 "to add to the other women's organizations that existed because we were a group of about 50 women who were active in various political parties but felt we needed to create a space where we could act and support each other concerning the status of women."[85] Benachir noted that while the women were strong members of their political parties, "we did not have space in our parties. So we wanted to take action within a different framework. While we initially had about 50 members, we chose an Executive Board of about thirteen women."[86]

The founders of Bridges hoped to truly offer a cross-party and non-party venue for women who wanted to focus on improving the status of Moroccan women. Additionally, Benachir recalled that, "The women who founded Joussour wanted to insure that women's issues were part of the national discourse of reform as agitation for reform was present throughout Morocco. They also wanted women's direct participation in governance to be included in the country's democratic reforms."[87]

Again, these Moroccan women activists recognized the need for continued discursive intervention into Morocco's political debates in order to keep women's concerns and the woman's question on the agenda. They also understood that 1995 offered conditions that now allowed for a truly national women's organization. Finally, with democratic reforms being proposed, they also were keen to advocate for women's participation in decision making.

Over the years, Joussour would found one of Morocco's first hidden shelters for women and their children who were victims of violence. Joussour would also be a major voice in promoting the issue of combating violence against women. The organization's leadership strategized to promote women's direct participation in government but also to build momentum for major issues of concern to women.

Utilizing new organizational forms and self consciously contributing discursively to national debates had served Moroccan women activists well. Creating yet another organization without any ties to a political party, without its membership or executive board being tied to any one party, strategically seemed to be a useful next step.

Changing Rules and Paths within Institutions and the Creation of Discursive Initiatives to Alter Morocco's Gender Discourses

The success of the Moroccan women gender activists in intervening discursively in Morocco's political dialogues and building new institutional forms and pathways yielded success in effecting change to the Moudawana and in creating pathways for the women to contribute to decision making regarding women's issues across the country.

The women's discursive interventions took a variety of forms. First they sought to bring their debates and study groups to their student organizations and political parties. During this period they honed their skills, developing their own ideas, proposals, and presentation strategies. Later, they founded national magazines to offer an alternative logic and narrative about Moroccan women to the alert public who would read such publications.

Still later, the one million signature campaign to improve the status of women required more than one million discussions of human rights and women's rights in order to secure the signatures. The signature campaign required that not just an alert public to national issues would be engaged in discussion, but that Moroccan women in the baths, at the supermarket, at work, in schools, all would be discussing the possibilities of altering the Moudawana and the changes needed in the status of Moroccan women. These were women who joined the discussion because they were approached, not because they sought out discussions about the status of women in Morocco.

These actions to intervene discursively created new political activities for Moroccan women activists in an expanded public space. Additionally, as the women acted discursively over the years, the legitimacy of their actions became accepted as commonplace, and not unusual.

The founding of women's organizations furthered Moroccan women activists' discursive interventions in their country as well as affected the decision making structures discussed below. The new women's organizations allowed Moroccan women activists to interface with professionals from across Moroccan society. Judicial, religious, economic, journalistic, sport, and political professionals all could be invited to meetings for exchanges and dialogue and information. Gathering such actors in society who serve as opinion leaders helped the women to reach those who regulate and distribute societal values in a variety of ways. This, in turn, helped socialize those who would make policy decisions and/or those who would make demands of policy makers.

The contacts the women developed and the legitimacy they earned led to expectations that their work was newsworthy. Thus, over time the women were able to keep alive their issues in the national dialogue through the media. Of course there were times of relative quiescence, as when the women waited for the palace to take a decision, and so they chose to continue their self education, to continue to strategize, and to more discretely conduct their advocacy.

Moroccan women also created new organizational forms that influenced both Morocco's gender institution and Morocco's political decision making institution. The creation of new organizational structures and the work of their members created new pathways that allowed women to take decision making positions without consulting male political leaders. The new organizations also created parallel forms for determining strategies to advocate for policies.

Creating new organizational forms outside their parties was one of the most powerful actions taken by Moroccan women. However, some of the women remained within their parties and so they also created new pathways and linkages (to the parties). Other Moroccan women cut ties with their parties though they maintained ties to individuals in their parties that largely were based on personal relationships.

By creating new forms of organizations, the women were able to act for themselves without clearing words or deeds by their parties or party leaders. Additionally, when King Hassan II looked for ways to consult leaders on the "women's question," Moroccan women's organizations provided women leaders with the legitimacy to speak on behalf of Moroccan women.

Because the palace was accustomed to making decisions through the pathways of consultative sessions and committees, not through parliament, when the women activist leaders were asked to participate in the existing structures of the Palace's consultation, they in effect moved into an entirely new realm of influence. Now they were at the table arguing their case, not on the outside lobbying others to speak on their behalf.

An additional advantage to the creation of new common organizations for women was that Moroccan women leaders avoided the pitfall of balkanizing their country's women's movement according to political parties or ideologies. Rather, the new forms allowed Moroccan gender activists to come together and determine their goals and strategies and then speak with common references and arguments. Only after they accomplished their common work, did they return to their parties to mobilize support for women's activities based on the common work they had completed in their new organizations. Thus, the new organizational structures reversed the direction of activity for many politically active Moroccan women. Rather than mobilize others to support their party and hope that women's issues would be addressed, now the women activists addressed women's issues and took these issues to their parties to mobilize support. Although this approach did not always work perfectly, it certainly was the frame that allowed the women to collect the one million signatures in several months' time.

The new women's organizations also played another role. They allowed women who wanted to advocate for women's issues, but not to join a political party, to have a political space in which to participate. Additionally, for the younger women who would come after them, the organizations founded by the pioneering Moroccan women activists would offer a logical space for those attracted to investigating the possibilities of action on behalf of women.

Political organizations have staying power; they are "sticky" as social scientists note, and they send a message that activists and their ideas and their agendas will continue into the future. Thus organizations both legitimize the political endeavors of the organization's members and also provide a socialization effect on members of society that the issues of concern to the members of an organization will remain part of the national political landscape and are to be taken into account. This organizational change, in effect, has the impact of helping to change the norms of a society which, in turn, contributes to changes in the institutions of society.

Initially, Moroccan women were able to accomplish what they did with support from allies, their families, their own reserves of energy, and from their own and family financial resources. As we shall see in the following chapter, chapter five, resources are important to activists. Thus, for Moroccan gender activists, as their goals expanded, the programs and initiatives that the women hoped to undertake required additional resources and resources on a scale that were not readily available to the women. The range of resources needed and how these were secured is the focus of the next chapter.

Notes

1. Eva Wegner, *Islamist Opposition in Authoritarian Regimes* (Syracuse: Syracuse University Press, 2011), 5.

2. Laurie Brand, *Women, the State, and Political Liberalization: Middle Eastern and North African Experiences* (New York: Columbia University Press, 1998), 60. This paragraph is based on Brand's research.

3. Brand, *Women, the State, and Political Liberalization,* 60.

4. Jane Gabriel, "In Rabat, Morocco, Speaking to Latifa Jbabdi and Fatima Outaleb," Open Democracy Net, http://www.opendemocracy.net/audio/jane-gabriel/feminism-and-fatwas-it-all-began-on-march-8th and Femmes du Maroc, Website with short bios of 100 active women in Morocco. http://www.femmesdumaroc.com/Magazine/Dossier/Les100quiontchangelaMoudawana

5. Loubna H. Skalli, *Through a Local Prism: Gender, Globalization, and Identity in Moroccan Women's Magazines* (Lanham, MD: Lexington Books/ Rowman and Littlefield Publishers, 2006), 62.

6. U.N.CEDAW/SP/2008/3 Appendix Committee Member resumes. http://www2.ohchr.org/english/bodies/cedaw/docs/CEDAW.SP.2008.3.pdf.

7. Fatima Outaleb, quoted by Gabriel, "In Rabat speaking to Latifa Jbabdi and Fatima Outaleb." Jbabdi and Outaleb are UAF activists.

8. The Soviet Union's anti-monarchist history made Marxist adherents a target for monarchs throughout the Middle East.

9. Skalli, *Through a Local Prism,* 63.

10. "Moroccan Women's Roundtable Discussion with First Lady Hillary Rodham Clinton and others," Marrakech, Morocco, March 30, 1999. http://www.library.cornell.edu/colldev/mideast/hilround.htm.

11. [About Islam] http://islam.about.com/od/basicbeliefs/p/intro.htm.

12. Nezha Alaoui, interview with authors, Casablanca, Morocco, July 20, 2009.

13. Latifa Jbabdi, quoted by Gabriel, " In Rabat speaking to Latifa Jbabdi and Fatima Outaleb."

14. Brand, *Women, the State and Political Liberalization*, 51. Brand and numerous Moroccan authors cite 1987 as the date this organization was founded. However, other authors record that this organization started in 1988.

15. Aicha Afifi and Rajae Msefer, "Women in Morocco: Gender Issues and Politics," in *Women and Politics Worldwide*, ed. Barbara Nelson and Najma Chowdhury (New Haven: Yale University Press, 1994) fn. 9.

16. Ghizlan Benachir, interview with authors, Rabat, Morocco, November 23, 2007.

17. U.S. State Department, Bureau of Democracy, Human Rights, and Labor, *Morocco Country Reports on Human Rights Practices 2001* (March 2002), 26.

18.Malika Zeghal, *Islamism in Morocco: Religion, Authoritarianism, and Electoral Politics*, translator (George Holoch (Princetown: Marcus Weiner Publishers, 2008), xxvi.

19. Zeghal, *Islamism in Morocco,* xxvi.

20. Zeghal, *Islamism in Morocco. Religion, Authoritarianism, and Electoral Politics*, xxvi.

21. This discussion is taken from Gregory W. White, Mark A. Tessler, and John P. Entelis, "The Kingdom of Morocco," in *The Government and Politics of the Middle East and North Africa*, ed. David E. Long and Bernard Reich (Boulder, CO: Westview Press, 2002), 4th ed., 392-396.

22. Gregory White, *A Comparative Political Economy of Tunisia and Morocco* (Albany: SUNY Press, 2001), 124.

23. Joel Migdal, *Strong Societies and Weak States* (Princeton: Princeton University Press, 1988).

24. James Sater, *Morocco: Challenges to Tradition and Modernity* (London: Routledge, 2010),8.

25. Zakia Salime, *Between Feminism and Islam: Human Rights and Sharia Law in* Morocco (Minneapolis, Minnesota, University of Minnesota Press, 2011).

26. Brand, *Women, the State, and Political Liberalization*, 47.

27. Brand, *Women, the State and Political Liberalization*, 47.

28. Fatima Sadiqi and Moha Ennaji, "The Feminization of Public Space: Women's Activism, the Family Law, and Social Change in Morocco," *Journal of Middle East Women's Studies*, 2, no. 2 (Spring, 2006), 95.

29. Oriana Wuerth, "The Reform of the Moudawana: The Role of Women's Civil Society Organizations in Changing the Personal Status Code in Morocco," *Hawwa Journal of Women of the Middle East and the Islamic World* 3, no. 3. (2005), 314.

30. Fatima Mernissi, *Doing Daily Battle: Interviews with Moroccan Women.* Translator, Mary Jo Lakeland (New Brunswick: Rutgers University Press, 1988). First published in *Le Maroc Raconté par ses Femmes* (1984).

31. Fatima Mernissi, *Beyond the Veil* (Cambridge, MA: Schenkman, 1975).

32. Zeghal, *Islamism in Morocco*, xv.

33. Will D. Swearingen, "Morocco's Agricultural Crisis" in *The Political Economy of Morocco*, ed. I. William Zartman (New York: Praeger Publishers, 1987) 165.

34. Swearingen, "Morocco's Agricultural Crisis," 163.

35. White, *A Comparative Political Economy,* 133.

36. White, *A Comparative Political Economy,* 133.

37. White, *A Comparative Political Economy,* 133.

38. Aiche Ech-Chenna, Presentation, "Leadership Féminin au Maroc: Enjeux et Perspectives," workshop sponsored by the Middle East Partnership Initiative (MEPI) Alumni Network, Rabat, Morocco, November 22, 2007.

39. "More Deaths Reported in Morocco Food Riots. Rabat, Morocco, Jan. 24 [1984]," *New York Times*, January 25, 1984.

40. Stephen O. Hughes, *Morocco Under King Hassan* (Reading, UK: Ithaca Press, 2001), 210.

41. *United Nations Arab Human Development Report,* 2005.

42. The first UN conference on women was held in Mexico City in 1975, the year designated as the Year of the Women. 1975 began the UN Decade for Women.

43. *United Nations Decade for Women 1976-1985* (United Nations Publication, 1985). The Free Library:
http://www.thefreelibrary.com/United+Nations+decade+for+Women+1976-1985%3b+%27really +only+a+...-a03838336">United Nations decade for Women 1976-1985; 'really only a beginning'.

44. Khadija Errebbah, interview with authors, Casablanca, Morocco, July 2009.

45. Errebbah, interview with authors, 2009.

46. Errebbah, interview with authors, 2009.

47. Brand, *Women, the State, and Political Liberalization,* 50.

48. Rachida Tahiri, interview with authors, Rabat, Morocco, November 23, 2007.

49. Tahiri, interview with authors, 2007.

50. Khadija Errebbah and other women in AFDM had come to see the value of rethinking their political party affiliations. Information provided by Khadija Errebbah, interview with authors, 2009.

51. Alaoui, interview with authors, 2009.

52. Alaoui, interview with authors, 2009.

53. Maria F. Curtis, "Moroccan women's rights advocate; founder of L'Union de L'Action Féminine (UAF)" http://www.answers.com/topic/latifa-jababdi.

54. Alaoui, interview with authors, 2009.

55. Brand, *Women, the State, and Political Liberalization,* 50.

56. As explained to the authors in the interview with five women from UAF, Casablanca, Morocco, July 2009.

57. *Arab Human Development Report 2005*, 131.

58. Brand, *The State, and Political Liberalization,* 69.

59. Vital Voices interview with Latifa Jbabdi, "A New Approach for Women's Rights."
http://cc.bingj.com/cache.aspx?q=million+and+Moudawana+and+1992&d=4978769085596441&mkt=en-US&setlang=en-US&w=41fcf9e6,539419d2.

60. Brand, *Women, the State, and Political Liberalization,* 72, citing Zakya Daoud, *Féminism et Politique au Maghreb* (Casablanca: Éditions Eddif, 1993) as a general reference for the account of this period.

61. Vital Voices, interview with Latifa Jbabdi.

62. U.S. Department of State, Background Notes: Morocco, 1994, 8.

63. [Moudawana Reform] www.geographic.org
http://www.theodora.com/wfb/1992/morocco/morocco_people.html.

64. Fatima Harrak, "The History and Significance of the New Moroccan Family Code," Working Paper No. 09-002 (Institute for the Study of Islamic Thought in Africa (ISITA), Buffett Center for International and Comparative Studies, Northwestern University, March, 2009), 3.

65. Harrak, "The History and Significance of the New Moroccan Family Code," 3.

66. The above quotes are taken from PBS, "Hopes on the Horizon" (Backside Inc., February 16, 2001).

67. The above quotes are taken from PBS, "Hopes on the Horizon" (Backside Inc., February 16, 2001).

68. Salime, *Between Feminism and Islam*, 46.

69. Salime, *Between Feminism and Islam*, 47.

70. Salime, *Between Feminism and Islam*, 49.

71. Salime, *Between Feminism and Islam*, 51-52.

72. Salime, *Between Feminism and Islam.* The sentences in this paragraph reflect Salime's account of what transpired at the time of the one million signature campaign.

73. "WAR IN THE GULF; Huge Morocco March Supports Iraq in War," *New York Times*, February 4, 1991. http://www.nytimes.com/1991/02/04/world/war-in-the-gulf-huge-morocco-march-supports-iraq-in-war.html.

74. Michael J. Willis, *Politics and Power in the Maghreb* (London: Hurst & Company, 2012), 304-306.

75. Willis, *Politics and Power in the Maghreb,* 304-306.

76. Yahia Zoubir, "Reactions in the Maghreb to the Gulf War" *Arab Studies Quarterly* 15, no.1 (1993), quoted in Willis, *Politics and Power in the Maghreb.*

77. Willis, *Politics and Power in the Maghreb,* 305.

78. The above quotes are taken from PBS,"Hopes on the Horizon" (Backside Inc., February 16, 2001). The text not quoted is the author's insertions.

79. Harrak, "The History and Significance of the New Moroccan Family Code," 3.

80. Harrak, "The History and Significance of the New Moroccan Family Code," 3.

81. The changes in the Moudawana identified here are based on the work of Harrak, "The History and Significance of the New Moroccan Family Code."

82. Sadiqi and Ennaji, "The Feminization of Public Space," 103.

83. Brand *Women, the State, and Political Liberalization,* 75.

84. Vital Voices Global Partnership 2009 interview with Latifa Jbabdi http://vitalvoices.org/vital-voices-feature/he-latifa-jbabdi.

85. Ghizlan Benachir is a member of USFP and a municipal official from Suisse district of Rabat. Information is from Benachir, interview with authors, 2007.

86. Benachir, interview with authors, 2007.

87. Ghizlan Benachir, interview with authors, Rabat, Morocco, July 21, 2009.

Nadia Tahiri

Nezha Alaoui

Nouzha Skalli

Zahra Chaggaf

Milouda Hazib

Ghizlane Benachir

Amina Ouchelh

Kadija Errebbah (L) Houdna Bennani (R)

Women of the Union de l'Action Fèminine (UAF) including: (back left to right) Fatima Outaleb, Nezha Ameziane; (front left to right) Nezha Alaoui, Latifa Jbabdi

Chapter Five
Resources

Moroccan women activists advocating for changes in the status of women in their country and for making changes in the Moudawana drew upon many resources, mostly domestic, in their early years of activity. And, as this chapter will demonstrate, in subsequent years, their need for resources expanded. Below we identify some of the major resources upon which the women drew. Such resources made their work both possible and effective so that they could position themselves and their allies to alter the institution of gender in Morocco.

Our earlier discussion of both institutional and feminist theories led us to the proposition that active Moroccan women would find resources through relations within their country and external to their country to pursue the changes they demanded in their country's gender institution. From the narrative of their struggles, it is obvious that the resources that Moroccan women drew upon first were local and then broadened to include support from international donors. This allowed them to have an impact beyond what their domestic resources would have allowed.

The formation and maintenance of important political alliances was an early resource for Moroccan women. We shall return to this variable when we consider the ascension to the throne of King Mohamed VI who replaced his father, King Hassan II in 1999. But during the years of their coming of age politically, Moroccan women activists relied on the formation of important political alliances mainly with their male relatives and colleagues. These alliances were the women's primary resources for entering the public sphere and engaging in political activity. These alliances gave the women permission to engage politically and also encouraged them to learn and strategize about issues. Eventually, as was demonstrated in the previous chapter, many of the women moved on, generally without the support of most of their male political mentors and allies and formed their own organizations and coalitions in which women led, prioritized, and strategized about the issues that concerned them. These women still needed family support to attend meetings even if they no longer needed party leaders' permission to take a position on a topic or undertake some political initiative.

But in addition to the cultural resource of male family support by which a woman could attend meetings, the activities of these women's organizations and their coalitions cost money. It took resources to publish, travel domestically, rent halls, make and distribute documents for meetings, and host conferences. Additionally, attending international conferences outside of Morocco also required money. And such conferences were important to Morocco's women activists and their gender work, as we demonstrate in this chapter.

We can see an early example of the need for real expenditures by a Moroccan women's gender activist organization following the Islamists counter attack against the one million signature campaign. In response, the UAF women determined to expand their knowledge and contacts concerning gender practices and strategies in order to better protect themselves from attacks and also to win more support. The women created their first Court for Arab Women which then met annually and offered intellectual resources. To this "court" came both female and male researchers, legal experts, practitioners, journalists, and policy makers. The annual court, with its study sessions, identifications of best practices, and the carefully researched documents it published, had the effect of not only educating the women in Morocco (and their male allies), but also of building transnational bridges to Arab experts and practitioners in foreign countries who focused on women's issues and who came and participated in the Moroccan women's court. The work of this court also provided solidarity and support for Arab women and their allies across many countries. Additionally, these annual courts kept the issues of concern to Moroccan women on the national agenda in Morocco at least while the court was in session and often afterwards due to some of the documents that were produced and distributed as well as due to the media attention the gatherings attracted.

A slightly earlier example of utilizing transnational intellectual resources through the use of international donor funds occurred in 1991 when the ADFM invited other women from organizations in Algeria and Tunisia to come to Rabat to create the Collectif 95 Maghreb Egalitè. Collectif 95 was to be a regional organization of gender activists who worked to improve the status of women. Being from a common region, though different countries, the women shared a civilization, language, and history that promoted "real unity" among them even though, over time, reaching consensus on issues—their adopted decision making rule—proved a lengthy process.[1] With the 1995 United Nations Fourth World Conference on Women to be held in Beijing, China, a few years away, the women set themselves important tasks. They determined that they should attend the Beijing conference and contribute an overview of the gains that women had made in their region since the last United Nations conference in 1985 (Nairobi, Kenya). They first began by working to identify metrics by which to assess the status of the women in each of the three Maghreb countries and then to identify which gains had been achieved, which had not, and where efforts had been made to push for change but no progress had occurred. From this assessment they produced an initial document.[2]

Their second task was to produce a paper that identified the status of international conventions relating to women's rights in each of the three Maghreb countries. They contrasted the women's rights they had identified in their first assessment against those found in the international covenants. Then they set their third task as one that would propose specific egalitarian family and personal status laws throughout the Maghreb. These proposals were published in a document titled, *Cent Mesures et Dispositions* (*One Hundred Steps, One Hun-*

dred Provisions).[3]

The ADFM women were not the only ones preparing for the Beijing conference. Many of Morocco's women activists prepared themselves through work with their civic associations. Others took part in the officially endorsed preparatory meetings held in Amman, Jordan.

Foreign donors, in this case, especially the Friedrich Ebert Stiftung of Germany, helped to underwrite the work of the ADFM. The Friedrich Ebert Stiftung has continued to be a stalwart supporter of ADFM women's activities even into the twenty-first century.[4] The foundation has provided financial resources that allowed the ADFM to play a leading role in advancing the status of Moroccan women, especially in the political and legal sectors.

Both the Konrad Adenauer Stiftung and the Friedrich Ebert Stiftung, foundations affiliated with political parties in Germany, provided critically important resources to Moroccan civic associations and to Morocco's feminist scholarship. Friedrich Ebert, for example, supported the work of Moroccan sociologist, Fatima Mernissi, and also underwrote conferences to explore the role of civic associations in the Arab world as well as to support the work of Moroccan members of civil society.

In many ways, Fatima Mernissi's work has been a national resource to all Moroccan women and their allies who have sought to improve the status of women in Morocco. Mernissi had already published works in the 1970s and 1980s important to the discursive interventions of Morocco women in their national debates. Then in 1988, Mernissi published *The Veil and the Male Elite* in French, which in 2014 she describes (on her website) as, "A feminist interpretation of women's rights in Islam." [5] The book was later translated into nine other languages. As a reinterpretation of women and Islam and the wives of the prophet Mohammed, the book was banned in Morocco following its publication in France.[6] Also in 1988, Mernissi published *Sheherazad is Not a Moroccan, Otherwise She will be a Salaried Worker.* In 1990, she published *Forgotten Queens of Islam.* In 1992 she published *Islam and Democracy*. In 1993 Mernissi published *Women's Rebellion and Islamic Memory*, and in 1994, *Dreams of Trespass Tales of a Harem Girlhood.*[7] All of these works examined the agency and the constrained agency of Moroccan women past and present.

In response, in 1994, 140 Moroccan religious leaders and intellectuals signed a petition citing Mernissi's work as blasphemous and as work that was "tarnishing Islam's image."[8] It would not be until 1997 that Mernissi published again, when she published *Rural NGOs of the High Atlas* and this time her subject matter was an entrepreneurial male Moroccan who returned to his roots to work with the rural populations to establish sewer systems and sell the rural producers wares on the internet.

The Western donors' resources provided those like Mernissi and those working in Morocco's democratization and human rights organizations with the ability to build knowledge about the role of Islam and various aspects of democratic practices. For example, in November 1996, the Friebert Ebert Stiftung identified its interest in sponsoring a conference on civil associations in the Arab world by beginning its announcement, "The emergence of civil societies in Muslim countries is partly the reaction to a fast process of modernization but also an answer to soft states which have not fulfilled their post-independence promises."[9] It continued, "We would like to meet and hear about individuals who function as role models in today's Muslim world. Such role models openly represent civil courage and the values of tolerance and pluralism."[10] Rather than host a conference to say here is how civic associations work best from other regions of the world, the Stiftung sought to allow Moroccans, Jordanians, Egyptians, and others to identify their best practices and through them to build knowledge about civil society in the Arab world.

Other international donors were also becoming increasingly active in Morocco during the 1990s because King Hassan's efforts at creating a political opening made foreigners willing to undertake support for political activities in Morocco if they could find appropriate Moroccan partners. The United States Agency for International Development (USAID), for example, which had operated in Morocco, since 1957, expanded its activities from its previous concentration in the agricultural sector helping provide technical assistance to turn semi arid land into farmland through irrigation and improved water practices and combating locusts. USAID now gave attention to assisting Morocco with its increasing energy demands. Additionally, Moroccan women benefitted from USAID's family planning initiatives during the 1990s and from its microfinance programs for family production and businesses that included women.

It was also believed that as USAID assisted Morocco with its economic liberalization program and Morocco created a new free market business climate, that this would attract new foreign investors and employment would trickle down to all Moroccans, including Moroccan women. Additionally, the argument was made that for modern, foreign companies to come to Morocco, all of their staff had to feel comfortable working there, including their female managers. A variation on this argument also would be utilized in 2001 when Moroccans debated whether or not to guarantee women's election to the parliament. [11] As we discuss in chapter six, there were those who argued that for Morocco to be attractive as an EU member or to attract foreign businesses that employed women managers, having Moroccan women be visible in the country's highest political legislature would reassure foreign companies and their female employees.

Amideast, a U.S. based non-profit that began work in 1951 with a mission of encouraging dialogue between Americans and the peoples of the Middle East as well as supporting educational exchanges to learn about each other's societies, expanded its activities in Morocco in the 1990s having done work there since 1960. For its major young women's initiative, Amideast partnered with USAID to fund and service rural schools with a major focus on retention of, and learning by, Moroccan girls. The United States Information Service (USIS), a cultural arm of the U.S. government, began routinely including Moroccan women in their programs and trainings in Morocco, back in the United States, and in some third country venues where the women wanted to participate.

Additionally, during the 1980s when U.S. President Ronald Reagan was concerned with militarily confronting the Russians across the globe to demonstrate strength, the U.S. Congress decided it wanted another component to its foreign policy. Congress founded the National Endowment for Democracy (NED) and agreed to partially fund initiatives by two U.S. party affiliated entities. The National Democratic Institute (NDI) and the International Republican Institute (IRI) were affiliates of the Democratic Party and the Republican Party respectively. All three democracy organizations were populated by those who hoped to assist—where and when invited—with democracy initiatives abroad. NDI established an office in Rabat in 1998, focusing at first on parliamentary support and skill building, as well as on programs for Government ministries and later, as we shall discuss, on providing Moroccan women with skill building when they chose to run for public office. NDI also created an active program for civil society assistance. IRI, too, arrived in Morocco but chose over time not to continue any major programs there and instead shifted to focus its efforts in Jordan, Egypt, Lebanon, Libya, and Pakistan. During this same period, the U.S. also created the Center of International Private Enterprise (CIPE), and the International Solidarity Center that works with labor unions.

International donors were not flooding into Morocco when King Hassan took his first steps of political opening. For certainly, the huge sea changes in the status of countries in Eastern Europe were grabbing the attention and support of many international donors. But enough donors were beginning to investigate and work in Morocco that the Moroccan women's organizations began to find connections and apply for programs that the donors would fund. The support of external donors for Moroccan government and civil society programs that supported an improvement in the status of women began in a major way in the 1990s for Moroccan women and it continued into the first half of the 2000 decade. And when the donors came to Morocco, unlike in some other countries, they found highly organized, politically savvy, Moroccan women leaders with a strong work ethic who would use their funds effectively. Thus as we posited in chapter one, the leadership of Moroccan women and the organizational structures that they had created assisted them in garnering donor support.

But in addition to foreign assistance from donors and foundations, United Nations conferences on women and UN treaties and conventions have provided important resources for women activists and for improving the lives of women globally. As Eve Sandberg's analysis of the contributions of UN conventions to women's organizations elsewhere has noted, UN conventions have provided women around the world with "resources, legitimacy, and alternative political advocacy models."[12] Additionally, "multilateral conferences have often been the very catalyst that has sparked women's, especially elite women's, political mobilization."[13]

The United Nations as a Resource for Women Globally and for Moroccan Women Gender Activists

The United Nations (U.N.) has long championed women's rights, recognizing such rights under the umbrella of human rights. For example, the U.N. Commission on the Status of Women (CSW) which began in June1946 as a full committee, had upgraded from a subcommittee created in February 1946 of the Commission on Human Rights.[14] However, a Section on the Status of Women of the United Nations Secretariat was created within the Human Rights Division to provide "secretariat functions."[15] Both the subcommittee and the upgrade were due to active promotion and advocacy by women in the post World War Two era who already were creating transnational networks. And when the Commission on the Status of Women began its work in 1947, meeting at Lake Success New York, all of the fifteen representatives from the member states (Australia, Byelorussian Soviet Socialist Republic, People's Republic of China, Costa Rica, Denmark, France, Guatemala, India, Mexico, Syria, Turkey, Union of Soviet Socialist Republics, United Kingdom, USA, and Venezuela) that were assigned to the commission were women.[16]

One of the commission's first successes was to review the proposed United Nations' Universal Declaration of Human Rights and insert more gender inclusive language into the Declaration. Doing so successfully, despite some resistance from those who originally drafted the document linked the commission's work on women's rights with human rights at an early stage and also signaled that there were knowledgeable and articulate women prepared to advocate for issues of concern to women at the United Nations and internationally.

In 1949, the CSW began work to formulate the Convention on the Political Rights of Women which the U.N. General Assembly adopted in December 1952. Later, the CSW would add modifications to the Convention on the Political Rights of Women and it also identified specific areas where the international member states needed to take action to protect women on issues that did not seem to be covered within a general framework of human rights, but rather were specific to women.

For example, the work of the CSW led to the UN General Assembly adopting important treaties/conventions that protected women in the areas of marriage, an area in which men's protections generally were not lacking. The Convention on the Nationality of Married Women was adopted by the UN General Assembly in January 1957, and the Convention on Consent to Marriage, Minimum Age for Marriage and Registration of Marriages was adopted in November 1962. Later, the CSW worked to refine the 1957 treaty of the Recommendation on Consent to Marriage, Minimum Age for Marriage and Registration of Marriages and these refinements were in November 1965.

For some, the major accomplishment of the CSW came when in December 1963 the General Assembly adopted resolution 1921 that instructed the Economic and Social Council (ECOSOC) to invite the CSW to prepare a draft declaration on the equal rights of men and women. Rather than bring forward items by themselves over time or convention by convention, many General Assembly members wanted a single document that identified the rights of men and women equally and women within the UN system (as well as outside of the U.N. system) had been advocating for such a document. After several years of research and consultation, it took additional years for the CSW to complete the draft of such a declaration. Thus, it was not until November 1967 that the General Assembly adopted the CSW's Declaration on the Elimination of Discrimination against Women.

The declaration was a guide and was not binding. However, in 1968, ECOSOC began the practice, which soon became a common practice, whereby ECOSOC invited member states of the United Nations to self report on the conditions of women in their countries with respect to the Declaration. Even though the reports were voluntary, they were a useful resource, as we discuss below, to women activists who came to utilize these reporting sessions as leverage for lobbying their national leaders who were self reporting to ECOSOC and had to demonstrate some advancement in the status of women in their countries.

But these reports were voluntary and the Declaration was not binding. Additionally, in the early 1970s, research on women, especially research by Ester Boserup whose work had an impact on development practitioners and officials at the United Nations, revealed that even some of the development programs of the United Nations and some of the development programs of well meaning donor states were contributing to the maintenance and expansion of the inequalities between women and men in many settings, but especially among the rural poor. Women within the United Nations system and women in non-governmental organizations outside the UN came to realize that a binding statement, not just a declaration, was needed.

Thus calls began to create a United Nations convention that would prevent the discrimination of women and would be binding on the member states when the convention was signed into force. But that convention took years to craft and it took years before it was signed into force. It was 1979 before the Convention for the Elimination of All Forms of Discrimination against Women (CEDAW) was adopted. And Morocco would not ratify the Convention for the Elimination of All Forms of Discrimination against Women (CEDAW) until 1993, and then it would do so with reservations. When Morocco ratified the convention, its government representatives stated that the provisions of Article 2 would apply to the extent that they would not conflict with shari'a law, and that Article 16 of CEDAW regarding marriage and its dissolution was considered to be incompatible with shari'a law and so the Moroccan government would not be bound by that article. But by signing CEDAW, even with reservations, the Moroccan government obligated itself to make reports on the progress of improving the status of Moroccan women to the CEDAW review committee that received such reports.

As noted above, the UAF women, together with experts from across the

Arab world, concentrated on exploring ways to find the compatibility of women's rights with Islamic laws, while the ADFM devoted itself to working with women across the region to determine how women's rights in each Maghreb country measured up to the international standards established by the United Nations' covenants and treaties. But when the 1995, Beijing China Fourth World Conference on Women convened by the United Nations approached, both the Moroccan government and Moroccan women's non-governmental organizations began their preparations. Regardless of their primary missions, many women's groups also took on the task of devoting themselves to preparing for this historic international gathering.

The UN Commission on the Status of Women, discussed previously, served as the preparatory committee for the Beijing conference.[17] And, as Rabèa Naciri's research has demonstrated, despite the "ambivalence of the state" as it moved back and forth on women's issues, it was clear that Moroccan women activists had gained "political recognition" when King Hassan asked for women representatives from Moroccan women's non-governmental organizations to be involved in "the formulation of the national report" for the upcoming convention.[18] And Morocco's entire political establishment observed this.

Naciri, like other researchers, credits the women's movement for its ability to retain allies in the political parties where many of the women, especially those in the UAF remained active. Additionally, the demonstration of Morocco's women's groups working across the boundaries of their own organizations and coordinating with other associations such as human rights groups and professional and civic associations, argues Naciri, gave the women the legitimacy and the capacity to negotiate.[19] For our purposes, we argue that the international women's convention in Beijing functioned as a resource for women to again assert their legitimacy and take part in the consultative processes of public decision making in Morocco.

Additionally, the upcoming United Nations conference provided Moroccan women with an opportunity to continue to chip away at the discrimination they faced. Laurie Brand reports that the USFP's activist, Badia Skalli (one of the two Moroccan women first elected to Morocco's parliament in 1993) recalled that the USFP and PI women and their male allies were able to bring to Morocco's parliament a bill and pass it as legislation arguing that the upcoming Beijing conference required that Morocco take some steps to improve the status of women. The bill that was passed into law repealed the practice that forbade married women from signing commercial contracts without their husbands' permission.[20] Skalli and those lobbying said it was a small thing that did not violate sharia law because it had its roots in French penal practices and it would give the Moroccan women something to take to Beijing.[21] Though the women did not succeed in some of the other issues they hoped to achieve before the conference, they were able to use the conference to gain one new right. And, of course, it was believed at the end of the UN Conference in Beijing, many rights for women would be enumerated.

But at the end of the Beijing convention, King Hassan and his representatives did not endorse all of Beijing Platform for Action. Instead, the Morocco delegation reserved its "position on paragraphs 96 and 106 (k) of the Platform for Action, whose content is in contradiction with the precepts of Islam and is not in conformity with its spiritual values and cultural traditions. Morocco also expresses its reservations on paragraph 232 (f), which refers to paragraph 96, and on paragraph 274 (d)."[22] Additionally, the King had not allowed a woman to represent the government even to this gathering on women's issues. Rather, Abdelhadi Boutaleb, one of King Hassan's male advisers, led the women's delegation to Beijing.[23]

Yet, the Beijing conference served as an importance resource for Moroccan women. In addition to providing Moroccan women gender activists with support and solidarity for the battles they had to fight, it also acquainted them with some of the international political debates and actors who could harm them as well. As Jane Bayes and Nayereh Tohidi have explored in their research, the Beijing conference offered a coalition of conservative Catholics and Muslims the opportunity to unite to oppose many rights for women that many women around the world felt they were entitled to, including the right to control their bodies (just as men are entitled to this right). Bayes and Tohidi trace the actions of Pope John Paul II and his sending of ambassadors to Muslim Kingdoms to oppose the policies that U.S. President Bill Clinton and U.S. Vice President Al Gore had campaigned on, in 1992, with regards to a woman's right to control her own body. From the Vatican, the Pope forged a coalition that he couched in anti-imperialist and anti-Western rhetoric. And when the Clinton-Gore administration began funding family planning clinics, the Pope charged that the U.S. and other Western donors were using foreign assistance to practice population control in non Western countries. Additionally, the conservative coalition opposed any marriage that was not between a man and a woman.[24]

At the Beijing conference, the Catholic-Muslim coalition consisted of Iran, Sudan, Libya, Egypt, Kuwait, Guatemala, Honduras, Ecuador, Peru, Bolivia, and the Philippines.[25] But by the year 2000, at the New York United Nations conference titled, Beijing Plus Five, other Muslim countries had joined the conservative coalition. These included Morocco, Algeria, Syria, and Pakistan.[26] Clearly while the United Nations conferences provided women, including Moroccan women, with powerful resources to continue their work at home demanding an improvement in the status of women, the conference also offered a venue to those who opposed their work. Additionally, when Morocco joined the conservative coalition, Moroccan women activists were forced to worry about the depth of support they could count upon from the Palace and parliament.

Pope John Paul II had dedicated himself to improving relations with Muslim populations around the world. And while this was viewed by almost everyone as a good initiative, the Pope's efforts to build a conservative coalition that would deny women decision making over their own bodies was a problem for many women activists who hoped to improve the status of women, including some of the Moroccan activist women.

Jerry Filteau's analysis of Pope John Paul II's outreach to Muslims, observes that one of the Pope's first trips abroad (in 1979) was to Turkey.[27] While in Turkey and when addressing Catholics there, the Pope preached respect for the values of Islam. He also visited a sanctuary that had been a great mosque and a great church during different periods of history—Santa Sophia.[28]

Further, the Pope had visited Morocco in 1985. Because King Hassan II is Morocco's religious/spiritual leader as well as its King, his invitation to the Pope meant this Pope was the first to receive an invitation to visit an Islamic country by the country's religious leader. In Morocco, the Pope met with thousands of young Moroccans in Casablanca and emphasized that Catholics and Muslims both believe in one God. Then, in 2001, John Paul II became the first Pope to visit an active Muslim mosque, when he entered the Umayyad mosque in Damascus, Syria.[29] Such outreach to Muslim countries was greeted enthusiastically across the MENA region. This made it even more difficult for Moroccan women gender activists, as well as women's activists in other countries, to counter the Pope's activities to limit women's control over their own affairs. The Pope sought the good will of Muslim populations even as he worked to activate local church groups to join with Islamists to oppose certain of the activities of women gender activists at Beijing and in their home countries.

As can be seen by the discussion above, the UN Conference in Beijing and its NGO parallel conference offered outstanding opportunities for Moroccan women activists. During the preparations for the meetings, women in Morocco, as elsewhere, were included in the consultation process. Through their regional preparations in Amman, Jordan, or within the smaller Maghreb region, they formed important connections and benefitted from the solidarity of working with others as well as from the substantive information they learned. The same was true of the conference itself where hundreds of simultaneous sessions took place and there was much to learn and many with whom to share the Moroccan experience.

And when they had been planning for the upcoming UN conference, Moroccan women also gained some leverage by which to enact a small, but important piece of legislation for a Moroccan woman who might hope to conduct commercial business. Finally, many of the Moroccan women attending the Beijing conference learned more about the international donor world than they had known previously. The UN women's conference in Beijing was an important event for many Moroccan women activists and the United Nations hearings and gatherings would continue to be important resources for Moroccan women during the coming decades.

As we discussed in a previous chapter, in 1996, the ADFM women sent representatives to the United Nations hearings that reported on how countries were implementing the Convention for the Elimination of Discrimination Against Women (CEDAW). At those United Nations hearings, ADFM women presented an alternative report on the status of Moroccan women that differed from the report which had been submitted by the Moroccan government. The ADFM women drew upon the research they had conducted through their Maghreb work and from the issues they had learned about through their own work as well as through their work collaborating with other women's organizations.

Making a presentation that contrasted with their government's account was an unusual move for any Moroccan organization's representatives. However, for many it demonstrated that Moroccan women were organized, articulate, and deserving of support. Among the Islamist community, however, it demonstrated that Western based institutions and ideas were continuing to challenge the traditional beliefs of the Islamists.

Then, in 1997, Moroccan women found ways to reach out to donors outside Morocco to secure their assistance that went beyond the proclamations offered by the United Nations. For example, in 1997, a cohort of Moroccan women's civil society organizations visited with a World Bank representative to inquire about how Morocco might adopt programs that would advance the goals identified at the 1995 United Nations Fourth World Conference on Women in Beijing.[30] As a result of that meeting, it was determined that Morocco's women's civil society organizations should collaborate to create a long term national plan that would integrate Moroccan women into the country's development programs.[31]

Additionally, the World Bank itself realized it needed to devise a strategy for its own activities within the Middle East North African (MENA) region. According to the World Bank's account:

> ... the World Bank conducted a MENA Gender Training Workshop for Bank staff in Washington in late June 1998, where the idea for a consultative council for women originated. The workshop brought women active in women's organizations from ten MENA countries to share their experience with Bank staff. During this workshop and again at MDF2 in Marrakesh, women from the MENA region expressed the need for a more pro-active Bank engagement in gender issues. To facilitate this, they suggested the establishment of a regional consultative and evaluation body. The MENA Consultative Council on Gender which consists of a core group of professional women from the MENA region, was formalized in January 1999.[32]

The follow-up workshop in Marrakesh enabled many of Morocco's women's organizations to offer input specifically regarding the Moroccan situation.

Having discovered the international donors as a resource for legitimacy, solidarity, financing, and skill building, Moroccan women's organizations would soon routinely turn to external donors in Europe, the United States, and elsewhere, to provide resources that would assist them to achieve the agendas that they had established for themselves and their organizations. Additionally, over the next few decades, but especially during the reign of King Hassan II's son, King Mohamed VI, international donors would begin to work with government officials to explore ways to improve the status of women in a wide range of sectors: education, agricultural, microfinance, and gender budgeting within Morocco's national ministries.

The European Union as a Resource for Moroccan Human Rights Activists, Political Party Democratizers and Moroccan Women Gender Activists

Throughout the 1990s Moroccan women in civil society and political parties continued their gender advocacy and their activities within Morocco. As noted earlier in this study, the domestic context of the women's struggles included other actors pressing for democratic reforms and improved economic conditions in Morocco. These pressures prompted King Hassan II to consider women's issues as one of many factors in his political calculations.

To understand Morocco's situation within the post Cold War era of the 1990s, Francesco Cavatorta argues that several changed phenomenon need to be understood. Morocco's socialist parties could no longer rely on "any ideological legitimacy conferred by socialism" to rally new supporters.[33] Additionally, international powers like the United States, which hoped for the kind of stability provided by King Hassan in a MENA country, would be unlikely to press the King seriously to democratize. Thus by the later part of the 1990s, this put pressure on the left parties to come to terms with the King and to accept offers to govern in a parliament that was restricted in its abilities even during the King's program of "alternance."[34]

Additionally, the economic hardships caused by the structural adjustment programs that Morocco enacted (beginning in the 1980s) for the International Monetary Fund (IMF) in order to secure significant loans that were needed to maintain Moroccan security forces in the Western Sahara and to pay the state's bills, help to fuel discontent and riots that Islamic movements elsewhere have used to gain legitimacy and power and which Morocco's Islamic movements also capitalized upon by offering neighborhood support to those in need as well as conducting education campaigns.[35] In keeping with structural adjustment policies, King Hassan devalued Morocco's currency and liberalized foreign trade hoping to promote investment in exports. The King also enacted austerity measures that sharply reduced subsidies for education, agriculture, health care, and food staples, while raising interest rates to curb inflation. He also privatized several state-led sectors of the economy. The average Moroccan suffered and there were bread riots and resistance.[36]

The unpopular foreign policy decision taken by King Hassan to support the Gulf War in 1991 and send troops has already been discussed and it contributed to undermining the legitimacy of the Palace. This issue was especially utilized by the Islamists as they sought for leverage vis-à-vis other parties and the King. And it was clear that they made inroads in mobilizing young unemployed Moroccan males to demonstrate against the government and the King's foreign policy.

And, as Said Haddadi has argued when King Hassan's outreach to build a regional organization with his neighbors failed, the King looked instead almost exclusively to Europe. During the late 1980s and early 1990s, Algeria was in turmoil. Additionally Algeria accelerated its opposition to Morocco's interests in the Spanish Sahara. Thus came the collapse of any hope for an Arab Maghreb Union or for any regional pact both because Algerian relations with Morocco deteriorated and then also because Libya was targeted by international sanctions and so there was little to be gained economically through affiliation with that country. King Hassan had to look to Europe for economic development possibilities and also economic assistance, both of which were linked to the perception of the King and his governance.[37]

Competition among Algeria's leadership as well as resistance from university activists aligned with Islamists saw the eruption of mass protests in Algeria in 1988. These protests were followed by a military crackdown on the demonstrators and quickly the Algerian government lost all legitimacy. In response, an Islamic Salvation Front (FIS) was forged, given legal status, and made significant gains in both the 1990 municipal and 1991 parliamentary elections. With runoff elections scheduled and the FIS poised to achieve a major victory, the Algerian military staged a coup and ousted the president, arrested or killed Islamist leaders and fought battles with Islamist fighters for the next decade during which time about 200,000 Algerians were reported killed.[38] When Morocco imposed visa restrictions on Algerian nationalists after terrorist attacks in the Western Sahara, Algeria's military closed its border with Morocco and expanded its opposition to Moroccan claims in the Western Sahara.[39]

In 1984, King Hassan had applied for membership in the European Union and been turned down, but EU officials arranged for technical and development assistance programs to focus on Morocco. The third round of funding for Morocco occurred between 1987 and 1991 and represented a significant increase in the funds committed. But King Hassan sought membership, and so he reapplied again to EU in 1987. When he did, King Hassan offered three areas of improvement that would make Morocco's entry into the EU possible. The King noted that Morocco was committed to developing a liberal economy. Unlike some other applicants, Morocco already had close ties with several European states. Third, Morocco was undertaking the "democratization of its domestic political life."[40] Morocco's application was again rejected. But it was clear that King Hassan recognized the metrics by which he and Morocco would be measured. And if he did not, they came into sharper focus when the EU's European Council adopted a Declaration on Human Rights in 1991 for use in determining the EU's foreign affairs.[41]

It is not lost on observers therefore, that King Hassan began taking steps at home to offer some measures of progress to those in the EU and elsewhere who were watching Moroccan affairs. In December 1988, King Hassan reversed his previous ban on the new human rights organization in Morocco that had been founded a few months earlier, the Organisation Marocaine des Droits de l'Homme (OMDH). In 1990, the King created a Royal Consultative Council on human rights and in June 1991 King Hassan released 300 political prisoners.

But the conditions of, and the stories from, the pardoned political prisoners were so horrific and Morocco's refusals to oblige UN Resolution 660 on the Western Sahara were viewed with such dismay that the European Parliament was prompted to withhold the fourth round of Morocco's EU foreign assistance funding.

King Hassan responded angrily and so ended negotiations with the EU over fisheries that were desired by European interests. Then, in June 1992 a Euro-Maghreb Partnership was initiated to address issues of democracy and human rights as well as development and Morocco was brought into a larger protocol though Morocco received no financing until the project was renewed in 1995 with the announcement of the Barcelona Declaration.

Many believed that the King's decision to hold an election in 1992 to ratify a new constitution and to choose local municipal officials and then to hold parliamentary elections in 1993, the first since 1984, was the result of the EU actions.[42] And King Hassan's offer in 1993 of key ministries to the opposition parties when their leaders charged the elections had been fraudulent, appeared designed to find some way to convince external as well as internal observers of his desire to reach out to the opposition parties.

The world was changing for King Hassan II. His task, according to many, when he took over from his father Mohammed V was to strengthen the unity and national identity of all Moroccans for their state and their King. He had done this and he also had survived two coup attempts. His miraculous escapes from both had given King Hassan II a reputation of being divinely protected. This was a reputation he nourished, according to Anouar Boukhars and other authors who have written on the King's strategy for governing. Boukhars also noted that as times changed, in 1993, the King shared with Èric Laurent, his biographer, the King's perspective that for his citizens to remain faithful to their king he had to defend their faith, their rights, and their national territory.[43]

If the EU's actions, coupled by internal pressures, helped move the King to initiate some reforms, it assisted not only Moroccan political party leaders, but also Moroccan women activists. For, as we noted in our discussion of resources in chapter one, exogenous events also provided new opportunities and allies for Moroccan women. The EU's new concern with democratization and human rights, including women's rights, helped create in Morocco a climate of expectation and legitimacy for women activists.

In the 1992 election, 75 women were elected nationwide of the 1,086 women candidates that ran in a field of 93,000 candidates for 22,820 municipal positions.[44] In the previous municipal elections in 1983, 54,165 candidates had run for office of which 306 were women and 34 of the 15,423 officials elected were women.[45]

Then in the 1993 elections the first women ever elected to parliament in Morocco won seats. Badia Skalli of USFP was placed high enough on her party's list and the party did well enough that she became a Member of Parliament.

Similarly, Latifa Smiress of the Istiqlal Party was also successful. However, the King did not include any women in the new government's ministries. Nor, when the elections were rejected by an important left political party and the King had to appoint a technocrat to head the parliament rather than a party leader, did the new Prime Minister seek to include any women in his government. As Stephen Hughes has noted, despite the King's and the parties' attempts to begin to include women in their decision making affairs, it would be 1999 before a woman was included in Morocco's government at the cabinet level.[46] However Hughes also notes that a UNDP study in 1995 noted that Morocco placed 85th of 170 states in the number of women that were appointed to administration and senior executive posts such as mining engineer, Amina Benkhadra, who was appointed Morocco's director of the government's mines division.[47]

The political openings and newly scheduled elections also provided the Islamists with opportunities to demonstrate support for their causes and to advocate that their positions should be adopted. Those Islamists who had formed political parties could now anticipate running for office with credibility and without facing attacks. However, not all Islamists chose to participate in elections. But in the late 1980s and throughout the 1990s efforts continued to coopt the leadership of Morocco's religious community by legitimizing their schools and supporting their activities through the efforts of the Director of the Ministry of Religious Affairs, 'Abd al-Kabir 'Alawi al-Mdaghri, who occupied that position from 1984 to 2002.[48]

Malika Zeghal notes that in 1988, for the first time, advanced studies in religion were now permitted in mosques and ten years later in 1998 these schools had a cohort of 200 students completing advanced studies whose curriculum was determined by religious leaders, instead of state officials.[49] Zeghal also notes that 'Abd al-Kabir 'Alawi al-Mdaghri's strategies of cooptation were roundly criticized following the 2003 bombings in Casablanca as some claim his support of a range of Islamist activities strengthened and expanded the Islamist movement in Morocco.[50]

In addition to supporting formal educational initiatives for the Islamists, al-Mdaghri began receiving religious leaders at the Ministry. Beginning in 1989 he facilitated Islamic Awakening gatherings across Morocco during the summer and in the early 1990s he began arranging for foreign visitors as well as local religious leaders to come to the Palace where they were able to meet with King Hassan II.[51] Morocco's Islamist community, while far from united, found ways to communicate and to coordinate. And Zeghal informs us that al-Mdaghri believed he could bring together the radical Abdessalam Yassine who had refused to recognize the King's special role in Morocco with, for example, the political Party of Justice and Democracy (PJD) that was willing to participate in electoral politics and publicly acknowledged the King's role. Al-Mdaghri believed that he could bring them into the King's circles through dialogue and inclusion.[52] Whatever al-Mdaghri's hopes, the continuous publicized warmth between Islamic leaders and the Palace gave Moroccan gender activists pause. To many of the Morocco's women activists, it appeared that King Hassan II was playing them off against the Islamists even as he had done with the left parties previously.

It would therefore become clear, upon the death of King Hassan II in 1999, and on the assumption of the throne by his son Mohamed VI, that one of the greatest resources for Morocco gender activists was an enlightened King. And Mohamed VI would demonstrate himself to be exactly that in the early years of his reign, as chapter six reveals. Advocacy theorists have long argued that for an idea to succeed, the grassroots have to capture elite decision makers. In Morocco there is no greater decision maker and no individual who is more elite than Morocco's King.

Notes

1. Collectif 95 Maghreb Egalité, *One Hundred Steps, One Hundred Provisions,* 3. http://www.wluml.org/sites/wluml.org/files/import/english/pubs/rtf/misc/100-steps.rtf.

2. Collectif 95, *One Hundred Steps,* 3.

3. Collectif 95, *One Hundred Steps,* 3-4.

4. Conversation with Khadija Errebbah, President of ADFM, during the Oberlin Alumni Association tour of Morocco. Khadija Errebbah, conversation with Sandberg, translator Harry Bichsel, Casablanca, March 31, 2012.

5. Fatima Mernissi's webpage http://www.mernissi.net/books/chronological_overview/index.html.

6. Martin Kramer, "Politics and the Prophet. Where are the Arab-Muslim Liberals" *The New Republic* (October 2009). http://www.geocities.com/martinkramerorg/Politics and Prophet.htm (accessed April 24, 2014).

7. Due to the many different languages in which Fatima Mernissi has published, dates for her books differ significantly in different sources. We have gone to Mernissi's own website for the definitive dating. Mernissi's webpage: http://www.mernissi.net/books/chronological_overview/index.html.

8. Stephen O. Hughes, *Morocco Under King Hassan* (Reading, UK: Ithaca Press, 2001), 306.

9. Friedrich Ebert Stiftung, http://www.fes.de/kommunikation/islam/index_gr.html.

10. Friedrich Ebert Stiftung, http://www.fes.de/kommunikation/islam/index_gr.html.

11. Both authors were in Morocco in 2001 during the national debates on whether or not to adopt a gender quota for the parliamentary elections of 2002. Several of the Moroccan women who worked with Eve Sandberg relayed this argument to her.

12. Eve Sandberg, "Multilateral Women's Conferences: the Domestic Political Organization of Zambian Women" *Contemporary Politics* 4, no. 3, (1998).

13. Sandberg, "Multilateral Women's Conferences.

14. Short History of the Commission on the Status of Women http://www.un.org/womenwatch/daw/CSW60YRS/CSWbriefhistory.pdf.

15. Short History of the Commission on the Status of Women.

16. Short History of the Commission on the Status of Women.

17. International Institute for Sustainable Development (IISD), "Daily Report on The Fourth World Conference On Women." *Earth Negotiations Bulletin* 14, no. 21 (18 September 1995), http://www.iisd.ca/vol14/enb1421e.txt.

18. Rabéa Naciri, *The Women's Movement and Political Discourse in Morocco*, Occasional Paper 8, United Nations Research Institute for Social Development, United Nations Development Programme (UNDP), Geneva, March 1998, 18.

19. Naciri, *The Women's Movement and Political Discourse in Morocco*, 18.

20. Laurie Brand, *Women, the State, and Political Liberalization: Middle Eastern and North African Experiences* (New York: Columbia University Press, 1998), 61.

21. Brand, *Women, the State, and Political Liberalization,* 61.

22. Platform for Action http://www.vrouwen.net/vweb/wcw/reserv.html (from the Dutch blog, Womannet).

23. Hughes, *Morocco Under King Hassan,* 310 Fn. 4.

24. Jane Bayes and Nayereh Tohidi, *Globalization, Gender, and Religion* (New York: Palgrave MacMillan, 2001). The paragraph is attributed to Bayes and Tohidi and is based on Chapter One.

25. Bayes and Tohidi, *Globalization, Gender, and Religion,* 3.

26. Bayes and Tohidi, *Globalization, Gender, and Religion,* 4.

27. Jerry Filteau, "Pope Made Important Overtures to Non-Christian Religions," *Catholic News Service* (2005) http://www.catholicnews.com/jpii/stories/story04.htm.

28. Filteau, "Pope Made Important Overtures to Non-Christian Religions." The information in this paragraph is based on the article by Filteau.

29. Filteau, "Pope Made Important Overtures to Non-Christian Religions." The information in this paragraph is based on the article by Filteau.

30. Marvine Howe, *Morocco: The Islamist Awakening and Other Challenges* (Oxford: Oxford University Press, 2005).165.

31. Howe, *Morocco: The Islamist Awakening and Other Challenges, 165.*

32. MENA Consultative Council on Gender [CCG] – World Bank hht://web.worldbank.org/WBSITE/EXTERNAL/COUNTRIES/MENAEXT/EXTMNAREGTOGENDER/0,,menuPK:493344~pagePK:51065911~theSitePK:49333,m00.html.

33. Francesco Cavatorta, "The International Context of Morocco's Stalled Democratization," *Democratization 12, no. 4* (August 2005), 560.

34. Cavatorta, "The International Context of Morocco's Stalled Democratization," 560.

35. Cavatorta, "The International Context of Morocco's Stalled Democratization," 560.

36. Eve Sandberg and Seth Binder, "The Moroccan Spring and King Mohammed VI's Economic Policy Agenda: Evaluating the First Dozen Years," in *Une Jeunesse Révoltée,* ed. Mohsine El Ahmadi (Rabat: Marsam Editions, 2014 forthcoming). English language edition *The Birth of the Arab Citizen and the Changing Middle East*, ed. Mohsine El Ahmadi and Stuart Schaar (Northampton, MA: Interlink Publishing, 2014 forthcoming). The profile of Morocco's IMF program is taken from this work by Sandberg and Binder.

37. Said Haddadi, "Two Cheers for Whom? The European Union and Democratization in Morocco," *Democratization* 9, no. 1 (2002), 149-169.

38. Alexis Ariell, *Algeria. Current Issues,* Congressional Research Service, November 18, 2013. This paragraph is based on this work.

39. Ariell, *Algeria. Current Issues,* Congressional Research Service. November 18, 2013.

40. Haddadi, "Two Cheers for Whom?" 151. This paragraph is taken from Said Haddadi.

41. Haddadi, "Two Cheers for Whom?" 152.

42. Haddadi, "Two Cheers for Whom?" 151. This paragraph is taken from Said Haddadi.

43. Anouar Boukhars, *Politics in Morocco* (London and New York: Routledge, 2011), 41.

44. Khadija Errebbah, "Women's Political Participation: The Moroccan Example," in *The Arab Quota Report: Selected Case Studies* (Stockholm, International Institute for Democracy and Electoral Assistance (International IDEA), *The Arab Quota Report: Selected Case Studies*. Stockholm 2007, 57.

45. Errebbah, "Women's Political Participation," 57.

46. Hughes, *Morocco Under King Hassan,* 305.

47. Hughes, *Morocco Under King Hassan,* 307.

48. Malika Zeghal, *Islamism in Morocco. Religion, Authoritarianism, and Electoral Politics,* translator, George Holoch (Princeton: Markus Wiener Publishers, 2008), 170-171.

49. Zeghal, *Islamism in Morocco,* 170-171.

50. Zeghal, *Islamism in Morocco,* 171.

51. Zeghal, *Islamism in Morocco,* 172-173.

52. Zeghal, *Islamism in Morocco,* 172-173.

Chapter Six
The Sum Is Greater Than Its Parts

In the late 1990s, the ideas of democratization and the improvement of human rights were world-wide forces for change. In Morocco, youth, women, Berbers and the vast majority of Morocco's population who are poor (in both the rural areas and on the urban streets) all hoped for improvements in the economic, political, and social sectors. All yearned for a better life. However, when King Hassan II died at age 70 in July 1999, and a youthful King Mohamed VI, aged 35, assumed the throne, few knew what to expect. As the third King of Morocco since independence, and at a time when monarchy as an institution had lost its appeal in much of the world, Moroccans wondered what the future held for their King and for themselves.

In the last years of King Hassan's life, his son, Mohamed, had represented Morocco in foreign capitals but he had not been publicly seen in domestic political contexts exercising any real authority. Mohamed was young, and few knew how close he might have been to governance and what lessons in governing he might have learned. He was known to favor surf boarding and mixing with commoners. A prince who would surf board and mix with commoners appealed to younger Moroccans. Whether he could effectively govern a nation and a country were unknowns.

The new King had completed his undergraduate work in Morocco but his graduate work was completed in France where he had written his thesis on trade relations between the EU and Morocco. The thesis focused largely on economic exchanges and the concept of democracy is mentioned only a few times and then briefly. However, the King would have had to have learned about—even if he did not write about—the expectations of the EU member countries concerning the improvement of the status of women, of human rights, and of democratic practices within any state that hoped to become a member of the EU, whether in Eastern Europe or in North Africa. Additionally, the fact that King Mohamed VI had resided outside of Morocco and was exposed to global notions of democracy and had lived in an advanced industrial country and witnessed the commercial and economic benefits available even for the working poor, had to color his world view and how he viewed Morocco.

Therefore, when King Mohamed VI assumed the throne and immediately embraced some personal choices that improved the status of women, Morocco's gender activists allowed themselves to become cautiously optimistic. When he assumed the throne, the new monarch made significant moves to show that he supported women and valued contributions that they could make. His first speeches addressed the issues of improving the status of Moroccan women. He appointed the first woman royal advisor, appointed a woman at the head of an oil research company, and appointed several more women to head important sectors in Morocco such as tourism and women's affairs.

Mohamed VI also was the first King of Morocco to introduce his wife—a commoner who had a degree in engineering—to the public. Pictures of the King's wife were available in print and through audio-visual media for the first time in Moroccan history. Previous queens were hidden away with almost no public visibility whatsoever and certainly their faces were always covered. We can only speculate that the King's own orientation coupled with Moroccan women's lobbying for change helped the King to embrace the notion of an expanded role for women in all manner of public spheres. Indeed, prominent women in Morocco were talking and writing articles prior to the King's marriage in which they wished that the King would elevate the image of women by introducing his own wife to the public and allowing her to be involved in state activities.

After his installation as King, the new monarch began meeting with women's leaders and with leaders from other civil society groupings concerned with issues of democratization. From our institutional analysis it is important to note that the fact that such organizations existed was a testament to the tenacity of Moroccan women who continued to organize and carry out their service activities for years even when they received little or no encouragement and had made uneven gains during their years of organizing.

It was also believed in Morocco that the King consulted with his sisters on various issues and took their views into account. The new King had lived the alternative logics that Moroccan gender activists hoped to bring to Morocco and in his first months as monarch, King Mohamed VI was recasting the role of women simply through his own personal actions. Some argued that the King's father had already started on such a path so he could make the argument that he was merely proceeding down that path.

Also the final elections that had taken place under King Hassan II marked an enormous democratic departure from all elections held previously in Morocco. First, King Hassan had announced that he now believed that a government of "alternance" in which coalitions led by alternating parties would be a good thing for Morocco. Parliament should no longer be dominated by a single party. In 1997, three coalitions of parties contested the parliamentary elections: the Koutla bloc which won 102 seats in the election, the Wifaq bloc which won 100 seats, and the Centre bloc which won 97 seats. But in the election, none of the coalitions won a clear-cut majority to enable it to govern. The socialist party USFP, led by Abderrahmane Youssoufi, had won the most seats (57) of any party. In a surprise move, King Hassan appointed socialist Youssoufi as Prime Minister in this new era of reform.

The choice of Youssoufi was a lightning bolt across Morocco's political landscape. Abderrahmane Youssoufi had been an independence activist against the French as a member of the Istiqlal party. He had left the Istiqlal party to join those further on the left, eventually becoming a leader in the USFP. But following the assassination of Ben Barka, Youssoufi had gone into exile from 1965 to 1980 working as a human rights lawyer often for immigrants in France from

Morocco and also playing a prominent role in establishing (with other lawyers) human rights organizations across the Arab world. Not only was Youssoufi a leader of an opposition party, he was a distinguished leader on the left and among those who had fought the Palace for democratization and human rights. On being appointed Prime Minister, Youssoufi declared his intention to support the promotion of women's equality. He called for further revisions to the Moudawana, Morocco's family code.

Just as Youssoufi's ascent to the post of the Prime Minister of Morocco signaled the democratic winds of change blowing, so too did the 1997 elections themselves. Moroccan women party activists convinced their parties to support their candidacies and allow them to contest parliamentary seats during the 1997 elections. Sixty-nine women from sixteen parties competed for parliament in the 1997 election.[1] Two women were elected and entered the parliament following the 1997 national elections: Badia Skalli and Fatima Belmoudden both of USFP. (The first two Moroccan women ever to have entered Parliament was in 1993: Badia Skalli (USFP) and Latifa Bennani Smiress (Istiqlal)) These two nationally elected women, however, comprised only 0.62% of Morocco's parliamentary seats. But beyond serving as role models of diligent and competent Members of Parliament, these two lone women in a sea of male Members of Parliament, and men who were all jockeying to advance their own positions, could do little for women's legislation. As MPs, they were important role models for women, but they mostly had to work within the confines of their parties' agendas vis-à-vis other parties.

The hopes for the new opposition parties that ruled in parliament and for the women that had been elected were undermined by reports that there had been vote buying and other illegal, non-democratic activities during the campaign. Thus, under King Hassan II, even his democratic opening was tainted by accusations of interference and corruption.

In 1999, upon the death of his father, when King Mohamed VI inherited the throne, one of his first acts as King was to remove the Minister of the Interior, Driss Basri, who was accused not only of corrupting Morocco's elections, but also of overseeing the brutal repression of Morocco's political opposition party activists and civic leaders. This act by itself raised expectations for the new monarch and one could hardly find a person in Morocco who did not rejoice that the powerful, violent Basri had been removed from office and could no longer wield power.

King Mohamed VI and the Women's Question

King Mohamed VI had ascended his throne against a backdrop of lobbying for and against a proposed revision to the Moudawana that was championed by Prime Minister Youssoufi. The National Plan of Action for Integrating Women into Development was the outcome of Moroccan women gender activists activating their connections to Moroccan leftist and other parties in the 1997 Parliament. Using old connections and personal relations to create new pathways for promoting legislation, Morocco's multitude of women's organizations both contributed to the substance of the proposals of the National Plan of Action and also lobbied their affiliated parties to make certain there was support for the program when it came before the Parliament. The prospect of such a program, however, created a huge backlash from the Islamic activists, including the government's own Minister of Islamic Affairs.

In an effort to promote the plan, Youssoufi's government had incorporated it into a World Bank presentation that stressed the integration of women into development planning in Morocco. The Minister of Islamic Affairs, Abdelkebir Alaoui M'Dghari, objected strenuously. And there were a number of Moroccan women gender activists who believed the plan should go still further as it did not propose full equality for both Moroccan men and women.

Thus, on assuming his position as King, Mohamed VI appointed a commission to study and propose reforms to the family code. He also announced his intent to integrate women into Morocco's national development plans. Once again Moroccan women coordinated and reached out to allies, now in the leadership of the political parties within parliament, to advance their agenda. And so, just after international women's day in March 2000 "tens of thousands, representing women's groups, human rights movements and political parties (and at least six government ministers), marched in the capital Rabat in support" of Youssoufi's plan or an improved version of it.[2] But the Islamists had organized as well. In Casablanca, about one million demonstrators called for no changes in the Moudawana. And there was an enormous women's contingent among the Islamist activists who chanted, "No to the international conventions on women's rights."[3]

Morocco's gender activists, however, were coordinating to reach out to old allies and to educate to gain new supporters. About thirty women's civil society organizations created "Le Printemps de l'Egalité," or the "Equality Spring" to organize, educate, lobby, and demonstrate for major changes in Morocco's family code. The number of member organizations increased over time.

The two major Islamist organizations for women (Jamāʻat al-ʻadl wa-l-ihsāne (Justice and Spirituality) and Harakat al-tawhīd wa-l-islāh (Movement of Unification and Reform) consisted of large networks whose religious women had been working for years to counter the programs of reform that they saw as Western inspired departures from their faith.[4] These Islamist activist women conducted face-to-face outreach to other women in neighborhoods all across Morocco to educate and bring the neighborhood women into an acceptance of the Islamists' worldview. When it was time to mobilize to oppose the National Action Plan, the work these women had done was evident for all to see as hundreds of thousands of women appeared in Casablanca to oppose the proposed reforms.

But two new resources that the gender activists could now rely upon were the new Prime Minister and the new King. On March 8, 2001, "the King, the Prime Minister, and several other ministers met with 40 representatives of women's organizations at the Royal Palace."[5] Then in April 2001, the King created a Consultative Commission for the Moudawana.

Five months later, however, in September, while the Commission was still working on its tasks, the ADFM and nine other Moroccan women's organizations who were members of the Equality Spring issued a communiqué that no changes to the Moudawana had yet occurred and this was very disappointing.[6] Additionally, they offered recommendations to be adopted by the Commission.[7]

But the Consultative Commission reported no news to the public and so again on October 17, the ADFM brought media attention to the issue and offered another statement in support of the recommendations offered the previous month (though its members declared there was no need to come again and testify before the commission). As of January 2002 the Consultative Commission still had made no public statements.[8] It was now eighteen months after the major demonstrations in Rabat and Casablanca that had the divided the country and "modernists" and "traditionalists," as the sides were being called, continued to organize and reach out to gather more support.

Three women served on the The Royal Consultative Commission for the Reform of the Moudawana. Nouzha Guessous (-Idrissi) was a professor at Casablanca's faculty of medicine and pharmacy. She was a founder of Morocco's major human rights organization, the Organisation Marocaine des Droits Humains. She believed that women's rights were integrated into human rights.[9]

Zhour Al Horr was the second woman on the Consulative Commission. She taught Arabic for ten years before she joined the legal profession as a lawyer, though she had received a law degree years earlier. She was the first Moroccan woman appointed as a court judge (in El Jadida in 1979) and she worked as a representative at the social and labor court in a district of Casablanca.[10] Zhour Al Horr was a known women's activist who later became chief justice at the new family court at Al Fida Derb in Casablanca. In December 2011, Al Horr was awarded the Ibn Zohr award for her activities in the Moroccan courts by Morocco's national division of Amnesty International.[11] The third woman to serve on the Royal Commission was Dr. Rahma Bourquia, who was the first woman appointed to head a Moroccan University. She served as President of the Hassan II University in Mohamedia.[12]

The Equality Spring coalition members were careful to utilize the work that the UAF women had been doing for years, identifying how the Koran supported women's claims and demonstrating that their goals were not Western inspired but in accordance with the Koran. Additionally, the ADFM women who had been reaching out across the Maghreb and other parts of the Arab world also offered their understandings of where and how Moroccan women's claims for an improved status of women overlapped with Islamic laws. The ADFM women promoted the work of the Equality Spring coalition viewing it as a major task for ADFM activists.

On October 13, 2001, while waiting for the Consultative Commission to complete its work, twenty women's organizations thinking proactively about the upcoming 2002 parliamentary elections raised the topic of a gender quota for

Morocco's national election at a Spring of Equality meeting held in Casablanca. The topic had been raised previously.

In 1996, the ADFM was among a group of women's organizations that advocated for a 20% quota of seats guaranteed for women in Morocco's Parliament. Nouzha Skalli was one of the early spokeswomen for this issue. In 1999, a Moroccan draft law addressing women in development had proposed a 30% quota for women in Morocco's parliament. Moroccan women raised the idea within their parties. So when in 2001 the twenty women's organizations called for 33% of parliamentary seats to be set aside for women through elections as well as a similar quota for professional bodies, unions, and the executive boards of the political parties be set aside, they did so within a context in which they had been discursively intervening for some time.

On the big issues of the Moudawana and national elections, Morocco's multitude of women activists and their organizations were coordinating their activities, utilizing the media to intervene discursively into national political debates, utilizing new pathways to newly placed decision makers, and actively seeking resources from domestic and foreign sources. Moroccan women activists were pushing the walls of the gender institution that constrained their lives. And now there were hundreds of them and the sum was greater than its parts. With each news release, each demonstration, each meeting, the socialization process necessary to change Morocco's family law was advanced.

Moroccan women activists turned to international donors to help finance a number of projects they hoped to undertake, organizing around the upcoming elections. The United Kingdom provided financial assistance for the ADFM and others to produce a pamphlet targeting rural women and the importance of voting. The ADFM also approached the National Democratic Institute (NDI), the democracy building organization whose Chairman was Madeline Albright, the former U.S. Secretary of State for President Bill Clinton. NDI's support and mission had evolved over time and NDI had come to function as a non-profit, nonpartisan, non-governmental organization partnering with local civic associations and political institutions in every region of the world. NDI's staff in Morocco responded to the request to conduct workshops that would help women who hoped to run for office and professionalize their approach to campaigning. (Full disclosure: both authors were involved with the NDI-ADFM initiatives. Kenza Aqertit as an NDI staff member in Rabat helped to organize these workshops. Eve Sandberg was one of about fifteen team members lead by Seattle-based political consultant Cathy Allen of the Connections Group and the University of Washington's Center for Women and Democracy. Allen had already led workshops for ADFM and she continued to lead a series of workshops in Morocco over the next decade.)[13]

For the parliamentary women's campaign training initiative in 2001-2002, 121 women from the major and many minor political parties attended the trainings. Even the religious Justice and Development Party (JDP) sent their women for parliamentary campaign trainings. [Sandberg was also part of Allen's group that held additional trainings in targeting and messaging for the (mostly male) executive boards of Morocco's political parties and Aqertit helped to organize these sessions as well.] And NDI's work in Morocco was not simply the work of women. It was possible also because of male allies such as NDI President, Kenneth Wollach, and NDI MENA Regional Director, Les Campbell.

The campaign trainings not only offered a transfer of skills, but they also kept women's issues on the front pages of the newspapers and on Moroccan national television. And they allowed the Moroccan women to meet one another across party lines. For many participants this was one of the most exciting aspects of the program, to meet and discuss with other Moroccan women political issues of the day and also their concerns for women in Morocco's political parties.

By May 2002 there was no movement on the issues of the Moudawana and the parliamentary elections were fast approaching. So when the new election law was to be read in Parliament, there was intense concern on the part of the women as to whether or not the new law would include a section on the quota for women. Morocco's women's groups accelerated lobbying their own political party colleagues as well as any member of parliament that they could find in order to urge passage of a gender quota section in the new election law.

Women in the public gallery and those watching on national television listened intently when the Minister of the Interior, Driss Jettou, read the new election law to the country's parliamentarians on May 6, 2002. The law, which now had enough support for passage, would ensure Morocco's first fair and free elections in the country's history. Additionally, the new law, as presented, included that special clause of interest to Moroccan women and to those concerned with the status of women globally. The general particulars of the bill that would move the country into its first free and transparent elections included: the use of indelible ink; moving from seventeen easily manipulated ballots to a single, secret ballot; severe sanctions against anyone caught interfering with or undermining the new democratic processes; the mandate that all candidates must present a written declaration of their legal and ethical worthiness for office based on their past and present activities; the relocation of voting polls to accommodate voters; and regularized national hours for voting. All these reforms suggested that Morocco hoped to become a new model of democratic politics.

Most important to the women listening that day, and to their male allies, however, was the clause that described what the new law would enable Moroccan women to do politically. According to the new election law, in addition to a national slate of 295 candidates running (locally) for the parliament, a new, separate slate of 30 additional parliamentary seats was announced. In the coming September 2002 election, the percentage of votes gained by the parties in the national election as they ran locally and in which the parties would campaign vigorously, would determine how many of the 295 seats each party earned in Parliament and it would also determine how many of the 30 seats on the women's list each party earned. Each party was to create a candidate list of thirty in addition to those on their regular slate. Each party pledged only to place female candidates on the top of the new, 30-seat national list. Thus if a party earned 10 percent of the seats in parliament, its top three women candidates on the 30-seat list (or ten percent of the list) would now also take their places in the parliament alongside those elected from the 295 candidate balloting. In the sitting Parliament that heard the bill read, there were only two women parliamentarians. Thus, following the September 27, 2002, elections, Morocco would likely advance from its .01 women representation in parliamentary (2 women out of 325 representatives) to a little less than 10% of women's representation (30 seats out of 325). As the bill was being read, Morocco's ranking of women in parliament was one of the worst in the world. But for the many Moroccan women in the gallery and watching at home that was about to change.

Moroccan women would be able to run on the regular ballot as they had in the past; but women on the new, separate 30-seat ballot in this coming election would run at the top of the list so that women would be certain to be those elected. The government had determined that it could not dictate that *only* women would be on the gender quota ballot because that would violate the country's non-discrimination clauses in the constitution. So an informal agreement among the political party leaders guaranteed that women would occupy the top spots on the gender quota ballot for the 30 seats and men would occupy the slots toward the bottom of the gender slate. Since, in the past elections, political parties rarely even attained thirty percent of the vote that meant only the top candidates on any party's gender quota slate had an opportunity to win.

For the major parties, the top woman on their gender ballot would most likely enter parliament. Perhaps a second woman from a large party that won a lot of votes would enter parliament as well. But it was unlikely that any party would attract enough votes so that three or four women of their party women would enter parliament. Thus, party women had to be thinking about their designated place on the slate (determined by the executive board or leader of each party) and this likely began to introduce some competition among the women within a party. But mostly, the women party activists were so excited for their country at the historic prospect of a substantial increase in the number of Moroccan women Members of Parliament (MPs) that they supported the gender slate with enthusiasm.

To be in Morocco's Parliament as the Minister of the Interior read, and the parliamentarians passed, the new election law with its section for women was exhilarating both for its proponents and for observers. The muted red and gray patterned carpets and the plush green (for ministers) and plush red (for parliamentarians) upholstered broad wooden chairs provided a rich backdrop to the dark wooden paneled walls and speakers' boxes. White plaster sculpted in geometric patterns provided light and added to the cultural markings and the grandeur of the hall. National television cameras carried the session live to a national audience and an electronic voting board could be seen on either side of the Chairman's box.

Morocco's parliament is a thoroughly modern building that is adorned by traditional images and crafts, seemingly a metaphor for the new political system. The parliament meets in a grand chamber and the building hosts elegant resting and caucus areas decorated with traditional art as well as modern art containing traditional Islamic themes. A superb dining room and outdoor terrace restaurant provide meals and respite for the parliamentarians during long working days when parliament is in session. Here, as in the resting areas, the MPs chat, waiting for the bell that will call them to vote, while members of their parties enter remarks (often after a bill has been voted upon) in the official chamber.

The parliament also has its share of portraits of national heroes and gifts from other parliaments, national assemblies, and congresses around the world. But it is the refined committee meeting rooms, each with state of the art technology and a supporting research library for all parliamentarians that offered a bright future of legislative activity for Morocco's political party caucuses and coalitions.

And while Moroccan women waited to see whether or not the women's quota section of the bill would remain in the bill when it came to a full vote, the speeches offered by various party members continued for hours. As one executive board member of the country's founding Istiqlal Party explained in the week following the passage of the historic legislation, "In Morocco, if you have little to say, people believe that you are not capable of thinking important thoughts or capable of being a leader. A leader is someone who can hold forth for a long, long time on any topic, even if the speaker says many things that have already been said."[14]

As the new election bill demonstrated, however, politics in Morocco was changing. As the Minister of the Interior declared in his summary of the legislation, the new democratic practices of this bill were historic. These were to be the procedures for the "first election held during the reign of King Mohamed VI and they would be watched nationally and internationally."[15] Further, he stressed that the reforms had been crafted by the Committee of the Interior after much consultation with, and feedback from, all political parties. All the parties had been consulted whether in group sessions or through individual leaders from the parties. The President of the Interior Committee and his staff as well as the Minister of the Interior himself had sought to fashion the reforms in a way that would benefit the nation as a whole, not any leading parties at the time, the Minister assured his multi-party audience.[16]

When the section on the new 30-seat slate which everyone knew was for women was voted upon favorably, many in the packed public gallery and in the national television audience understood that a major step in attaining new status for Moroccan women had been taken. One of the two sitting women parliamentarians rose from her seat, made her way from the well of the chamber up to the public gallery where your authors and the parliamentarian's allies were seated to greet and thank everyone. Morocco's female MP thanked everyone for the work they had done: those who had lobbied for the bill for years, those Moroccan women who had stepped forward to prepare themselves to serve as candidates in the upcoming historic 2002 parliamentary elections, and those allies who had supported Moroccan women in their efforts to change the election law.

Though there continued to be silence on the issues of the Moudawana, party campaigning swung into high gear for the Parliamentary elections. And while for Moroccan activist women it was an historic election, for many other Moroccan citizens they had long ago given up on any election process in Morocco. Many Moroccans did not believe that the 2002 elections would be fair and free and they did not believe that it mattered who was elected to Parliament. For a great number of Moroccans, Parliamentarians had little power and so its members did little but collect large salaries and utilize special privileges.

To encourage voting, the Minister of the Interior and the election officials encouraged international observers to watch and validate that this election process would be honest. Additionally, as election day 2002 approached, there was something exciting in the air, especially for women opinion leaders, and it provided many Moroccans with the hope, that just perhaps, their new King Mohamed VI and his new Minister of the Interior, Driss Jettou, would make certain that the parliamentary elections were honest.

On Morocco's 2002 national election day, 51.6% of Morocco's eligible voters turned out to vote. Over twenty parties contested in the elections. While the socialist USFP's share of votes declined from the 1997 election total (from 57 seats to 50 seats) it nonetheless earned the largest number of votes, 13.9% of the electorate.[17] The Istiqlal Party (Independence Party) earned 13.2% or 48 seats (an improvement from its 1997 allocation of 32 seats) in the 2002 election. But in a warning to those who worried about Islamist activists determining rules for all Moroccans, the Justice and Development Party (PJD) came in third with 42 seats. Since the PJD had earned only 9 of 325 seats in the previous legislature, this represented an enormous surge in demonstrated popular support. The RNI earned 11.1% of the vote, the Popular Movement earned 10.3% and the Constitutional Union earned 10.2%. All the other parties earned below the 10% threshold.

Additionally, and to some, astonishingly, four women won their seats through the regular slate process, not on the gender slate. It seemed as though, in the political representative realm of politics, Moroccan women had arrived. In the coming months, the thirty-four women taking their place in the national parliament and being seen on television and in the print press, was an important component of the socialization process of Moroccan society. Moroccan acceptance regarding women's participation in public elections grew, especially for younger Moroccans who came of age during this period. And the 2002 election unleashed the aspirations of thousands of other women who dared to run for municipal office in 2003. Clearly an important anchor of Morocco's gender institution had been altered, that of having women directly participate in the legislative decision making processes at the national and municipal levels, taking part in the decision making processes that would affect them as women.

There were those who claimed that adding women's leadership to that of men in the parliament and in the municipal councils would do little for poor and uneducated women. Women's entry into decision making arenas, some critics argued, was a success only in the view of Western liberals who believed that elections mattered. And in fact, it turned out that the Moroccan women elected to parliament did not work so well across their party lines during their first term in the legislature. There were personal rivalries, party rivalries, and differences of opinion on agenda setting for new legislation. Male colleagues demanded to know why their party women were not getting as much or more press attention than women from other parties. Male colleagues also became jealous when some women leaders attracted more press attention than the male leaders could garner.

Those thousands of Moroccan women activists not contending with a new electoral office position continued to work in the exploding civil society sector to provide services to women and others as well as to continue to advocate for changes in the Moudawana. Now, however, women parliamentarians, and following the 2003 elections, women municipal leaders, could help such calls gain press attention. But even those women who worked in Morocco's civil society represented only a fraction of Morocco's population. This is true in countries around the world, and so even civil society activists have been accused of being elitist, for they are part of a small group of activists and leaders.

The 2005 Civicus civil society index and report on Morocco noted that when most Moroccans participate in civil society organizations (CSOs), they join sport, education, or cultural organizations. In the Civicus index, women's advocacy organizations are categorized together with other political advocacy organizations as human rights organizations. The Civicus index estimated that of those Moroccans who volunteered with CSOs, only 1.4% participated in human rights civil organizations (this sector includes the women's organizations).[18]

In 2003, as the newly elected parliamentarians entered government, with little news of the Royal Commission's work on the Moudawana, and with the municipal elections scheduled for June 2003, many activist women were working with their political parties or assisting those women whom they supported in their campaigns for municipal office.

The Casablanca Bombings by Islamist Extremists

Then, on May 16, 2003, five simultaneous suicide bombings in Casablanca killed 45 and injured nearly 100. Targets of the attacks were mostly members of the Moroccan Jewish community but the victims included Moroccan Muslims as well. All of the victims were merely going about their business and the attacks shocked Moroccans' sense of national stability and the country's pride in its religious tolerance.

Eventually it was learned that fourteen of the attackers were Moroccan and believed to be part of a local extremist group, As-Sirat al-Mustaqim, the Righteous Path. The group operated throughout the slums of Casablanca. It was also believed that the attackers were tied to al-Qaeda and received external funding and training. It was widely reported that in a 2002 audiotape, Osama bin Laden had included Morocco on a list of the countries that were "ready for liberation." Press and foreign attention was also given to the rumors that the group had targeted "unbelievers," as determined by this extremist group, and that similar "unbelievers" had been being assassinated in the neighborhoods of Casablanca for some months.[19]

The standing of Morocco's Islamist communities within Moroccan society plummeted. The PJD decided to restrict its contestation in the municipal elections so as not to invite attacks and to wait until the popular mood shifted. King Mohamed VI postponed the national elections scheduled for June until September so the government could investigate the bombings and take precautionary steps to safeguard the elections. The Casablanca bombings were a blow to the PJD just when it had anticipated a major electoral victory in the municipal elections.

Then, King Mohamed VI who had been working assiduously to improve Morocco's human rights performance seemed to borrow a leaf from the book of his father, King Hassan, and joined with parliamentarians to act. Quickly, over 1000 people were arrested as suspects. Sixteen were sentenced to death and fifty were incarcerated for life. Human rights groups protested that the trials lacked legitimacy and transparency. Some wondered if Morocco would now backtrack on democracy. But most Moroccans believed that swift action was needed to both punish the culprits and to deter any further attacks in Morocco.

The Casablanca bombings demonstrated both that there remained some who would use violence to achieve their goals, and that there were some who deeply opposed the political reforms of the Monarchy and parliament. The media also portrayed the young bombers as dismayed over the government's inability to create jobs, and so they had no stake in the existing Moroccan system.

Another consequence of the bombings was that in light of the concerns raised that this King would turn to violations of human rights as his father had done and because the young monarch hoped to achieve legitimacy in his own right, King Mohamed VI then made an extraordinary gesture as a sitting Monarch. On January 7, 2004, at the request of the King, Morocco established an Equity and Reconciliation Commission charged with investigating the reign of King Hassan II in order to "close the file on past human rights violations."[20] This was an extraordinary action and muted much of the criticism of King Mohamed VI's actions towards the bombing suspects.

In the first years of King Mohamed's reign, the Monarchy and the Parliament did not slow democratization reforms. And the King traveled widely and displayed his charitable works, as his father had done before him, because the Monarchy had to attend to the concerns of all Moroccans, including those in the rural areas that were the most religious and who historically had most supported the Crown. Also the new King promoted Berber rights as well as those of women. This, too, demonstrated a distinctive departure from his father, King Hassan II. Privately owned news media sprang up as it was perceived that more freedom of the press would be tolerated, although most editors and authors were careful to engage in self censorship because when some crossed a line, they were brought into court.

Revisions to the Moudawana

And when many Moroccan women gender activists had almost given up hope on the Royal Council producing anything to improve women's rights, in September 2003, the Monarchy proposed, and in February 2004, the parliament adopted by a unanimous vote, a new family code. The bombings in Casablanca had cast the Islamists in such a poor light that some believe it would have been difficult for their leaders to object to any reforms for women that the King proposed in September 2003. Moreover, King Mohamed VI saw that the changes to the Moudawana were legislated. This made them the law of the land and also signaled that the parliament had a role to play in the religious life of the country as well as the King. It also allowed history to view that all political parties, not just the King, had endorsed changes for Moroccan women.

And so the revisions recommended by the Royal Commission were adopted. According to the revisions, men and women together were responsible for their children. Women were not obligated to obey their husbands. Male polygamy was restricted. Women and men both could now ask for divorce and it was left to the secular judges to make determinations regarding divorce. Men could no longer simply renounce their wives, nor did women have to submit to vicious husbands. Widows and children were granted some inheritance rights. The children of Moroccan women who married foreigners were granted Moroccan citizenship just as had been the case for the children of Moroccan men who married foreigners. Any language that suggested women were inferior was omitted from the new family code.

While it would take much to get these reforms implemented—because many judges as well as common practices continued to undermine the reforms—a major component of Morocco's gender institution had been altered. In the following years (in the short term), the national debate about the Moudawana would address the enforcement of the new code. By the next decade, however, Moroccan women gender activists would be advocating to make changes in the Moudawana that protected women and children from violence.

There certainly remained other changes to work for such as increased inheritance and specific language about penalties for violence to women as noted above. But a unanimous vote for changing the Moudawana could not have been contemplated in the 1980s. In 2004, it became a reality. The difference was found in the work undertaken by Moroccan gender activists. Their leadership, their strategizing, their goal setting, the particular organizational dynamic they established of linking to political parties and then working across parties through coordination among women's civil society organizations, their discursive interventions into Morocco's national debates, all contributed to the success achieved in 2004. Moroccan women had formed new byways of decision making, had placed themselves at the decision making tables, and had sought and found new resources to help them work for change.

When King Mohamed VI finally announced the reforms to the family code, each reform was legitimated by a Koranic reference.[21] The King then chose to submit the proposed reforms to parliament for its vote. Unlike his father, King Hassan II, King Mohamed VI did not wrest from the new parliament decision making power—even in the issue area of religion and customary practices.

In 2006, King Mohamed VI would make another startling announcement. He announced that women religious leaders were to be identified, trained, and certified as guides for Moroccan society. These women were not recruited from gender activists groups. Rather, the recruits would be devout Muslims who had the aptitude for study, training, and leadership. As religious leader of the country, King Mohamed VI created positions for women to act as religious Islamic teachers and guides, called Mourchidats. Initially, fifty women were designated for training, certification, and employment as Islamic teachers. Over time, the numbers have increased. The women are assigned posts in schools, prisons, and hospitals. And these Mourchidats are no activists who have their own interpretation of the Koran. Most are very pious women who believe they, too, can spread the word of Islam. But the fact that women can now study, interpret, and teach the Koran, alters Morocco's gender practices in ways that altering only secular practices cannot. Women now can be seen as leaders in every sector of Moroccan society.

Morocco's Changing Foreign Policy Context

In 2002, when the United States invaded Iraq, the tide seemed to tip against democratic activists across the Middle East and certainly in Morocco it made it more difficult to be arguing in favor of what anyone could charge was Western ideas, including those for women. No one wanted to be associated with a U.S. foreign policy that used its army to invade a Muslim country without provocation. No one wanted to be accused of being pro-West after the United States invaded Iraq and then said it would establish a Western style democracy there.

Across the Arab world, there had been tremendous good will towards the United States after it was attacked on 9/11. There had been many protestations by Moroccan moderates, and others across the Middle East, that such attacks did not represent Islam. But following the U.S. invasion of Iraq, many Middle Eastern democracy activists ran for cover. Those in Morocco were no exception. Democratic activists across the Arab world limited their activities to avoid the charge of being seen as pro-West and associated with the U.S.'s unilateral actions in the Middle East. Women gender activists who previously were confronted with accusations of not being authentic Moroccans but instead merely pro-Western puppets, now took even more care not to be seen as too supportive of Western ideas.

On King Mohamed VI's first visit to Washington in 2002, President George W. Bush had praised the new, young Monarch and announced they would work together to defeat terrorism and that Morocco and the United States would form an economic free trade pact. In addition to the anticipation of extended trade with the United States, a new phase of Morocco's relations with the European Union (that had begun with the Barcelona Process in 1995) took effect in 2000. It seemed that in addition to his democratizing efforts on the political front, the King was determined to liberalize some of Morocco's economic structures as well. And by doing so, Foreign Direct Investment to Morocco began to improve in 2004 and 2005, also doing well in 2006, 2007, and in 2008.[22] But investment in sectors such as bringing luxury goods to Morocco often does not translate into gains for Morocco's middle and lower classes who cannot afford such goods and do not benefit from the purchases of such items. By contrast, investments in tourism that will attract paying customers and provide jobs for Moroccans are more desirable. Moroccans, including women, wanted jobs.

But in the early and mid 2000s, Morocco was mainly an agricultural producing country. And if it could not export its goods to Europe due to perceived competition by countries in the EU like Greece, Spain, and Portugal, which tend to grow similar products to those grown in Morocco, then Morocco's economy would not expand quickly. Morocco was, and continues to be, dependent on rains, low oil prices for energy, and markets that it cannot generally reach or control.

Morocco's King Mohamed VI had to be keenly aware that most analysts of Moroccan affairs began their account with the high levels of unemployment and poverty found across the country. So in his May 18, 2005, speech, King Mohamed VI signaled to the country that he was committed to maintaining a social safety net while at the same time finding ways to advance human development. The King launched the National Initiative for Human Development. In his 2005 speech, the King promised to "attack the social deficit by making the basic social services more accessible, promote activities likely to create employment opportunities and stable incomes, adopt an imaginative action towards the informal sector," and help people suffering with vulnerabilities as well as "those with specific needs."[23]

The King also began professionalizing the state ministries and departments to make Morocco a better place for commercial activity for both Moroccans and foreigners. The banking sector was largely privatized. Years later, in an account of the King's economic programs from his ascension to the throne until the Arab Spring, Sandberg and Binder would argue that,"under King Mohamed VI, important macro-economic structures and practices were altered and additionally progress was made to establish the meta-institutional conditions that support development, but that the payoff in the daily lives of Moroccans has yet to be realized and that such lack of economic advancement for Moroccans 'in the street' diminishes the King's legitimacy" as well as support for his policies.[24] The point here is that even in 2005, the King faced economic challenges that did not enhance the legitimacy of the monarchy. And so any bold political initiatives were that much more difficult because the King did not work from a strong position economically.

Morocco's Evolving Domestic Politics

Morocco's political gains also continued to need care in order to be certain that they would take root. In the September 7th, 2007, national election, only four women managed to transcend the local lists: Yasmina Baddou of the Istiqlal party, Latifa Jbabdi of the Socialist Union of Popular Forces, independent candidate Fatiha Layadi, and Fatna Lkhail of the Popular Movement. Thirty women were again elected on Morocco's national gender slate. Thus, 34 women took their place in parliament but there was no increase in women's representation. And the parties did not return all the same women, so some of the experience that the first female parliamentarians had gained, was lost.

It appeared that those in the palace also had come to believe that the political process needed something to safeguard improvements that had been made and to make additional improvements that were needed. In 2008, the King's adviser and friend from his college days, Fouad Ali El Himma, created the Movement of All Democrats. El Himma was a former Deputy Minister in the Interior (for security) where the King could be certain that a loyal friend was observing the most sensitive ministry in the country. Then, in the 2007 elections El Himma ran for parliament and won his seat. It was a logical next step that he would look for partners and found a new political party in the 2008 parliament.

It seemed El Himma's aim was to infuse energy into the political landscape and to secure support for the King's programs in the face of increasing opposition from the Islamist forces. Also, Moroccan voters had grown cynical watching the existing parties do business as usual. In 2008, El Himma formed the Party for Authenticity and Modernity (PAM) and over one hundred parliamentarians left their parties or decided to merge their parties with PAM during the mid session. Suddenly PAM was the major party in parliament and El Himma looked like the face of Morocco's political future.

To coordinate such a coalition, however, required not just important political leaders but also skilled administrators. El Himma, therefore, turned to one of Morocco's women parliamentarians, Meluda Hazib, who had entered Parliament on the first gender slate in 2002 and had proved herself a leader in the National Assembly. Hazib came from a small party that did not win enough votes for her to return to the Parliament. But her skills were well known and prior to serving in parliament she had run a successful tourism business. Hazib was tapped to serve as Advisor to the Caucus of Modernization and Authenticity that represented the new coalition of political leaders and parties. The new caucus sought to energize the parliament and offer new legislation on a range of issues of importance to Moroccan citizens.

In the next three years, El Himma would continue to build his party. The 2009 municipal elections saw PAM sweep the opposition, including the Islamist Justice and Development Party. As a result, some observers hoped that Moroccan political parties, which were perceived as needing to demonstrate leadership abilities to Morocco's eligible voters or face continued declining voter turnout, would now obtain some legislative achievements because PAM's numbers and prestige were increasing. Others worried that PAM was too close to the King and the parliament would be seen as lacking independence from the King.

And when the winds of the Arab spring of 2011, swept Morocco, it seemed that the second view prevailed. The Arab spring saw Moroccan protesters arguing that El Himma was too close to the King and the country needed independent parties. El Himma was also charged with being too close to those around the King who were thought to be corrupt. Coupled with an upsurge in support for the Islamist Justice and Development Party among the electorate most likely to vote, El Himma handed the party off to Ilyas El Omari whose task was to keep members from bolting the party while fashioning an identity for the party that moved beyond the perception of a party with a leader like El Himma having access to the King.

Earlier, King Mohamed VI had watched the 2007 elections closely and, as we reported in chapter three, everyone in Morocco's top political circles noticed when the consummate parliamentarian and long-time women's gender activist, Nouzha Skalli, was denied a top spot on her party's ballot and other women with no or little party experience were placed in slots in front of Skalli and other party women who had long worked for the party and also might have been tapped. But Skalli continued to campaign for those in her party in whom she believed and she did not resign from her party. After the elections had concluded, King Mohamed VI reached over her party's male leadership to offer Skalli a cabinet position. In the ensuing years, King Mohamed VI would appoint women to dozens of important posts across Morocco. And in 2014, the King appointed Zineb El Adaoui as governor of the region Gharb-Chrarda-Beni Hssen, in the the province of Kenitra. She was the first woman to receive such an appointment in Moroccan history. Moroccan women were visible as leaders in all walks of Moroccan life, especially its political life. For the moment, women's appointments and gains no longer were connected to debates concerning Western foreign affairs.

Morocco's Gender Institution in Motion

In December 2008, King Mohamed VI took another step that would contribute to the transformation of Morocco's gender institution. King Mohamed VI retracted Morocco's reservations concerning CEDAW. Morocco's women gender activists were ecstatic. No longer could there be legal objections in Morocco to the principles of the United Nation's Convention for the Elimination of Discrimination Against Women. Although there would be few quick changes that resulted from this retraction, the hard work of now choosing cases and issues to pursue legally, now that the objections were retracted, could begin.

Then, another notable gain for women occurred that Moroccan gender activists hoped would contribute to an evolving Moroccan gender institution. There was a significant increase in the number of women elected to municipal councils in 2009. In fact, women's representation increased from 0.5% to 12.3%. And while the government had established a 12% quota for women in the 2009 municipal elections, women managed to exceed this quota. And, as most political analysts know, to achieve higher office, one is likely to do better if one can build on successful experiences in lower offices first. So for some women political leaders, the future looked bright as they anticipated climbing the political ladder.

Programs to advance women's education and health care also were promoted throughout the decade of 2000. International development experts had come to conclude that in order to accelerate economic development, the economic position of women, not just men, had to be improved. Women provided for their families and so when women had access to resources, the entire family benefitted. Many of those advising King Mohamed VI, and perhaps the King himself, came to embrace these findings.

Moroccan women's illiteracy was at unacceptable levels when King Mohamed VI assumed the throne in 1999. Although female illiteracy rates had improved from 1960 when they stood at 96%, in 2000, 62% of Moroccan women were still illiterate. (Male Moroccan illiteracy rates in 2000 stood at 37%.) It is no wonder that Morocco's women's movement is considered an elite movement. In 2001, Morocco's National Charter for Education and Formation was adopted as the basis of the government's program for improving education for girls and for making primary education compulsory.

To attack the problems facing women across Morocco who suffered from little or no educational opportunities, employment, or health services, Morocco's Ministry of Family Affairs, Solidarity and Social Work adopted (with King Mohamed VI's permission and likely with the encouragement of the Prime Minister) and implemented the best practices for incorporating women into development that had been developed by the United Nations. In 2003, the Ministry began exploring how to implement "gender mainstreaming" in policies and program at the national level that would incorporate women's development needs into every sector of Moroccan society.[25]

However, it would not be until 2006 that Morocco would begin to draft a gender budget statement and present it as an annex to the Finance Bill. Then in 2009, key ministries began to pilot the gender budgeting processes. And it would take until January 2014 for parliament to pass a law (in an Islamic PJD-led coalition parliament) stipulating that "gender equality must be taken into account in the definition of objectives, results and indicators of performance of the line budgets." Further, the 2014 law institutionalized the Gender Report as an official document that is part of the annual Finance Ministry bill.[26]

There was no doubt, by 2014, that even though change came slowly and millions of Moroccan women still labored outside of the modern developing Morocco, and even though many changes were still needed, Morocco's gender institution was changing. In the space of twenty five years, Morocco's gender activist women had created a new evolving Moroccan institution of gender.

And so, when the Arab Spring swept across Morocco and King Mohamed VI responded by offering a new constitution that reportedly was overwhelmingly endorsed by those Moroccans who voted in the 2011 constitutional referendum, the new constitution included improved protections for Moroccan women. Article 19 of Morocco's new constitution of 2011 declared that "men and women enjoy on an equal footing civil, political, economic, social, cultural and environmental rights and freedoms." Morocco's previous "democratizing" constitution of 1996 had specified that "Men and women shall enjoy equal political rights" and that "All Moroccan citizens shall be equal before the law."[27] But the previous wording had left open the possibility for some to argue (and they did) that the guarantees of equal political rights only referred to voting. And women and men might be equal before the law but the laws could be different for women and men. The new Article 19 changed any such interpretation.

But the Arab spring also swept into power a Moroccan parliament in which the Islamist party, the Justice and Development Party (PJD), won the most votes in the November 2011 parliamentary elections. PJD voters were motivated to vote in order to give their party the leadership of the country for the first time in its history. And they did, taking 107 out of the 395 parliamentary seats. The new constitution stipulates that the King may no longer appoint any person whom he wishes as Prime Minister, but rather must appoint the leader of the party that earned the most seats. And so the Secretary General of the PJD, Abdelilah Benkirane, became Morocco's Prime Minister in a parliament with new powers that former parliaments lacked. The Istiqlal Party joined the PJD's coalition.

Morocco's women gender activists, who had been encouraged by the new constitution were now filled with foreboding at the prospect of an Islamist led government. But then, in 2012, the media publicized the stories of two tragedies for young women who were forced to marry their rapists. Forcing these young women into marriage was supposed to protect their honor, the honor of their families, and allow the rapists to avoid prosecution. Amina Filali was sixteen years old when she was forced to marry Moustapha Fellak whom she charged had raped her. Fellak was about twenty-five years. Filali then reported that in the ensuing seven months of her marriage Fellak physically abused her, which he denied. Amina Filali swallowed rat poison and died a painful, tortured death to escape her forced marriage.[28]

Then there came to light the case of a young woman who is given no family name in the press. Safae from Tangiers, was raped and impregnated when she was fourteen years old. A Moroccan judge and a Moroccan prosecutor forced her mother and Safae, who had filed a complaint in court, to consent that she should marry her rapist, which she did. Safae's rapist was therefore spared prosecution and soon disappeared while Safae gave birth to a daughter. Her life was so hurtful at this point that she attempted suicide twice.

Media coverage of these and other cases caused an uproar across Morocco. Moroccan gender activists and even some Islamist women joined in a coalition that began protesting that the Moroccan government needed to change Article 475 of the Penal Code that protected rapists and forced women victims of violence into marriage with those who had assaulted them.

In 2010, the ADFM had already called for the launch of a new coalition, the Springtime of Dignity, to fight for legislation to protect women from violence.

The UAF had also launched and participated in many demonstrations to end violence against women. Countless other (many of them new) Moroccan women's organizations also had supported the call for an end to violence against women and for legislation that would protect women who were assaulted and prosecute the men who assaulted them.

In 2011, a national study found that almost 63 percent of Morocco women ages 18 to 64 had suffered some form of violence during 2010, with most being victimized by their husbands.[29] Then, following the 2012 media reports of the two cases discussed above, and after years of Moroccan women waging a national campaign, the parliament finally amended the law on January 22, 2014, by a unanimous vote. But Moroccan women's work was still not done.

In March 2014, after seeing that the Islamist government was doing little to enforce the new legislation or take seriously the 2011 constitution that guarantees Moroccan women equality with Moroccan men, a Civil Coalition for the Application of Article 19 was formed and it was reported that about 500 NGOs joined the coalition. On April 13, 2014, about 800 women marched from the center of Rabat to the Parliament building to demand that the government apply and enforce Article 19 of the constitution.

The new activism of the women's groups organizing around the constitution and against violence against women has brought some young, new women into the movement. And just in time. Morocco's gender activists who bravely began fighting the battles of the 1980s are aging and they are tired. As one well-known Moroccan activist said in confidence, "Our generation in Morocco is almost burnt out. We want others to take up the struggle." But then she added quickly, "But who can be tired when they are fighting for democracy." They surely must be tired. But when these Moroccan women look around and see how they have changed the institution of gender in Morocco, they must also feel great pride.

Today, young women in Morocco who have the fortune to go to school, can aspire to be leaders in every profession. They see corporate women leaders and they see political leaders. They see women journalists and judges, they see women religious leaders. It is true that the number of Moroccan women leaders in each field is not large. And certainly it is true that there is much to be done to improve the lives of the vast majority of Moroccan women (and men). Yet, Morocco's gender institution continues to change. It is now an evolving institution; it is not immovably rooted in the past. And it is up to the next generation of Moroccan women and men to defend the advances that have been made and to continue the processes of reform.

Notes

1. The Inter Parliamentary Union http://www.ipu.org/parline-e/reports/arc/2221_97.htm.

2. Wendy Kristianasen, "Hard-Won Change in Iran and Morocco," *Le Monde Diplomatique* (February 4, 2004) http://mondediplo.com/2004/04/02islamicwomen.

3. Zakia Salime, *Between Feminism and Islam: Human Rights and Sharia Law in Morocco* (Minneapolis: University of Minnesota Press, 2011), xiii.

4. Salime, *Between Feminism and Islam.* Salime offers an analysis of how these women organized themselves and their outreach activities and how sometimes they knew they were being promoted to be the face of the religious opposition but yet lacked real participation in the agenda setting activities of the men's religious organizations.

5. U.S. Department of State, Bureau of Democracy, Human Rights, and Labor, *Morocco Country Reports on Human Rights Practices 2001*, March 4, 2002.

6. U.S. Department of State, *Morocco Country Reports*, March 4, 2002.

7. U.S. Department of State, *Morocco Country Reports,* March 4, 2002.

8. U.S. Department of State, *Morocco Country Reports*, March 4, 2002. This account is largely taken from the U.S. Department of State account.

9. Wendy Kristianasen, "Hard-Won Change in Iran and Morocco."

10. Women's Learning Partnership, "Morocco Adopts Landmark Family Law Supporting Women's Equality" February 4, 2004. http://play.learningpartnership.org/en/advocacy/alerts/morocco0204. The profile of Zhour Al Horr is taken from this story.

11. Women's Learning Partnership, "Morocco Adopts Landmark Family Law Supporting Women's Equality."

12. Program, "Family Laws In The Muslim World: Comparative Perspectives," December 11-13, 2007. Under The Royal Patronage of His Majesty King Mohamed VI: An International Conference Organized by The Esprit de Fès Foundation and The Protection Project at The Johns Hopkins University. http://www.wluml.org/node/4199.

13. The November 2, 2001, workshops were especially poignant as they followed the September 2001 attacks in the United States by al-Qaeda and Moroccans were seeing few travelers in the months that followed, which seriously injured the country's tourism earnings. The (mostly) American women flying to Morocco for the NDI trainings encountered few other passengers in airports during their travels. Both the Moroccan women and the US women in various ways felt that they were reaching out to each other as women in the midst of a bitter divide. Most of the Moroccan women were therefore quite shocked when the U.S. Ambassador to Morocco, Margaret Tutwiler (who had been welcomed in Morocco due to her special relationship with James Baker, who led the UN team to report on the Western Sahara crisis) announced that the Bush Administration did not look with favor upon quotas. The NDI workshop trainers, however, explained that in the United States, as in Morocco, positions differed on important political issues and women in the U.S. were not homogenous just as they were not in Morocco.

14. As explained to Sandberg in the week following the election law speeches by someone who asked that the information not be attribtued.

15. Morocco Minister of the Interior Driss Jettou, speech to the Parliament, Rabat, Morocco, March 6, 2002.

16. Jettou, Driss, Minister of the Interior, Speech to the Parliament, Rabat, Morocco, March 6, 2002.

17. No one knows for certain if the 1997 outcomes honestly reflected the parties' support or if the Minister of the Interior extensively intervened in those elections as well.

18. Civicus, *Civil Society Index for Morocco Analytical Country Report,* International Version May 2011, 25. http://www.cswatch.org/user/37/article/civicus-civil-society-index-country-report-morocco.

19. Freedom House, http://www.freedomhouse.org/report/freedomworld/2004/morocco#.U1wRO1c7Ygc.

20. The European Forum for Democracy and Solidarity, "Morocco" July 15, 2009 http://www.europeanforum.net.

21. Wendy Kristianasen, "Hard-Won Change in Iran and Morocco" quoting Nouzha Guessous, a Moroccan female professor at Casablanca's faculty of medicine and pharmacy and a founding member of the Organisation Marocaine des Droits Humains who also was one of the three women who served on the King's Consultative Commission.

22. Oliver Wyman, *Overview of Investment in Morocco* (Rabat: Kingdom of Morocco Ministry of Industry, Trade and New Technologies, 2010) 3.

23. His Majesty King Mohamed VI, speech on National Initiative for Human Development, Kingdom of Morocco Website. http://www.maroc.ma/PortailInst/An/MenuGauche/Major+Projects/National+Initiative+for+Human+Development/National+Initiative+for+Human+Development.htm.

24. Eve Sandberg and Seth Binder, "The Moroccan Spring and King Mohamed VI's Economic Policy Agenda: Evaluating the First Dozen Years," in *Une Jeunesse Révoltée,* ed. Mohsine El Ahmadi (Rabat: Marsam Editions, forthcoming). English language edition *The Birth of the Arab Citizen and the Changing Middle East*, ed. Mohsine El Ahmadi and Stuart Schaar (Northampton, MA: Interlink Publishing, forthcoming).

25. The Ministry of Family Affairs, Solidarity and Social Work, "Gender Mainstreaming in Policies and Programmes at the National Level, Case Study of Morocco," Workshop on Gender Mainstreaming, United Nations Economic and Social Commission for Western Asia, Beirut, Lebanon, December 6-7, 2003.

26. UN WOMEN, "Budgets respond to the needs of women in Morocco" March 27, 2014 http://www.unwomen.org/en/news/stories/2014/3/budgets-respond-to-the-needs-of-women-in-morocco#sthash.2rvYX6uS.dpuf.

27. "Moroccan Constitutional Backround" http://www.servat.unibe.ch/icl/mo00000_.html

28. Andrew Katz, "Morocco amends controversial rape marriage law," BBC News Africa January 23, 2014 http://www.bbc.com/news/world-africa-25855025

29. Tara Culp-Ressler, "Hundreds Of Moroccan Women Take To The Streets To Demand Gender Equality," *Think Progress* April 14, 2014. http://thinkprogress.org/health/2014/04/14/3426373/moroccan-protest-gender-equality/.

Chapter Seven
Conclusion

When we began our study, we asked how it was possible to alter Morocco's gender institution that was claimed to be immutable, rooted in both religious and common practices that would not change. We focused our investigation largely on the time frame that began in the mid 1980s and ended in 2004 when Morocco's Moudawana or family code was greatly reformed, and then we observed ongoing changes in Morocco's gender institution until mid 2014. We continued our study to demonstrate that the appropriate way in which to view Morocco's current gender institution is as an institution that is evolving. This does not mean that gains cannot be reversed or that progress in improving the status of women in Morocco will not continue to be slow. But it does mean that the multiple parts of Morocco's gender institution have now been revealed and that those who work with intentionality can continue to pursue and achieve positive changes for Moroccan women.

We began our study by synthesizing the institutional and feminist literatures. From this synthesis we derived our four variables and our study's methodology that systematically investigated the possibilities of change derived from the interaction of those four variables. Our methodology also demanded that we focus on Moroccan women and hear their voices and view their strategic actions. Further, our methodology required that we remain mindful of the divisions among Moroccan women according to class and education, as well as religion. And finally, our methodology required that we make clear where the authors served as participant observers to the events and activities that we analyze.

We hypothesized that our four variables form a template through which change can be achieved in a national institution of gender. And, in fact, our case study of Morocco has confirmed our hypotheses that this is possible. But it has also revealed that while, in the historical sense, a strongly rooted national gender institution can be transformed, for those who are living the change, they often see only incremental improvements over time.

We are also aware that while we have provided one "thick" study of the possibilities for changing a national gender institution, many others must contribute their work before we can ultimately determine if Morocco is an outlier, or, a model for institutional gender change. Research by colleagues may well tell us whether this template of institutional change will also work for other institutions in national life as well as for those of gender.

Thus below, we revisit our hypotheses that comprise our template for changing a national institution of gender and offer a summary of the evidence that the Morocco case has provided and that confirms our four hypotheses. We hope that this summary offers insight to those who would apply these hypotheses in practice or study these hypotheses in another case setting.

Our four hypotheses that were deemed necessary in order to change a national gender institution were:

* **Hypothesis one** projected that women in a given country must utilize their agency to make demands for change.

* **Hypothesis two** projected that the women advocating for improving the status of women within their country must find ways to create new structures for action and follow new rules, both informal and formal for themselves and for those in their country's decision making structures.

* **Hypothesis three** projected that these women and their male allies will engage in discursive initiatives designed with intentionality to engage the national alert public in a debate concerning the status of women and to offer an alternative logic to underpin a new national institution of gender.

* **Hypothesis four** projected that these active women would find resources through relations within their country and external to their country to pursue the changes they demand in their country's institution of gender.

Agency

We argued first that women in a given country must utilize their agency to make demands for change. As the Moroccan case has demonstrated, no matter how just was the Moroccan women's cause or how much they devoted themselves to working for their parties and for their male mentors, over time it became evident that no one other than the women themselves was going to dedicate themselves to putting women's issues on the national agenda. Moroccan women activists worked in their associations and their parties during the 1960s, through the 1970s, and into the 1980s before they came to the conclusion that only they could lead their struggle for change.

The agency of Moroccan women demanded personal courage on the part of each activist. In a society that frowned on women's activism in the public sphere, Moroccan women activists had to exemplify the dedicated wife and mother before they could justify their added political work on behalf of themselves, their daughters, and the world in which they hoped to raise their sons. If, in the rare instance, they chose not to follow the path of marriage, they had to have enormous resources of courage and dedication to justify their lives.

Moroccan women activists also risked violence in the face of fatwas and the chance that any self-appointed religious extremist could choose to attack at any time. They risked being belittled, overlooked and marginalized, and/or patronized by their male colleagues. But even if personally thwarted, they refused to give up their positions and they kept their ties with their parties and associations and they muted their disappointments no matter how painful. This was particularly evident in the case of USFP leader Badia Skalli who was passed over for an early leadership position so that a young man with little experience could play a leadership role. Then, after being the first woman to enter as an elected official to Morocco's parliament and serving two terms in the parliament prior to the creation of a gender slate, Badia Skalli was again passed over by her party when the party's gender slate was constructed.

Later, Nouzha Skalli, of the PPS, who for decades had dedicated herself to national reform, to women's rights, and to her party, was not included on her party's slate in the second round of elections in which the gender slate played a role. This time, King Mohamed VI, an ally of Moroccan women activists, reached out to right the wrong, making Nouzha Skalli a Minister in Morocco's executive cabinet.

As chapter three of this study demonstrated, Moroccan women's agency early on was made possible, in part, from male allies. In their early years, the women needed the permission and encouragement of male fathers, brothers, uncles, and teachers in order to enter the realm of the political and the public. But as the women matured, and as their skills increased, their agency came from their own determination and from their own dedication.

As we argue in this study, no one component of our template alone can change a national gender institution. And so as important as was the agency of Moroccan women, it had to be coupled with other aspects of our template for Moroccan women's agency to achieve the goals of Morocco's women gender activists.

Creating New Structures, Formal and Informal, and New Pathways of Rule Making

Our second hypothesis projected that women activists seeking to alter a national institution of gender must find ways to create new structures for action and follow new rules, both informal and formal. The Moroccan women in our case study did exactly that. First, they formed women's sections or bureaus in their political parties or student or human rights associations. Then, they formed their own organizations in civic society. A woman's relations with her previous associations and parties varied depending on the woman and her male and female colleagues who remained within the associations and parties.

The women then found ways to coordinate across their (sometimes competing) civic organizations. Rather than balkanize their efforts they found ways to unite and coordinate their advocacy.

Moroccan women gender activists earned seats for themselves, for other women of their time, and for the women who come after them, at the decision making tables of Moroccan legislative and other bodies. They entered the municipal councils and they entered the national parliament as decision makers. They served on Royal consultative councils, commissions, and committees. They served as representatives to international organizations and institutions preparing reports on issues of concern to Moroccans. Moroccan women joined the ranks of banks, of corporations, of the media, and of religious institutions.

Engagement In Discursive Initiatives Designed With Intentionality To Engage The National Alert Public In A Debate Concerning The Status Of Women And To Offer An Alternative Logic To Underpin A New National Institution Of Gender

Moroccan women gender activists created their own journals, magazines, and newsletters. They did the spade work of reaching out intellectually to challenge the alert public before they attempted to advocate for any policy changes. By founding *8 Mars, Kadima,* and other publications and organizational newsletters (and later websites), Moroccan gender activists offered an alternative logic to their present national gender institutional order. They offered reinterpretations of historic practices and they interpreted the goals of Moroccan gender activists within the context of their society and their religious traditions.

The research of Moroccan women academics, such as sociologist Fatima Mernissi, brought the status of Moroccan women to the attention of Moroccan readers. Over time, studies and reports by many gender activists published by their civic associations and based on their work of bringing together domestic, regional, and international experts, such as those who attended the UAF's court, or collaborated with the UDFM's Maghreb study group all combined to socialize Moroccans and to provide information and data for informed debate.

No one had a monopoly on the discursive work that was accomplished. And some who provided excellent research were aided by those who were excellent public presenters. The goal was to promote the ideas and the agenda that Moroccan women gender activists had determined.

The women also promoted their work in many venues. Some promoted their work in Morocco through publications. Some promoted their work outside of Morocco and allowed the Moroccan press to carry the message home. The women learned the skills of attracting media attention even in a country with a government-controlled media. They created their own publication outlets when they needed to and they utilized the national and international press when they found it was available to them.

The substance of what Moroccan women gender activists injected into the national debate was shocking to some Moroccans at the outset. But it became understandable to all Moroccans, over time, as ideas and policies were repeated, explained, and supported by an increasing number of Moroccan opinion leaders.

Finding Resources Through Relations Within Their Country And External To Their Country To Pursue The Changes They Demand In Their Country's Gender Institution

The most important resource that Moroccan women secured in their struggle to change their national gender institution was the support of their Moroccan male allies. Especially in the late 1990s and throughout the first decade of the twenty-first century, Morocco's USFP Prime Minister, Abderrahmane Youssoufi, and Morocco's King Mohamed VI would become critically important allies for Morocco's gender activists. Gaining these allies among decision makers provided important resources to Moroccan gender activists. But even their male allies sometimes would not, or could not, act as quickly or as broadly as Moroccan women gender activists had hoped. And so when their party leaders disappointed them, when male family members and colleagues refused to prioritize women's issues alongside other important issues of the day, the Moroccan women gender activists sought domestic and international resources to pursue their programs and their initiatives on their own.

International organizations and donors provided valuable resources for Moroccan gender activists. As chapter five demonstrated, visibility, legitimacy, and financial resources were provided in various ways to different Moroccan gender activists' groups when these groups approached outsiders as well as those in Morocco for support. Just as the Islamists received Saudi funds or diaspora funds or local funds, so too, did the women gender activists turn to both external and internal financing strategies.

Eventually under King Mohammed VI and through the Ministers in his cabinets, funds from national budgets were allocated to Moroccan gender activists' civic associations for the work they did in literacy, for maintaining shelters, for campaigns to educate about eradicating violence against women, for health care trainings, and for microfinance and employment trainings.

International conferences and gatherings offered Moroccan women gender activists an opportunity to secure knowledge resources as well as legitimacy. Importantly such international gatherings also offered the support of solidarity to Moroccan gender activists who were often exhausted and stretched.

International organizations also provided Moroccan leaders with the carrots needed to persuade them to offer Moroccan gender activists more support than otherwise they might have offered. For example, King Hassan's desire to enter the European Union and attract Western corporate foreign direct investment to Morocco likely played a role when he chose to offer (albeit limited) support to Moroccan women gender activists.

Similarly, international donors and foundations provided project assistance and also support for research and publications. The Moroccan gender activists learned how to approach the array of international donors in a multitude of languages for assistance and support. They learned how to identify and offer the metrics of accomplishment that the various donors favored. But Moroccan gender activists were surprisingly successful in securing money not for what donors believed was important, but rather to support the agendas that Moroccan women gender activists had established for themselves and their organizations.

Institutional Theorizing and the Moroccan Case

As we noted in chapter one, Peter Hall argued that institutions are "regularized sets of practices with a rule-like quality" which "structure the behavior of political and economic actors."[1] In a complementary understanding of institutions, Wolfgang Streeck and Kathleen Thelen defined institutions as "building blocks of social order . . . that represent socially sanctioned, that is, collectively enforced expectations" that "involve mutually related rights and obligations for actors."[2] If we think of these rights and obligations being enforced through expectations as well as through rule-like practices and structures of behavior, we certainly can understand the constraints and rights of a gender institution.

Both of these definitions are easy to apply to the Moroccan case after analyzing the simultaneous changes that took place across Moroccan society in judicial, legislative, economic, and family practices that affected Moroccan men and women. Such changes took place in Morocco's gender institution. What had seemed like immutable, regularized, common practices for men and women in Morocco gradually were transformed into new routinized practices with new sets of rights and obligations for Moroccan male and female citizens. In Morocco, it is quite easy, as we have done in this study, to identify when and where and why a rule or obligation or right for Moroccan women was changed.

But our findings also demonstrate that when one knows what was changed, and where and when it was changed, it is easier to argue for another rule change, and then another. This was the case as Moroccan women learned that Morocco's gender institution was not divine, but rather determined by a committee of religious writers in 1956. And while each victory was a partial victory, the trajectory of Morocco's gender institution was clear, it was moving toward accommodating the demands of Morocco's women gender activists.

Both proponents and opponents of Morocco's reforms for women have learned that both parliament and the municipal councils have been powerful venues in which Moroccan women gender advocates have made gains and have improved the status of women. At almost the mid-point of the second decade of the twenty-first century, however, many among Morocco's women gender activists believe that the left parties are all that stand between them and an Islamist state. These activists fear that should an Islamist party sweep into office in large numbers, it could then (alone) control the legislative pathways of rule making. Then through the legislative venues of the state, the Islamist representatives would roll back the gains that Moroccan women gender activists have attained in the last twenty-five years.

Others believe that the left parties in Morocco can never again sufficiently mobilize Moroccans. So perhaps new parties or coalitions must be established. New political organizations would have less historical baggage and perhaps could provide the new programs and the new hope that is necessary to persuade those Moroccans to vote who might support rival parties to the Islamist party. Younger voters also must somehow be recruited.

Still other Moroccan women activists worry about the changing role of the monarchy in Morocco and what that will mean for gender activists in the future. It is agreed that less powers for a monarch may bring benefits to parliamentarians and add to Morocco's democratic credentials. However, if the Monarch continues to act as an ally of Moroccan women gender activists, then a stronger Monarch will provide more benefits for Moroccan women, half the country's population. Such accountability should also be factored into evaluations of Morocco's democratic trajectory, argue some Moroccan gender activists.[3]

Many Moroccan gender activists also know with certainty that the gains for Moroccan women must be seen to benefit all Moroccan women and not only those in legislative bodies and upper middle class homes. Improved services and improved life opportunities must be offered to all Moroccan women so that they can take advantage of the changes in Morocco's evolving gender institution. And perhaps when they benefit they will feel a stake in defending Morocco's new (slowly) evolving gender institution. But to defend the gains and to further improve the status of Moroccan women will require that all with a stake in the outcome of the contests yet to come learn the rules and their rights and responsibilities even as they advocate for change.

Finally, Morocco's women gender activists who have fought so long and achieved so much also know that there must be younger Moroccans who will step up to take their places to advance the status of women in Morocco. While young Moroccans coming of age in Morocco in the last ten years assume that everyone, men and women alike, have certain rights and opportunities, they are less aware of those who wish to take away those rights and opportunities. And many of these young people have little focus on, or understanding of, how to organize to protect their rights. But while institutions are "sticky" and their practices have tremendous staying power, as we have just learned from this Moroccan case study, even an entrenched national gender institution can be altered if the right combination of factors comes into play. Thus the gains for Moroccan women in the last three decades can also be altered.

We have argued that there are four primary arenas in which activists must act in order to alter an entrenched institution. First, they must operationalize their own agency. Second, they must look for ways to change rules (both informal and formal), as well as structures of action, and paths within institutions where decisions are made. They must seek to build parallel paths and structures. Third, they must engage in discursive initiatives to influence the national debates and to offer alternative logics to the everyday practices of citizens. Fourth, they must actively seek resources domestically and internationally that will provide legitimacy, allies, and financing.

We hope that this case study has served as a convincing argument concerning the success that can be achieved when women gender activists work determinedly in those four arenas. We also hope that we have demonstrated the ways in which Moroccan women gender activists were brave, smart, and effective as they organized and sacrificed and dedicated themselves to changing Morocco's national gender institution.

Notes

1. Peter Hall, "Historical Institutionalism in Rationalist and Sociological Perspective" in *Explaining Institutional Change: Ambiguity, Agency, Power*, eds. James Mahoney and Kathleen Thelen (Cambridge and New York: Cambridge University Press, 2009).

2. Wolfgang Streeck and Kathleen Thelen, *Beyond Continuity: Institutional Change in Advanced Political Economies* (Oxford: Oxford University Press, 2005).

3. This line of thinking is further complicated when one considers that some Islamist women would likely support an Islamist party and state, not necessarily more powers for Morocco's King. Nor would they support the policies that the King likely would enact to improve the status of Moroccan women.

Bibliography

[About Islam.] Website. http://islam.about.com/od/basicbeliefs/p/into.htm (accessed April 24, 2014).

Abouzeid, Leila. *Year of the Elephant: A Moroccan Woman's Journey Toward Independence.* Translated by Barbara Parmenter. Austin, TX: Center for Middle Eastern Studies, University of Texas at Austin, 1989.

Afifi, Aicha and Rajae Msefer. "Women in Morocco: Gender Issues and Politics." In *Women and Politics Worldwide*, edited by Barbara Nelson and Najma Cowdhury. New Haven: Yale University Press, 1994.

Ahmad, Aijaz. "The Politics of Literary Postcoloniality." *Race and Class* 36, no. 3 (1995): 1-20.

Alaoui, Nezha. Interview with authors. Casablanca, Morocco. July 20, 2009.

———. Interview with authors. Casablanca, Morocco. November 20, 2007.

Ariell, Alexis. *Algeria. Current Issues.* Congressional Research Service. November 18, 2013.

Baba, Jouhara Filali. "To Lalla Radia, Our Eternal Lighthouse." In *Women Writing Africa: The Northern Region,* edited by Fatima Sadiqi, Amira Nowaira, Azza El Kholy, and Moha Ennaji. New York: Feminist Press at the City University of New York, 2009.

Badran, Margot. *Feminism in Islam: Secular and Religious Convergences.* Oxford: Oneworld Publications, 2009.

Baker, Alison. "History and Myth: Women's Stories of the Moroccan Resistance." *The Oral History Review* 22, no. 1 (Summer, 1995): 29-49.

Bayes, Jane and Nayereh Tohidi. *Globalization, Gender, and Religion.* New York: Palgrave MacMillan, 2001.

Benachir, Ghizlan. Interview with authors. Rabat, Morocco. July 21, 2009.

———. Interview with authors. Rabat. November 23, 2007.

Bordo, Susan. *The Flight to Objectivity: Essays on Cartesianism and Culture.* Albany: SUNY Press, 1987.

Boserup, Ester. *The Conditions of Agricultural Growth: The Economics of Agrarian Change Under Population Pressure.* Chicago: Aldine, 1965.

———. *Women's Role in Economic Development.* London: George Allen and Unwin, 1970.

Bouabdelli, Fatima. "Habiba Guessoussa: An Opening Speech." In *Women Writing Africa: The Northern Region*, edited by Fatima Sadiqi, Amira Nowaira, Azza El Kholy, and Moha Ennaji. New York: Feminist Press at the City University of New York, 2009. Nowaira, Azza El Kholy, and Moha Ennaji. New York: Feminist Press at the City University of New York, 2009.

Boukhars, Anouar. *Politics in Morocco.* London and New York: Routledge, 2011.

Brand, Laurie. *Women, the State, and Political Liberalization: Middle Eastern and North African Experiences.* New York: Columbia University Press, 1998.

"Budget Responds to the Needs of Women in Morocco." UN WOMEN. 27 March 2014. www.unwomen.org/ca/news/stories/2014/3/budgets-respond-to-the-needs-of-women-in-morocco (accessed April 24, 2014).

Cavatorta, Francesco. "The International Context of Morocco's Stalled Democratization." *Democratization* 12, no. 4 (August 2005): 548-566.

Chaggaf, Zahra. Interview with authors. Rabat, Morocco. November 22, 2007.

Charrad, Mounira. *States and Women's Rights: The Making of Postcolonial Tunisia, Algeria, and Morocco.* Berkeley: University of California Press, 2001.

Civicus. *Civil Society Index for Morocco Analytical Country Report,* International Version. May 2011. http://www.cswatch.org/user/37/article/civicus-civil-society-index-country-report-morocco (accessed April 24, 2014).

Collectif 95 Maghreb Égalité. *One Hundred Steps, One Hundred Provisions.* http://www.wluml.org/sites/wluml.org/files/import/english/pubs/rtf/misc/100-steps.rtf (accessed April 24, 2014).

Crawford, Sue E.S., and Elinor Ostrom. "A Grammar of Institutions." *American Political Science Review* 89, no. 3 (September 1990): 582-600.

Culp-Ressler, Tara. "Hundreds Of Moroccan Women Take To The Streets To Demand Gender Equality." *Think Progress.* April 14, 2014. http://thinkprogress.org/health/2014/04/14/3426373/moroccan-protest-gender-equality/.

Curtis, Maria F. "Moroccan women's rights advocate; founder of L'Union de L'Action Féminine (UAF)" http://www.answers.com/topic/latifa-jababdi (accessed April 24, 2014).

Daoud, Zakya. *Féminisme et Politique au Maghreb.* Casablanca: Éditions Éddif, 1993.

De los Ángeles-Crummett, María. "Rural Women and Migration in Latin America." In *Rural Women and State Policy*, edited by Carmen Diane Deere and Magdalena León. Boulder, CO: Westview Press, 1987.

Devault, Marjorie. "Talking and Listening from Women's Standpoint: Feminist Strategies for Interviewing and Analysis." *Social Problems* 37, no. 1 (February 1990): 96-110.

DiMaggio, Paul. "The New Institutionalism: Avenues of Collaboration." *Journal of Institutional and Theoretical Economics* 154, no. 4 (December 1998): 696-705.

Driscoll, Kathleen and Joan McFarland. "The Impact of a Feminist Perspective on Research Methodologies: Social Sciences." In *The Effects of Feminist Approaches on Research Methodologies*, edited by Winnie Tomm. Waterloo, Ontario: Wilfred Laurier University Press, 1989.

Ech-Chenna, Aiche. Presentation, "Leadership Féminin au Maroc: Enjeux et Perspectives." Workshop. Sponsored by the Middle East Partnership

Initiative (MEPI) Alumni Network. Rabat, Morocco. November 22, 2007.

Economist Intelligence Unit. *Celebrating 60 Years . . . with a Glimpse of the Future*. (London: Economist Intelligence Unit, Ltd, 2006): 7.

Enloe, Cynthia. *The Morning After: Sexual Politics at the End of the Cold War*. Berkeley and Los Angeles: University of California Press, 1993.

Errebbah, Khadija. Conversation with Eve Sandberg, translated by Harry Bichsel. Casablanca, Morocco. March 31, 2012. Oberlin Alumni Association tour of Morocco.

———. Interview with authors. Casablanca, Morocco. July 2009.

———. "Women's Political Participation: The Moroccan Example." *The Arab Quota Report: Selected Case Studies*. International Institute for Democracy and Electoral Assistance (International IDEA): Stockholm, 2007.

European Forum for Democracy and Solidarity, The. "Morocco," July 15, 2009. http://www.europeanforum.net (accessed July 19, 2005).

Evans, Peter B., Dietrich Rueschemeyer, and Theda Skocpol. *Bring the State Back In*. Cambridge and New York: Cambridge University Press, 1985. Femmes du maroc. Website with short biographies of 100 active women in Morocco. http//www.femmmesdumaroc.com/Magazine/Dossier/Les100quiontchangelaMoudawana (accessed April 24, 2014).

Fillali, Brahim. "Morocco: On Pre-Colonial Morocco." Ex-CLER (Morocco). Published in Morocco on October 11, 2005. Translated by Pat Murgah, Canada, 2008, edited by Michael Schmidt, South Africa, 2008. Posted by *tahriricn*, August 5, 2008. http://tahriricn.wordpress.com/2013/03/01/morocco-on-pre-colonial-morocco/ (accessed April 24, 2014).

Filteau, Jerry. "Pope Made Important Overtures to Non-Christian Religions." *Catholic News Service* (2005). http://www.catholicnews.com/ipii/stories/story04.htm (accessed April 24, 2014).

Fonow, Mary Margaret and Judith Cook, eds. *Beyond Methodology: Feminist Research as Lived Research*. Bloomington: Indiana University Press, 1991. [Freedom House.] http://www.freedomhouse.org/report/freedom-world/2004/morocco#.U1wRO1c7Ygc (accessed April 24, 2014).

Friedrich Ebert Stiftung. http://www.fes.de/kommunikation/islam/index_gr.html (accessed April 24, 2014).

Gabriel, Jane. Open Democracy Net. In Rabat, Morocco speaking to Latifa Jbabdi and Fatima Outaleb http:/www.opendemocracy.net/audio/jane-gabriel/feminism-and-fatwas-it-all-began-on-march-8th (accessed April 24, 2014).

Glacier, Osire. *Political Women in Morocco: Then and Now*. Translated by Valérie Martin. Trenton: Red Sea Press, 2013.

Haddadi, Said. "Two Cheers for Whom? The European Union and Democratization in Morocco." *Democratization* 9, no. 1 (2002): 149-169.

Hall, Peter. "Historical Institutionalism in Rationalist and Sociological Perspective." In *Explaining Institutional Change: Ambiguity, Agency, Power*, edited by James Mahoney and Kathleen Thelen. Cambridge and New York: Cambridge University Press, 2009.

Hankinson-Nelson, Lynn. *Who Knows: From Quine to a Feminist Empiricism*. Philadelphia: Temple University Press, 1990.

Harding, Sandra. "Introduction: Is There a Feminist Method?" In *Feminism and Methodology*, edited by Sandra Harding. Bloomington and Indianapolis: Indiana University Press, 1987.

———. *The Science Question in Feminism*. Ithaca: Cornell University Press, 1986.

Harrak, Fatima. "The History and Significance of the New Moroccan Family Code." Working Paper No. 09-002. Institute for the Study of Islamic Thought in Africa (ISITA), Buffett Center for International and Comparative Studies, Northwestern University, March, 2009.

Hazib, Meluda. Interview with authors. Rabat, Morocco. November 29, 2007.

His Majesty King Mohamed VI. Speech on National Initiative for Human Development, Kingdom of Morocco. http://www.maroc.ma/PortailInst/An/MenuGauche/Major+Projects/National+Initiative+for+Human+Development/National+Initiative+for+Human+Development.htm (accessed April 21, 2014).

Howe, Marvine. *Morocco: The Islamist Awakening and Other Challenges*. Oxford: Oxford University Press, 2005.

Hughes, Stephen O. *Morocco Under King Hassan*. Reading, U.K.: Ithaca Press, 2001.

International Institute for Sustainable Development (IISD), "Daily Report On The Fourth World Conference On Women." *Earth Negotiations Bulletin* 14, no. 21 (18 September 1995). http://www.iisd.ca/vol14/enb1421e.txt. (accessed, April 24, 2014).

Inter Parliamentary Union, The. http://www.ipu.org/parline-e/reportarc/2221_97.htm (accessed July, 30 2011).

Iraqui-Sinaceur, Zakia and Moha Ennaji. "'Al Fatat' on Young Women's Education." In *Women Writing Africa: The Northern Region*, edited by Fatima Sadiqi, Amira Nowaira, Azza El Kholy, and Moha Ennaji. New York: Feminist Press at the City University of New York, 2009.

"Islam: Shapely Agitator." *Time Magazine* September 23, 1957.

Jettou, Driss, Morocco Minister of the Interior. Speech to the Parliament, Rabat, Morocco. March 6, 2002.

Katz, Andrew. "Morocco Amends Controversial Rape Marriage Law." BBC News Africa. January 23, 2014. http://www.bbc.com/news/world-africa-25855025 (accessed April 24, 2014).

Katzenstein, Stephen. *Between Power and Plenty*. Madison: University of Wisconsin, 1978. Quoted in Kathleen Thelen and Sven Steinmo. "Historical Institutionalism in Comparative Politics." In *Structuring Politics: Historical Institutionalism in Comparative Analysis*, edited by Sven

Steinmo, Kathleen Thelen, and Frank Longstreth. Cambridge: Cambridge University Press, 1992.

Keohane, Robert. "Theory Talk #9: Robert Keohane on Institutions and the Need for Innovation in the Field." *Theory Talks.* 2008. www.theory-talks.org/2008/05/theory-talk-9.html (accessed Febru ary 24, 2013).

King Mohammed VI. Speech to National Initiative for Human Development, May 18, 2005.

Kramer, Martin. "Politics and the Prophet. Where Are the Arab-Muslin Liberals?" *The New Republic.* October 26, 2009. http://www.geocities.com/martinkramerorg/PoliticsandProphet.htm (accessed April 24, 2014).

Krasner, Stephen D. "Approaches to the State: Alternative Conceptions and Historical Dynamics." *Comparative Politics* 16, no. 2. (January 1984): 223-246.

Kristianasen, Wendy. "Hard-Won Change in Iran and Morocco." *Le Monde Diplomatique*. February 4, 2004. http://mondediplo.com/2004/04/02islamicwomen (accessed April 24, 2014).

Krook, Mona Lena and Fiona Mackay, eds. *Gender, Politics, and Institutions: Towards a Feminist Institutionalism.* London and New York: Palgrave Macmillan, 2011.

Landry, Donna and Gerald MacLean, eds. "Introduction: Reading Spivak." *The Spivak Reader: Selected Works of Gayatri Chakravorty Spivak.* London and New York: Routledge, 1996, 1-14.

Longino, Helen. *Science as Social Knowledge*. Princeton: Princeton University Press, 1990.

Lugones, Maria C. and Elizabeth V. Spelman. "Have We Got a Theory for You! Feminist Theory, Cultural Imperialism and the Demand for 'the Woman's Voice.'" In *Women and Values: Readings in Recent Feminist Philosophy,* edited by Marilyn Pearsall. Belmont: Wadsworth, 1986.

Mahoney, James and Kathleen Thelen, eds. *Explaining Institutional Change: Ambiguity, Agency, Power*. Cambridge and New York: Cambridge University Press, 2009.

March, James G., and Johan P. Olsen. "The New Institutionalism: Organizational Factors in Political Life." *American Political Science Review* 78, no. 3 (September 1984): 734-749.

"Matters of Principle." *Time Magazine.* September 14, 1953.

MENA Consultative Council on Gener (CCG). World Bank. http://web.worldbank.org/WBSITE/EXTERNAL/COUNTRIES/MENAEXT/EXTMNAREGTOPGENDER/0,,menuPK:493344~pagePK:51065911~piPK:51065916~theSitePK:493333,00.html (accessed April 24, 2014).

Mernissi, Fatima. *Beyond the Veil.* Cambridge, MA: Schenkman, 1975.

———. *Doing Daily Battle: Interviews with Moroccan Women,* translated by Mary Jo Lakeland. New Brunswick: Rutgers University Press, 1988.

———. webpage: hhtp://www.mweniaai.net/books/chronological_overview/index.html (accessed April 24, 2014).
Migdal, Joel. *Strong Societies and Weak States.* Princeton: Princeton University Press, 1988.
Ministry of Family Affairs, Solidarity and Social Work, The. "Gender Mainstreaming in Policies and Programmes at the National Level. Case Study of Morocco." Workshop on Gender Mainstreaming, United Nations Economic and Social Commission for Western Asia, Beirut, Lebanon, 6-7 December 2003. Unedited draft.
Mohanty, Chandra Talpade. "Under Western Eyes: Feminist Scholarship and Colonial Discourse" In *Third World Women and the Politics of Feminism*, edited by Chandra Talpade Mohanty, Ann Russo, and Lourdes Torres. Bloomington: Indiana University Press, 1991, 51-80.
"More Deaths Reported in Morocco Food Riots. Rabat, Morocco, Jan. 24 [1984]." *New York Times.* January 25, 1984. http://www.nytimes.com/1984/01/25/world/more-deaths-reported-morocco-food-riots-rabat-morocco-jan-24-ap-several-people.html.
[*Moroccan Constitution* 2011.] http://www/moroccoboard.com/news/5314-morocco-government-explains-new-constitution-english (accessed July 30, 2011).
["Moroccan Constitutional Background."] http://www.serbat.unibe.ch/icl/mo00000_.html (accessed April 24, 2014).
"Moroccan Women's Roundtable Discussion with First Lady Hillary Rodham Clinton and others." Marrakech, Morocco. March 30, 1999. http://www.library.cornell.edu/colldev/mideast/hilround.htm (accessed April 24, 2014).
"Morocco: 26 Matters of Principle." *Time Magazine*. September 14, 1953.
[Moudawana Reform.] www.geographic.org
———. http://www.theodora./wfb/1992/morocco/morocco_people.html (accessed April 24, 2014).
Naciri, Rabéa. *The Women's Movement and Political Discourse in Morocco.* Occasional Paper 8. United Nations Research Institute for Social Development. United Nations Development Programme (UNDP). Geneva, March 1998.
Nelson, Lynn Hankinson. *Who Knows: From Quine to a Feminist Empiricism.* Philadelphia: Temple University Press, 1990.
North, Douglass C. *Institutions, Institutional Change, and Economic Peformance.* Cambridge; New York: Cambridge University Press, 1990.
Offe, Claus. "Institutions' Role in the Distribution and Control of Social Power." Paper presented at the "Crafting and Operating Institutions" Conference, Yale University, New Haven, CT, April 11-13, 2003.
Opie, Anne. "Qualitative Research: Appropriation of the 'Other' and Empowerment." *Feminist Review* no. 40 (Spring 1992): 52-69.

Orren, Karen and Stephen Skowronek, "Regimes and Regime Building: Review of Literature on the 1940s." *Political Science Quarterly* 113, (Winter 1998-99): 689-702.

Ouchelh, Amina. Interview with authors. Rabat, Morocco. November 28, 2007.

Parpart, Jane L., Shirin M. Rai, and Kathleen Staudt, eds. *Rethinking Empowerment: Gender and Development in a Global/Local World.* Routledge/Warwick Studies in Globalization, 3. London and New York: Routledge, 2002.

PBS. Hopes on the Horizon. (Backside, Inc.). February 16, 2001.

Platform for Action http://www.vrouwen.net/vweb/wcw/reserv.html. From the Dutch blog Womannet (accessed April 24, 2014).

Program. "Family Laws in the Muslim World: Comparative Perspectives." International Conference, Fès, Morocco, December 11-13, 2007. http://www.wluml.org/node/4199.

Rothstein, B. *Social Traps and the Problem of Trust.* Cambridge: Cambridge University Press, 2005. Quoted in Schmidt, Vivien, "Discursive Institutionalism: The Explanatory Power of Ideas and Discourse." *Annual Review of Political Science* 11 (2008): 303-326.

Sadiqi, Fatima. The Image of Moroccan Women in Public Spheres." In *The Idea of the University,* edited by Taieb Belghazi. Rabat: Publications de la Faculté des Lettres, 1997.

Sadiqi, Fatima and Moha Ennaji. "The Feminization of Public Space: Women's Activism, the Family Law, and Social Change in Morocco." *Journal of Middle East Women's Studies* 2, no. 2 (Spring 2006): 86-114.

Salime, Zakia. *Between Feminism and Islam: Human Rights and Sharia Law in Morocco.* Minneapolis: University of Minnesota Press, 2011.

Sandberg, Eve. "Multilateral Women's Conferences: The Domestic Political Organization of Zambian Women." *Contemporary Politics* 4, no. 3, (1998): 271-284.

Sandberg, Eve and Amber Ault. "Our Policies, Their Consequences: Zambian Women's Lives Under Structural Adjustment." In *Feminist Frontiers IV: Rethinking Sex, Gender, and Society*, edited by Laurel Richardson, Verta Taylor, and Nancy Whittier. New York: McGraw-Hill, 1997, 493-496.

Sandberg, Eve and Seth Binder. "The Moroccan Spring and King Mohammed VI's Economic Policy Agenda: Evaluating the First Dozen Years." In *Une Jeunesse Révoltée,* edited by Mohsine El Ahmadi. Rabat: Marsam Editions, forthcoming. English language edition *The Birth of the Arab Citizen and the Changing Middle East,* edited by Mohsine El Ahmadi and Stuart Schaar. Northampton, MA: Interlink Publishing, forthcoming.

Sater, James. *Morocco: Challenges to Tradition and Modernity.* London: Routledge, 2010.

Seiz, Janet. "The Bargaining Approach and Feminist Methodology." *Review of Radical Political Economics* 23, nos. 1-2 (1991): 22-29.

Schmidt, Vivien, "Discursive Institutionalism: The Explanatory Power of Ideas and Discourse." *Annual Review of Political Science* 11 (2008): 303-326.

Schuler, Margaret, ed. *Empowerment and the Law: Strategies of Third World Women.* Washington D.C.: OEF International, 1986.

Shaarawi, Huda. *Harem Years: The Memoirs of an Egyptian Feminist 1879-1924.* Translated and edited by Margot Badran with an introduction by Margot Badran. New York: Feminist Press at the City University of New York, 1987.

Shepsle, Kenneth A. "Institutional Equilibrium and Equilibrium Institutions." In *Political Science: The Science of Politics*, edited by Herbert Weisenberg, 52. New York: Agathon Press, 1986. Quoted in Kathleen Thelen and Sven Steinmo. "Historical Institutionalism in Comparative Politics." In *Structuring Politics: Historical Institutionalism in Comparative Analysis*, edited by Sven Steinmo, Kathleen Thelen, and Frank Longstreth. Cambridge: Cambridge University Press, 1992.

Shohat, Ella. "Notes on the 'Post-Colonial.'" *Social Text* no. 31/32 (1992): 99-113.

Short History of the Commission on the Status of Women. http://www.un.org/womenwatch/daw/CSW60YRS/CSWbriefhistory.pdf (accessed April 24, 2014).

Skalli, Loubna H. *Through a Local Prism: Gender, Globalization, and Identity in Moroccan Women's Magazines.* Lanham, MD: Lexington Books/Rowman and Littlefield Publishers, 2006.

Skalli, Nouzha. Discussion with authors. NDI and ADFM campaign workshop for Moroccan women running for parliamentary seats. Rabat, Morocco. November, 2002.

———. Interview with authors. Rabat, Morocco. November 28, 2007.

Skowronek, Stephen. *Building a New American State.* Cambridge: Cambridge University Press, 1982.

Streeck, Wolfgang and Kathleen Thelen. *Beyond Continuity: Institutional Change in Advanced Political Economies.* Oxford: Oxford University Press, 2005.

Swearingen, Will D. "Morocco's Agricultural Crisis." In *The Political Economy of Morocco,* edited by I. William Zartman. New York: Praeger Publishers, 1987.

Tahiri, Rachida. Interview with authors. Rabat, Morocco. November 23, 2007.

Thelen, Kathleen, and Sven Steinmo. "Historical Institutionalism in Comparative Politics." In *Structuring Politics: Historical Institutionaism in Comparative Analysis*, edited by Sven Steinmo, Kathleen Thelen, and Frank Longstreth. Cambridge: Cambridge University Press, 1992.

Truong, Thanh-Damn. *Sex, Money, and Morality: Prostitution and Tourism in Southeast Asia.* London: Zed Press, 1990.

U.N.CEDAW/SP/2008/3 Appendix Committee Member resumes. http://www.2.ohchr.org/english/bodies/cedaw/docs/CEDAW.SP.2008.3.pdf (accessed April 24, 2014).

UN WOMEN. "Budgets respond to the needs of women in Morocco." March 27, 2014 http://www.unwomen.org/en/news/stories/2014/3/budgets-respond-to-the-needs-of-women-in-morocco#sthash.2rvYX6uS.dpuf.

United Nations Arab Human Development Report. 2005.

United Nations Decade for Women 1976-1985. United Nations Publications, 1985. The Free Library http://www.thefreelibrary.com/United+Nations+decade+for+Women+1976-1985%3b+%27really+only+a+...-a03838336>United Nations decade for Women 1976-1985; 'really only a beginning) (accessed April 24, 2014).

U.S. Department of State. *Background Notes: Morocco.* 1994.

U.S. Department of State. Bureau of Democracy, Human Rights, and Labor. *Morocco Country Reports on Human Rights Practices 2001* (March 2002).

Vital Voices Global Partnership 2009 interview with Latifa Jbabdi. http://vitalvoices.org/vital-voices-feature/he-latifa-jbabdi (accessed April 24, 2014).

Vital Voices interview with Latifa Jbabdi. "A New Approach for Women's Rights." http://cc.bingi.com/cache.aspx?q=million+and+Maudawana+and+1992&d=4987690855964441&mkt=en-US&setland=en-US&w41fcf9c6.539419d2 (accessed April 24, 2014).

"WAR IN THE GULF; Huge Morocco March Supports Iraq in War." *New York Times*. Feb. 4, 1991. http://www.nytimes.com/1991/02/04/world/war-in-the-gulf-huge-morocco-march-supports-iraq-in-war.html

Waylen, Georgina. *Engendering Transitions: Women's Mobilization, Institutions, and Gender Outcomes*. Oxford: Oxford University Press, 2007.

Wegner, Eva. *Islamist Opposition in Authoritarian Regimes.* Syracuse: Syracuse University Press, 2011.

White, Gregory. *A Comparative Political Economy of Tunisia and Morocco.* Albany: SUNY Press, 2001.

White, Gregory W., Mark A. Tessler, and John P. Entelis. "The Kingdom of Morocco." In *The Government and Politics of the Middle East and North Africa,* edited by David E. Long and Bernard Reich. Boulder, CO: Westview Press, 2002.

Willis, Michael J. *Politics and Power in the Maghreb: Algeria, Tunisia, and Morocco from Independence to the Arab Spring*. London: Hurst & Company, 2012.

"Women, The." *Time Magazine*. January 23, 1956.

Women's Islamic Initiative in Spirituality and Equality. "Muslim Women Past and Present: Huda Shaarawi." Last modified 2013.

http://www.wisemuslimsomen.org/muslimwomen/bio/huda_shaarawi/ (accessed April 24, 2014)

Women's Learning Partnership. "Morocco Adopts Landmark Family Law Supporting Women's Equality." February 4, 2004. http://play.learningpartnership.org/en/advocacy/alerts/morocco0204 (accessed April 24, 2014).

Wuerth, Oriana. "The Reform of the Moudawana: The Role of Women's Civil Society Organizations in Changing the Personal Status Code in Morocco." *Hawwa Journal of* Women of the Middle East and the Islamic World 3, no. 3 (2005): 309-333.

Wyman, Oliver. Overview of Investment in Morocco. Rabat, Kingdom of Morocco Ministry of Industry, Trade and New Technologies. 2010.

Wyrtzen, Jonathan. *Constructing Morocco: The Colonial Struggle to Define the Nation, 1912-1956.* Ph.D. Diss., Georgetown University, April 15, 2009.

Zartman, I. William. "Political Pluralism in Morocco." In I. William Zartman, ed. *Man, State, and Society in the Contemporary Maghrib.* New York: Praeger Publishers, 1973.

Zeghal, Malika. *Islamism in Morocco: Religion, Authoritarianism, and Electoral Politics.* Translated by George Holoch. Princeton: Markus Weiner Publishers, 2008.

Zisenwine, Daniel. *The Emergence of Nationalist Politics in Morocco.* London: I.B. Taurus Publishers, 2010.

Zoubir, Yahia. "Reactions in the Maghreb to the Gulf War." *Arab Studies Quarterly* 15, no. 1(1993): 83-103.

Index

About the Authors

Eve Sandberg has a Ph.D. in political science from Yale University and she is Chair of the Politics Department at Oberlin College. Sandberg is President of Strategic Research Inc. (a political consultancy firm) and she was elected and served two terms on Oberlin City Council. She has been a participant observer making presentations and conducting training workshops for candidates, parties, and non-governmental organization leaders on democracy and advocacy issues in Morocco, Jordan, Ethiopia, Namibia, South Africa, Zambia, and in the United States. She is the author of Eve Sandberg, ed. *Perspectives in Comparative Politics* (New York: CourseWise Press, 2000) and Eve Sandberg. ed. *The Changing Politics of Non-Governmental Organizations and African States* (Westport, CT: Praeger Publishers, 1994).

Kenza Aqertit is NDI/Nepal Country Director. She has worked with NDI for more than 14 years and brings substantial field experience and expertise in managing and implementing democracy building programs in the Middle East and North Africa, West Africa, and Asia. In particular, Kenza has led programs in various NDI's functional areas including political party development, legislative strengthening, women's political participation and elections, in Morocco, Kuwait, Jordan, Liberia, and Nepal. She also contributed to NDI's programs in Algeria, Mauritania, Iraq and Egypt. Kenza served as Deputy Regional Director of Programs in charge of Asia and Latin America at the Canadian International Center for Human Rights and Democratic Development in Montreal from 2011 to 2012. She has a Master's Degree in Public and International Affairs on a Fulbright Scholarship from the University of Pittsburgh, and a Fellowship from Stanford. Kenza is fluent in Arabic, Berber, English, and French; intermediate in Russian and Spanish, and actively learning Nepali.